BRITAIN AT THE POLLS 2005

Edited by

John Bartle and Anthony King

CQ PRESS

A Division of Congressio
Washington,

CQ Press
1255 22nd Street, NW, Suite 400
Washington, DC 20037

Phone: 202-729-1900; toll-free, 1-866-427-7737 (1-866-4CQ-PRESS)

Web: www.cqpress.com

Cover design: Auburn Associates
Cover photo: EMPICS, A Press Association Group Company

♾ The paper used in this publication exceeds the requirements of the American
National Standard for Information Sciences—Permanence of Paper for Printed
Library Materials, ANSI Z39.48-1992.

Printed and bound in the United Kingdom

09   08   07   06   05   1   2   3   4   5

Cataloging-in-Publication Data available from the Library of Congress,
Washington, D.C.

ISBN 1-933116-63-3

Contents

Preface

This is the eighth book in the Britain at the Polls series, which has been published after each general election since February 1974, with the exception of 1987. Its purpose is to provide general readers, students of British politics and professional political scientists alike with up-to-date analyses of the major social, economic and political developments prior to the election, an assessment of the impact of these developments on the election outcome and some reasoned speculations about the future of British politics.

Britain at the Polls 2005, like its predecessors, contains relatively little on the formal four-week campaign. Most elections, including the May 2005 election, are largely won and lost over the long haul, with the formal campaign largely reinforcing decisions taken and loyalties formed long before polling day. Readers desperately interested in the 2005 campaign, however, need not feel deprived: British election campaigns are among the best documented of any in the world. Those who yearn for a blow-by-blow account of the campaign proper can refer to *The British General Election of 2005*, written by David Butler and Dennis Kavanagh, two of the doyens of British election studies; *Britain Votes, 2005*, edited by Pippa Norris and Christopher Wlezien; and *Political Communications: The General Election Campaign of 2005*, edited by Dominic Wring, Jane Green and Roger Mortimore. Those wishing to know the details of the constituency-by-constituency results are referred to the invaluable *Times Guide to the House of Commons*. Finally, those wanting to explore the available survey data for themselves can visit the British Election Study (BES) website at the University of Essex and download the pre-election, post-election and "rolling thunder" campaign data. As editors of *Britain at the Polls 2005*, we naturally believe that the present volume has an additional dimension to all these other volumes, providing readers with analyses of long-term and macro developments unavailable elsewhere.

Britain at the Polls 2005 contains many of the features associated with previous books in the series. Thomas Quinn in chapter 1 provides a detailed narrative tracking the course of British politics from 2001 to 2005, a period that—as a direct consequence of the attacks of September 11, 2001, and the wars in Afghanistan and Iraq—witnessed a marked shift in the domestic agenda toward security issues. Anthony King in chapter 7 provides a detailed analysis of why Labour won the election and why the Conservatives failed to capitalise on the opportunities for electoral advancement that Tony Blair and

New Labour gifted them. Ivor Crewe in chapter 9 takes the story a stage further in examining the strategic problems facing the major parties in the run up to the next general election.

In contrast to previous volumes in this series, *Britain at the Polls 2005* contains little bearing directly on political and organisational developments within the Labour and the Liberal Democrat Parties. The reason is simply that very little changed within these two parties between 2001 and 2005, and what little did change had only a negligible impact on either the course of politics during those years or the eventual outcome of the election. The Conservative Party, however, chopped and changed personnel, produced lots of new policies and managed to go through three leaders in four years. Philip Norton in chapter 2 provides a detailed analysis of the Conservative Party's fumbled attempts to respond to the challenge posed by Tony Blair's New Labour. The Conservatives' failure to adapt to changed circumstances gave the period an air of unreality: the Labour government was far from popular, but few voters, commentators or journalists seriously doubted that it would be returned to office, nor, indeed, did Prime Minister Tony Blair, who called the election one year short of a full parliamentary term.

The decision to omit detailed discussion of the Labour and Liberal Democrat Parties provides us with an opportunity to examine more important long-term developments in British politics. Nicholas Allen in chapter 3 explores evidence of widespread discontent and restlessness among the electorate. David McKay in chapter 4 examines how Europe became a major issue in the 1990s but had become a virtual non-issue by 2005. Iain McLean in chapter 5 provides an update on Britain's ongoing experiment in devolution, something that many even in England know little about but that is already producing profound changes in how the various parts of the United Kingdom relate to each other. John Bartle in chapter 6 goes on to analyse how developments in the relationship between politicians and journalists influenced the pre-2005 political debate as well as the election outcome. E. J. Dionne Jr in chapter 8 provides an analysis of what remains (to many Britons and other Europeans) one of the most curious aspects of recent British politics: Tony Blair's fascination with the United States and his support for George W. Bush's foreign policy. Dionne, a widely read columnist for the *Washington Post* and a scholar at the Brookings Institution, provides a well-informed and acute North American perspective on the 2005 election.

The editors would like to acknowledge the support of several people in connection with the present volume. Charisse Kiino at CQ Press initially commissioned the book and supported the editors throughout production. Her enthusiasm, good humour and professionalism have been greatly appreciated by the editors. Thanks should also go to Steve Pazdan and Robin Surratt at CQ Press for ensuring that we stuck to a tight production schedule. Sue Miller of Oxford Publicity Partnership provided excellent advice on marketing. Finally, we would like to thank Heather Bliss for subjecting the manuscript to a rigorous copy-editing.

Contributors

Nicholas Allen is a PhD candidate at the University of Essex. He is currently researching the regulation of parliamentary standards.

John Bartle is a senior lecturer in government at the University of Essex and the co-editor of *Political Communications Transformed: From Morrison to Mandelson* (2001).

Ivor Crewe is vice chancellor of the University of Essex and professor of government. He is the author of numerous books and articles on British politics and the co-author of *SDP: The Birth, Life and Death of the Social Democratic Party* (1995). He is a regular commentator on British elections for television and radio.

E.J. Dionne Jr is a senior fellow at the Brookings Institution, University Professor at Georgetown University and a columnist for the *Washington Post*. He is the author of *Why Americans Hate Politics* (1991), *They Only Look Dead: Why Progressives Will Dominate the Next Political Era* (1996) and *Stand Up, Fight Back: Republican Toughs, Democratic Wimps, and the Politics of Revenge* (2004).

Anthony King has contributed to Britain at the Polls since the first book in the series appeared in 1974. He is the Essex County Millennium Professor of British Government at the University of Essex and contributes regularly to BBC election night broadcasts.

David McKay is professor of government at the University of Essex. He is the author of *American Politics and Society* (2005) and *Designing Europe: Comparative Lessons from the Federal Experience* (2001) and the co-author of *The New British Politics* (2004).

Iain McLean is professor of politics and director of the Public Policy Unit at Oxford University. He previously worked at Newcastle and Warwick Universities and held visiting professorships at Washington and Lee, Stanford, Yale and the Australian National Universities. His specialties include devolution in the United Kingdom, electoral systems and social choice.

Philip Norton is professor of government at the University of Hull and director of the university's Centre for Legislative Studies. He is the author of *Parliament in British Politics* (2005) and co-author of *Politics UK*. He sits in the House of Lords as Lord Norton of Louth.

Thomas Quinn is a lecturer in government at the University of Essex. He is the author of *Modernising the Labour Party: Organisational Change since 1983* (2004) as well as articles in *Party Politics*, *The British Journal of Politics and International Relations* and *Political Studies*.

1

Tony Blair's Second Term

Thomas Quinn

On September 11, 2001, Tony Blair was due to deliver an eagerly awaited speech to the Trades Union Congress (TUC), where he was expected to receive a bumpy ride from delegates opposed to his plans for public-sector reform. Minutes before the prime minister was due to speak, news of a series of major terrorist attacks on the United States filtered through to the conference. Blair hurriedly cancelled his speech to rush back to London to prepare his response to what was evidently the beginning of a new and highly dangerous era in global affairs. The events of that afternoon at the TUC symbolized the abrupt change of priorities forced on his government. Although Labour was returned to office in 2001 promising to improve public services, the enduring memory of its second term will be of the steadfast support that Blair offered a Republican US president and the wars that he helped prosecute. The government undoubtedly made progress on public-service delivery and reform, sometimes producing fierce opposition from within the Labour movement. Its principal legacy, however, will almost certainly lie in the field of foreign affairs, particularly its decision to go to war in Iraq.

This chapter begins with an account of the Iraq War, the key event in Labour's second term. The war and its aftermath damaged the reputation of the prime minister and coloured attitudes to his government's domestic performance. Nevertheless, domestic policy loomed large in British politics, especially as voters' attentions drifted from the continuing bloodshed in Iraq to more immediate concerns. The second part of the chapter examines the government's record on delivering public services and on "security" issues such as crime and immigration. The final part looks at the discord that emerged within the governing party and the effects that the resulting loss of cohesion had for New Labour in office.

Foreign Policy: From 9/11 to the Iraq War

In its first term Labour had developed a liberal-interventionist foreign policy, supporting military action in Kosovo and undertaking another humanitarian mission in Sierra Leone. It also assisted in the ongoing US containment of Iraq. The attacks of September 11, 2001, ensured that foreign policy would dominate much of Labour's second term. Members of Osama bin Laden's al-Qaeda organization hijacked four civilian airliners and crashed two of them into the World Trade Center towers in New York and another into the Pentagon outside Washington, DC. A fourth crashed in a field in Pennsylvania, after passengers tackled the hijackers. Bin Laden was sheltered by the fundamentalist Taliban regime in Afghanistan and after it failed to hand him over to the United States, war became inevitable. The global revulsion at the 9/11 attacks and the deaths of some 3,000 civilians ensured that the resulting war had widespread support including that of the United Nations (UN) and the North Atlantic Treaty Organization (NATO). Blair strongly supported it and supplemented the political case for regime change with a moral case for humanitarian intervention based on the penury and repression of Afghans under the Taliban. The Taliban were quickly overthrown and a new government installed, although bin Laden escaped.[1]

The consequences of 9/11, however, were far reaching. To Blair the assaults demonstrated a new form of nihilistic terrorism, unconstrained by morality and driven by no coherent political goal. He feared that groups such as al-Qaeda would not hesitate to use weapons of mass destruction (WMD)—chemical, biological, radiological and nuclear—if they could get hold of them. President George W. Bush declared a "war on terror", in which the United States would target groups it deemed to be terrorist and their state sponsors. That immediately brought into focus Saddam Hussein's regime in Iraq, an old foe of America since the Gulf War in 1991.

Although no convincing direct connection was ever discovered between Iraq and al-Qaeda's attacks, US policy-makers saw Saddam and his Ba'athist regime as a continuing threat that could no longer be tolerated in the post-9/11 world. Saddam's regime had a long history of seeking to acquire—and using—WMD; it harboured terrorists and paid money to the families of Palestinian suicide-bombers; it consistently ignored UN resolutions; and it remained one of the most tyrannical regimes in the world. The policy of containing Saddam was, moreover, disintegrating. UN weapons inspectors were effectively forced from the country in 1998 and the effects of sanctions were deflected towards ordinary Iraqis. Regime change in Iraq would remove a dangerous dictator who might one day supply WMD to terrorists, but it could also assist America's broader strategic goal of securing change in the Middle East, with Iraq becoming a democratic beacon for the whole region.

Tony Blair had long been concerned about the dangers of Saddam's regime and was quick to see the threat that rogue states posed after 9/11. Although he would have preferred a peaceful resolution to the crisis, he was prepared to commit British troops in the event of war, deeming it imperative to support the United States in order to maintain British influence. However, both the country and the Labour Party were deeply divided about Iraq. Blair desperately needed political cover in the form of UN support for military action.

The declared aim of the allies, and the eventual *casus belli* of the war, was the disarmament of Iraq. The full disclosure and destruction of Iraq's

WMD arsenal were the principal goals. Blair could not follow Bush in calling for regime change because the government's legal officers advised him that this justification would be contrary to British law. Blair believed that framing the dispute in terms of WMD might assist the effort to secure UN backing for military action. The government produced two dossiers of evidence on Iraq's WMD programme. The first (dubbed "the dodgy dossier") turned out to be largely plagiarized from an old doctoral thesis and added little new information. The second, published in September 2002 ("the September dossier"), was based on intelligence sources and contained some eye-catching claims, including the suggestion that Iraq could deploy WMD within forty-five minutes. Although the response to the dossier was mixed, there was little dispute—even among opponents of war, such as France and Russia—that Iraq *did* possess WMD.

The efforts of Blair and Jack Straw, his foreign secretary, to obtain UN support for any action against Iraq necessitated concessions to countries opposed to war. Iraq was given a chance to comply under the terms of UN resolution 1441, unanimously passed by the Security Council in November 2002, which declared Iraq to be in "material breach" of existing obligations to the UN, demanded the return of weapons inspectors and required Iraq to disclose the full extent of its WMD arsenal. Failure to comply would constitute "a further material breach" of Iraq's obligations and leave it facing "serious consequences", though these were not defined.[2]

Saddam begrudgingly allowed the weapons inspectors to return and provided documentation on WMD, but the United States dismissed his actions as falling short of what was demanded and turned its attentions to planning military action. Some in the Bush administration wished to withdraw from the UN process altogether but Blair persuaded the president—as a favour, for British domestic purposes—to seek a second resolution that would explicitly permit the use of force. Opposition to an invasion of Iraq was growing in Britain, and in February 2003 one million anti-war demonstrators marched through London. In the following month, however, France declared it would veto any second resolution "whatever the circumstances", and Blair was faced with his nightmare scenario: embarking on military action alongside the United States without explicit UN authorization. The attorney-general, Lord Goldsmith, argued that the use of force would be legal on the basis of resolution 1441, although his claim was contested by others. Robin Cook, the leader of the House of Commons and previous foreign secretary, resigned. Clare Short, another critic, remained in the government, but resigned after the war. Although the British prime minister can declare war without parliamentary approval, Blair decided to allow a vote in the House of Commons to demonstrate that he had the support of the country and his own party. On March 18, a government motion allowing "all means necessary to ensure the disarmament of Iraq's weapons of mass destruction" was passed by 412 votes to 149, with Conservative support. The Liberal Democrats backed a rebel amendment stating that the case for war had not been established, and they were joined by 139 Labour members of parliament (MPs). It was the largest revolt against any government by its own back-benchers since the mid-nineteenth century. The amendment, however, was defeated. Crucially for Blair's authority, a narrow majority of Labour MPs voted for the war, as did the chancellor of the exchequer, Gordon Brown, the other major figure in the government and Blair's rival. Without the backing of Brown (who was sceptical of the war) and a majority of the Parliamentary Labour Party (PLP), Blair would probably have resigned.[3] British forces joined the US-led coalition's invasion of Iraq on March 20, and on April 9 US troops entered Baghdad.

Relief at the quick military victory, however, was soon forgotten amid the problems that beset Iraq. A lack of planning for the post-war period meant that there was little security and few basic services after the collapse of the state apparatus. A bloody insurgency conducted by ex-Ba'athists and foreign jihadists gripped Baghdad and the so-called Sunni triangle area of central Iraq. Most crucially for Blair, no WMD were discovered and the media inevitably turned its focus on to the "September dossier". It was felt that some of the government's claims were expressed in ways that appeared to go further than the intelligence on which they were based warranted. A BBC journalist, Andrew Gilligan, claimed an "intelligence source" told him that Alastair Campbell, Blair's communications chief, had "sexed up" the dossier to make it sound more convincing and had included the forty-five minute claim knowing that it was probably untrue. The alleged source, later revealed to be a former weapons inspector named David Kelly who worked for the Ministry of Defence, committed suicide after intense questioning by a parliamentary committee. An independent inquiry into his death was set up under Lord Hutton, a law lord. His report, delivered in January 2004, cleared the government of wrong-doing and criticized the BBC, prompting the resignations of its chairman, its director-general and Gilligan himself.[4]

The prime minister was forced to concede another inquiry shortly afterwards, this time on the use of intelligence in the decision to go to war. The inquiry, chaired by the former cabinet secretary, Lord Butler, exonerated the government of the central charge that it had misrepresented intelligence to bolster the case for war. Butler decided that the politicians had faithfully reported the intelligence that the security services had provided even though much of that intelligence turned out to be inaccurate. However, he also found the intelligence as originally reported was accompanied by numerous caveats and that these had been removed from the government's "September dossier", transforming possibilities into probabilities. In particular, the forty-five minute claim should not have appeared in the dossier without clarification over what it referred to: battlefield weapons rather than long-range missiles, which had been the impression left by contemporaneous press reports. Nevertheless, Butler concluded that the dossier's claims "went to (although not beyond) the outer limits of the intelligence available".[5]

Figure 1.1 British Public Opinion on the Iraq War, 2003–2005

Q. Do you think the United States and Britain are/were right or wrong to take military action against Iraq?

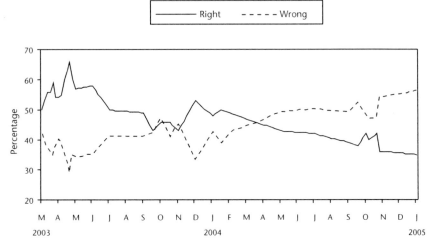

Source: YouGov, "Iraq War Right or Wrong?" tracker poll for various clients, http://www.yougov.com/archives/pdf/ TEL040101022_3.pdf.

The finding that Blair was a "sincere deceiver" (in the words of *The Economist*) was not met with universal acclaim.[6] Despite being cleared of the most serious allegations of falsifying evidence, trust in the prime minister fell sharply. There appears to have been little incentive for Blair knowingly to make false claims about WMD if an imminent invasion of Iraq would quickly prove them wrong. However, pre-existing concerns about the government's propensity for "spin" came back to haunt it, and they subsequently infected public opinion about everything it did. Indeed, it looked likely to remain thus for as long as Blair was in office, though the individual who personified spin more than anyone else, Alastair Campbell, announced before the Butler inquiry reported that he was stepping down.

Public support for the Iraq invasion was never particularly deep, though a big majority was in favour during its early stages. That fell back sharply, as the insurgency took hold (see Figure 1.1). The government's hope was that after Iraqi elections in January 2005, British voters' attention would move elsewhere, and for the most part it did. Yet there is no doubt that the Iraq War inflicted considerable damage on the government's popularity. Labour's poll ratings, already on a downward trend, fell further after the invasion, though discontent with domestic policy was also undoubtedly to blame. After being re-elected in 2001, Labour's support fluctuated around 45 per cent for eighteen months; after the war it rarely moved above the mid-to-high thirties range (see Figure 1.2).[7]

Figure 1.2 Monthly Opinion–Poll Ratings (Average of All Polls), 2001–2005

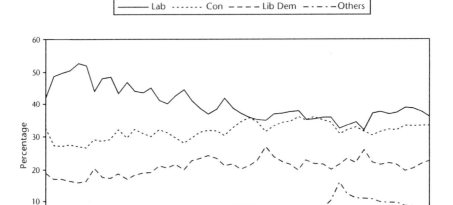

Sources: Gallup, YouGov, ICM, MORI, Populus, CommRes, Live Strategy, NOP, BPIX. First and last listings are results of the general elections of 2001 and 2005, respectively.

The government was fortunate, however, that the main opposition party, the Conservatives, had also supported the invasion. The Conservatives were unable to benefit from the government's problems over Iraq, unlike opposition parties in other countries that joined the "coalition of the willing". The most notable example was Spain, where the anti-war Socialists defeated the ruling Popular Party in 2004. The Spanish government had looked set for re-election, but a series of bomb attacks in Madrid by Islamist extremists three days before the poll focused attentions back on the war. By contrast, the British Conservatives saw only a modest improvement in their poll ratings, despite the Blair government's travails. Their leader in the 2005 election campaign, Michael Howard, claimed that had he known that the intelligence case for war was so weak he might not have supported it. That claim, together with his later charge that Blair "lied" about the intelligence, was widely viewed as opportunistic. Instead, the main winners were Britain's third party, the Liberal Democrats, who attracted the support of liberal-minded people and Muslims hostile to the war. In the six by-elections held during the 2001 to 2005 parliament (all in safe Labour seats), they obtained four swings of over 17 per cent from Labour, winning two seats—Brent East and Leicester South—with high concentrations of Muslim voters. The Conservatives saw their vote-share fall in all these seats. Yet it remained true that only they could hope to replace Labour in government. Conservative support for the war thus meant that they could not easily make political capital out of the post-war mess.

The failure to find WMD did not shatter trust in the government—if only because trust had ebbed before the war. From early 2000 onwards, those voters who thought the government was honest and trustworthy were always outnumbered by those who did not—a salutary lesson in the corrosive effects of "spin". The gap widened in Labour's second term, and by early 2003 barely 30 per cent of respondents in YouGov's tracker poll considered the government trustworthy, against about 65 per cent who did not. Nevertheless, the war's aftermath deepened distrust and ensured that the government's rating for trustworthiness remained stuck at about 25 per cent. It was a similar story with Blair's personal approval ratings. During his first two years as prime minister the proportion of voters satisfied with his performance rarely fell below two-thirds. Towards the end of his first term, it slipped below 50 per cent and by the beginning of 2003 it was down to a third, where it remained for the rest of his second term.[8] One consequence of this fall in esteem was a disinclination by voters to believe anything that ministers said about domestic-policy achievements.

Labour's only consolation was that voters were even less impressed with the Conservatives. In YouGov's tracker poll of who would make the best prime minister, Blair was chosen by 30 per cent after the Iraq War, while Iain Duncan Smith, who led the Conservative Party between 2001 and 2003, was usually below 20 per cent. His lacklustre performance led to his replacement by Michael Howard, but Howard's rating in turn never rose above 30 per cent, and by late-2004, he trailed Blair by 10 points. The rating of Charles Kennedy, leader of the Liberal Democrats, was usually in the mid-teens.[9]

The political damage that Iraq inflicted on the government, therefore, was serious but not terminal. Faced with demands to apologize for his mistakes, Blair felt able to stand his ground and defend his decision to take the country to war. In his speech to Labour's 2004 annual conference he admitted:

> The evidence about Saddam having actual biological and chemical weapons, as opposed to the capability to develop them, has turned out to be wrong. . . . And the problem is I can apologise for the information that turned out to be wrong, but I can't, sincerely at least, apologise for removing Saddam. The world is a better place with Saddam in prison not in power.[10]

These words were unlikely to convince those who had long opposed the war; but Blair's hope was that they would persuade others that he had acted sincerely and that it was time to move on.

Domestic Politics and Policy

Foreign affairs loomed large during Labour's second term and there was always the risk that its ambitious domestic policies would be overshadowed. In fact, as people became weary of the daily bloodshed in Iraq, their thoughts focused on things that directly impacted on their own lives. Labour's priori-

Table 1.1 Salient Political Issues in the United Kingdom, 1997–2005

Q. What would you say is the most important issue facing Britain today?
Q. What do you see as other important issues facing Britain today? (Unprompted; combined answers)

	First term					Second term					1st term mean	2nd term mean
	1997	1998	1999	2000	2001	2001	2002	2003	2004	2005		
Health	46	42	39	51	44	51	53	42	36	39	44	44
Defence/Foreign affairs/Terrorism	2	7	10	3	3	27	22	36	38	28	6	31
Education	40	35	30	31	33	34	31	29	27	27	33	29
Crime	24	18	18	22	23	22	29	23	25	28	20	25
Race relations/ Immigration	5	4	7	11	14	18	21	30	29	33	8	26
Europe/Euro	26	23	28	22	19	17	11	11	9	7	24	11
Economy	16	19	13	10	10	13	9	12	10	11	14	11
Pensions/Welfare	13	13	11	14	12	9	10	10	12	13	13	11
Unemployment	34	34	22	16	12	12	8	8	7	8	24	8

Source: MORI, "Political Monitor: Long Term Trends—The Most Important Issues Facing Britain Today", http://www.mori.com/polls/trends/issues.shtml.

Notes: The table shows the annual average percentage of respondents citing each issue in reply to the above questions in monthly polls. Only the most frequently cited issues are included.

For 1997 the monthly polls included one from June to December. For 2001, the polls from January to April are included in the first term, and those from June to November in the second term. For 2005 the polls included one from January to March.

ties in domestic policy changed between its first and second terms. The former saw considerable constitutional change and only limited improvements in public services.[11] In its second term, the government was less active on constitutional matters. It failed to complete reform of the House of Lords, while its policy of creating English regional assemblies was still-born after a crushing defeat in a referendum in the North-East. Nevertheless, the government did introduce the Freedom of Information Act and promised that a supreme court would replace the House of Lords as the highest court in the land. It also tried, and failed, to abolish the office of lord chancellor when the proposal caused outrage among the legal profession.

The main domestic priorities in Blair's second term were the economy, public services, crime and asylum.[12] Polls indicated that these were the issues that largely interested voters (see Table 1.1). Health and education regularly topped the list, but crime, immigration and terrorism rose up the political agenda in the aftermath of 9/11. Economic issues were mentioned less frequently, possibly as a result of relatively benign economic conditions. Nevertheless, the economy continued to have the potential to halt the government's progressive agenda, as it had for Labour governments in the past, so the government continued to place great emphasis on economic stability.

The Economy

Ever since Labour returned to government in 1997 its trump card in elections had been its management of the economy. During its first term, Labour was concerned to establish its reputation for competence, which it did by immediately announcing the operational independence of the Bank of England to set interest rates in pursuit of an inflation target. Gordon Brown, the chancellor, also committed the government to maintain the strict spending limits set by the previous Conservative government for the first two years. That decision left little room for immediate increases in funding for public services, but Labour went into the 2001 general election promising to improve those services if it won again. It pledged not to raise the basic rate of income, but refused to rule out a rise in the rate of national-insurance contributions (NICs).[13] Once re-elected, Brown predictably increased the rate of contributions from 10 per cent to 11 per cent in the 2002 budget, insisting that the extra money was needed to improve the National Health Service. This rise, together with other tax increases in the budget, boosted revenue to the Treasury by £22 billion over three years. Initial polling evidence suggested that this move was popular, though it risked damaging Labour's standing in the long run if improvements in services were not forthcoming.[14]

Britain's economic performance was steady rather than spectacular. Although gross domestic product (GDP) grew continuously, this expansion had actually begun in 1992 under John Major's Conservative government and growth in Britain was slower than growth in the United States. Nevertheless, the British economy comfortably outperformed the euro zone in terms of growth (see Figure 1.3) and unemployment.[15] Higher growth helped to push unemployment below 5 per cent, half the rate in France and Germany. Consequently, unemployment was not the hot political issue in Britain (see Table 1.1) that it was elsewhere in Europe. Moreover, the tight labour market had little effect on inflation: throughout the second term the consumer price index remained below the government's target of 2 per cent. Britain's superior performance had the important political effect of further strengthening the position of those who opposed British adoption of the single currency. Midway through the parliament, the chancellor announced that the time was not right for Britain to join the euro zone (see below).

There were two major sources of Britain's economic growth in Labour's second term: one was the large increases in government spending; the other was a consumer boom fuelled by credit secured on the back of rising house prices. House-price inflation ran at 15–20 per cent or above, with prices trebling between 1997 and 2005. The soaring housing market was helped along by low interest rates: the Bank of England's base rate fell from 5.25 per cent when Labour was re-elected in June 2001 to 3.5 per cent two years later, before rising again to 4.75 per cent in 2004. The low cost of borrowing encouraged a credit splurge and consumer spending: the volume of retail sales grew at about 6 per cent a year for much of Labour's second term.

Figure 1.3 GDP Growth Rates, 2001–05

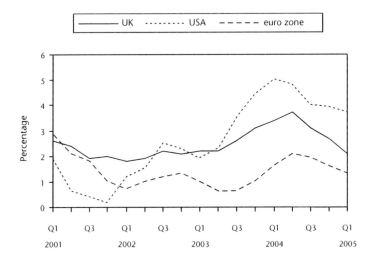

Source: Organisation for Economic Co-operation and Development, *Main Economic Indicators.*
Note: The figure shows the percentage change on the same quarter in the previous year.

Overall Britain became a noticeably wealthier country during Labour's first two terms. Britain's GDP per capita overtook that of France and Germany. People bought more (and bigger) cars: the number of new cars registered in 2004 was 18 per cent higher than in 1997.[16] Britons took 41.2 million holidays abroad in 2003, more than double the number in 1991. The country embraced new technologies: in 2002–2003, 45 per cent of households had internet access from home, a four-fold increase since 1998–99; 70 per cent had mobile phones, a four-fold increase since 1996–97; and a third of households owned DVD players.[17] The country as a whole looked more modern. London was seen throughout Europe as a city on the up, a centre of culture, art and fashion. Other cities, such as Manchester and Newcastle, long associated with urban decay, experienced dramatic rebirths. Britain's modern and wealthy image in 2005 contrasted with the country that was dubbed "the sick man of Europe" in the 1970s.

The government reaped political rewards for overseeing this upsurge in the country's economic well-being. Labour's lead over the Conservatives on economic competence rose significantly in the run-up to the 2005 election, after a lull that coincided with a temporary dip in house-price inflation and retail sales in 2003. The "feel-good factor", which summarized voters' optimism about household finances, was negative but improved noticeably in 2004–2005, having been around -30 in 2003 (see Figure 1.4). British elections are often won and lost on the economy: Labour's first-term accomplishment of establishing itself as the party of economic competence was preserved in its second term, with few opportunities for the Conservatives to make electoral capital.

As Labour's second term drew to a close, however, there began to appear worrying signs that the economy might worsen. The housing market started to cool and consumer spending was reined back. The public finances also went into the red after the substantial spending increases announced in the Treasury's comprehensive spending reviews in 2000 and 2004. Government expenditure was expected to account for 42.3 per cent of GDP by 2008, up from 37.4 per cent in 2000 (see Figure 1.5). Many economists predicted that the government would need to increase taxes if it were to stick to its "golden rule" of borrowing only to invest over the course of the economic cycle.[18]

The chancellor was sensitive to allegations that government spending was out of control and had not greatly improved front-line services. In August 2003 he announced that Sir Peter Gershon, former head of the Office of Government Commerce, would conduct a root-and-branch review of the civil service. Gershon's report, published in July 2004, suggested wide scope for effi-

Figure 1.4 Government's Perceived Economic Competence and the "Feel-good Factor", 2003–2005

Q1. If Britain were in economic difficulties, which party do you think could handle the problem best—the Conservatives or Labour? (Figures in chart are Labour scores minus Conservative scores.)

Q2. How do you think the financial situation of your household will change over the next 12 months? (Better/worse/same. "Feel-good factor" is percentage saying better minus percentage saying worse.)

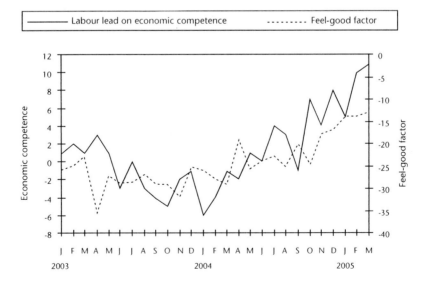

Source: YouGov, "Political Trackers 2003–2005", for the Daily Telegraph, http://www.yougov.com/archives/pdf/ TEL020101018_24.pdf.

Figure 1.5 Government Expenditures, 1997–2008

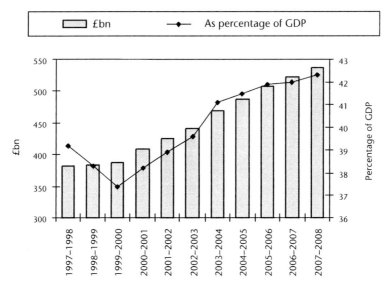

Source: HM Treasury, *2004 Spending Review,* Table A.11, p. 191.
Note: Figures from 2004–2005 onwards are for planned expenditure. Expenditure is shown in real terms, based on prices in 2004–2005.

ciency savings, by cutting a net total of 71,000 civil-service jobs and relocating posts outside London. It claimed that £21.5 billion a year could be saved by 2007–2008 as a result of such economies, of which £13 billion could be diverted into front-line services.[19] These economies were crucial if the government were to reassure voters that the extra spending had secured real improvements in the public services and to deflect Conservative claims that the public sector was rife with waste.

Reforming the Public Services

Labour knew that it had to deliver noticeable improvements in healthcare, education and law and order or risk losing the confidence of voters. "Delivery", therefore, permeated cabinet discussions, ministerial speeches and departmental press releases. A new Delivery Unit, directly answerable to the prime minister, was established to ensure that departments made progress on key manifesto pledges.[20]

There were two important developments in Labour's second term. There was first a huge injection of funds into the public services paid for by the taxpayer. There followed a tentative move away from the traditional top-down, command-and-control ethos of Britain's public services towards decentralized structures that were more responsive to "customers". The first approach was closely associated with the chancellor, while the second was championed by the prime minister. It was an indication of trouble at the top of government.

Healthcare. The National Health Service (NHS) is a socialized health-care system funded out of general taxation and free to patients at the point of delivery. However, years of underinvestment by previous (mainly Conservative) governments had left it struggling to cope with the demands placed on it by medical advances and an ageing population. In particular, the NHS was notorious for its long waiting lists and waiting times. Labour had to demonstrate clear progress on the issue that consistently topped voters' list of concerns (see Table 1.1).

Following the 2001 election, Gordon Brown commissioned a report by Derek Wanless, a former NatWest Bank group chief executive, into the NHS's long-term funding requirements. The Wanless Report made a case for a large injection of cash over the following twenty years, and in 2002 Brown announced huge funding increases for the NHS—7 per cent a year in real terms. Spending would rise from £68 billion in 2003 to £109 billion in 2008, by which time total UK health spending would amount to 9.4 per cent of GDP.[21] The extra money would be used to pay for new hospitals, medical facilities and thousands of doctors and nurses. To reduce waiting lists for those treatments that were longest, such as orthopaedics, the government created twenty-six NHS specialist treatment centres, offering routine surgery, with twenty more planned.[22]

With the extra money, facilities and staff afforded to the NHS, the number of people on waiting lists fell by a third, from 1.16 million to 822,000, between 1997 and 2005. In 2000, over 250,000 patients in England waited longer than six months for an operation, but the government set a target of reducing that figure to zero by December 2005 and was on course to achieve that target.[23]

Nevertheless, output increases in the NHS lagged behind the funding increases. Lower productivity meant that output rose by just 3.7 per cent a year between 1998 and 2003. Much of the extra money spent on health went in higher wages and salaries. The government decided that existing structures had to be reformed if the NHS were to improve and, furthermore, that market forces would play a role. A new payments system for elective surgery was introduced for hospitals in April 2005, replacing the old system of pre-determined block budgets with one in which hospitals were paid national tariffs for specific types of treatment. This system gave hospitals incentives to cut their costs and increase output, since resources followed patients, who had greater choice over which hospital to visit.[24] Controversially, the government decided to co-opt the private sector. It had already expanded the Private Finance Initiative (PFI), a scheme using private consortia to invest in public-sector capital projects such as hospital buildings. More significantly, in 2000 the government signed a concordat with private healthcare providers, where it paid them to treat NHS patients. Bids were invited for contracts in 2003.

NHS unions and some Labour MPs complained that the ethos of the NHS was being undermined.

Labour's most controversial reform was the establishment in 2004 of "foundation hospitals". These were to be high-performing hospitals whose managers would be granted greater autonomy from central government: they could borrow money from banks for capital expenditure, retain the proceeds of land sales and reinvest it in service provision, and pay employees above national NHS levels in order to attract the best staff. They would also be subject to fewer interventions and inspections from the centre. In effect, they represented a local form of public ownership.[25] Foundation hospitals would be run as independent not-for-profit trusts ultimately controlled by their staff, patients and local residents, who would elect a board of governors. According to their pioneer, the Blairite secretary of state for health, Alan Milburn, foundation hospitals would decentralize decision-making in the NHS, encouraging managerial innovation and the allocation of resources to match local needs.

The proposal to create foundation hospitals caused controversy within Labour ranks because it threatened to undermine the NHS's status as a properly *national* health service. The chancellor was concerned that giving such hospitals financial freedom would leave the government unable to control them, though it would still be bound to bail then out if they ran into difficulties. The NHS unions were worried about the trusts' freedom to set wages and the end of national pay scales; they feared the creation of a two-tier workforce, with employees of elite foundation hospitals on better pay and conditions than staff elsewhere. In November 2003 a huge rebellion by Labour MPs against the foundation-hospitals proposal saw the government's parliamentary majority slump from 167 to just seventeen.[26]

The government was undaunted and late in the second term it targeted another traditional feature of the NHS for reform: the top-down provision of services to passive recipients (patients). John Reid, who replaced Milburn as health secretary in 2003, set out ways of widening patient "choice", especially relating to which hospital they wished to be treated in. The idea was that funds would follow patients, who would choose better general practitioners (GPs) and hospitals—giving under-performers an incentive to improve. It was seen as a way of using market forces to drive up the quality of health care and dovetailed with moves to decentralize the service.

Despite their importance, the debates on foundation hospitals and patient choice had a limited impact on voters, who were more concerned with immediate improvements in the NHS. In that respect, there were worrying signs for the government. A YouGov poll for the *Sunday Times* in May 2004 found that one third of respondents thought that the NHS had got worse over the past few years (23 per cent thought it had got better). Moreover, 58 per cent believed that the extra money poured into the NHS was mostly wasted. Yet patients had a positive view of the service when they used it: 84 per cent of those who had visited a GP in the previous year were impressed with the service, as were 70 per cent of those who visited a hospital.[27] Ministers blamed this discrepancy on the media, which focused on "waste" and ran periodic health "horror stories", such as the spread of superbug infections in hospitals. Voters' ungenerous assessments of the government, however, also reflected their lack of trust in its declarations. Despite considerable progress in reducing waiting lists, the government's reputation for spin (announcing and re-announcing expenditure, policies or initiatives) ensured that it struggled to win plaudits.

Education. Education came second only to health on the government's list of public-service priorities after 2001. Whereas the main problem in health was one of quantity—lack of capacity—the principal problem in education, particularly in schools, was one of quality.[28] Accordingly, the government sought to improve the quality of schools through a combination of more money and reforms designed to raise pupils' performance. Funding per school pupil rose by 25 per cent in real terms between 1998 and 2004. Yet while this injection of funds was welcomed by the teaching profession, more controversy attended the government's plans for reform.

In primary schools (ages 5–11) first-term initiatives such as "numeracy" and "literacy" hours focused on the basic skills of reading, writing and counting arithmetic. Ministers had set a target of 85 per cent of 11-year olds reaching the expected level in English and maths by 2002. After initial improvements, progress levelled off. By the end of Labour's second term, a quarter of pupils were leaving primary school without the necessary skills in English and maths.[29]

In secondary schools (ages 11–16) the aim was to increase the proportion of pupils who achieved five good passes (grades A*–C) in subjects taken for the General Certificate of Secondary Education (GCSE) at the age of 16. Some progress was made in the first term when the proportion of pupils reaching this standard rose from 46.3 per cent in 1998, to 50 per cent in 2001. The government's target from 2002 was to achieve average annual increases of 2 per cent, but despite some progress—53.4 per cent of pupils achieved five good passes in 2004—this target was missed.[30]

Organizational reform played a significant role in the government's attempts to raise standards. During the post-war era, the British secondary schooling system moved away from academic selection to the egalitarian ideal of "comprehensive" education. Most people in the Labour Party saw comprehensive schools as a way of levelling the playing field. They believed that allowing schools to select children on the basis of academic ability meant consigning most children from poorer backgrounds to bad schools. The middle classes were better able to tutor their children and prepare them for entrance exams to the old elite grammar schools. Those who advocated the comprehensive system aimed to provide education for all regardless of background and facilitate social mobility.

In practice, however, there was always a wide variation in the quality of comprehensive schools. Those in middle-class areas tended to be very good whereas those in inner-cities were less impressive. Any move away from the comprehensive ideal was controversial in the Labour Party, so the government encouraged schools to specialize in some particular area, such as the arts, science, languages or sport. These specialist schools could select up to 10 per cent of their pupils on the basis of aptitude for these disciplines, but all would have to teach the national curriculum and offer a broad education to pupils. The theory was that excellence in one field (such as the arts) would spill over into academic attainment and push up standards. By 2004 60 per cent of secondary schools were such specialist schools. In the inner cities the government proclaimed new "city academies" as replacements for failing schools. These relied partly on private funding by business or religious organizations and would number 200 by 2010.[31]

The government also began to emphasize parental choice as a means of improving standards. Low-quality schools would not be able to attract enough pupils and would end up closing. Good-quality schools, by contrast, were encouraged to expand or take over failing schools. However, the notion of choice conflicted with Labour's taboo of academic selection, and critics feared it would be schools, not parents, who did the "choosing", with the middle classes benefiting. Moreover, most good schools were unwilling to expand because doing so might destroy the ethos that had helped them succeed.[32]

It was in the field of university funding, however, that the government faced one of its toughest battles. During its first term, Labour introduced flat-rate tuition fees for domestic students. These were set at a low level (a maximum of £1,125 per year in 2003–2004), and the government continued to subsidize students. However, the subsidy and fees covered only about half the cost of educating an undergraduate student. The top universities successfully pleaded that they were under enormous financial strain and that more money was desperately needed if the government were to achieve its target of getting 50 per cent of school-leavers to university by 2010. It was politically impossible to fund this expansion by raising taxes, so the government decided to allow universities to charge variable fees, up to a maximum of £3,000 per year.

Even with the maximum fee of £3,000 per year, the government would still be subsidizing the system to the tune of £4,000 per student. The policy was bitterly opposed, however, by the National Union of Students (NUS), the other main parties and substantial sections of the Labour Party. The NUS claimed top-up fees would deter students from poorer backgrounds, while the middle classes, who dominated the university system, believed that students had a right to free or cheap education.

Many Labour MPs, led by Nick Brown, a former minister and ally of the chancellor, were also unhappy. They extracted concessions that diluted the government's plans, including a promise that the maximum fee would not rise before 2009 and that parliamentary approval would be required before it was allowed to rise. Furthermore, non-repayable grants and bursaries would be available for poorer students, together with favourable loans for all. Fees would no longer be payable up-front, but instead would be repaid after graduation when the graduate started earning £15,000 per year. In the Commons vote in January 2004, seventy-two Labour MPs voted with the opposition, but the concessions proved just enough and the government squeaked home by five votes.

Public Services

Labour's approach to the public services combined a massive injection of funds and further market reforms. This combination was designed to avoid the danger of traditional tax-and-spend policies that might cause voters to question whether they were getting value for money. Such questions were asked with increasing frequency, however, during Labour's second term. In December 2003 a YouGov poll for the *Daily Telegraph* found dissatisfaction with Labour's performance. Fully 69 per cent believed that they paid too much tax and 79 per cent said that much government spending was wasted.[33]

By the middle of Labour's second term there was a striking difference between the positive news contained in government statistics and public perceptions about the public services. The slippage between the two was partly a product of media coverage which focused on "newsworthy" but unrepresentative issues such as hospital superbugs and disruptive schoolchildren. Noticeably less attention was devoted to genuine improvements in the public services, such as falling hospital waiting times. However, the slippage was also partly the product of the government's rhetoric. As Anthony King observes in Chapter 7, the government failed to find the right language to present its policies, using words such as "delivery" and "choice", which left many voters cold or confused. It also gained a reputation for spin and deceit, leaving others—even its own supporters—sceptical about government statistics purporting to demonstrate that things had got better.

Despite the government's problems with the public services, it was saved by the Conservatives' failure to capitalize on them. In the same YouGov poll cited above, only 22 per cent of respondents thought that taxes and services *should* be cut, which explained why the Conservatives sought to make a case for tax cuts funded by cuts in government waste. Voters were not convinced, however. Fully 60 per cent believed that taxes would also rise under a Conservative government.

Labour's market reforms in the public services attracted little attention among voters, though they sparked rows within the party. The decentralization and choice agenda in health and education questioned the egalitarian and statist ethos of Britain's public services. It is ironic that it was Labour—the party most associated with that ethos—that implemented these reforms, rather than the free-market Conservatives. Fears lingered among voters that the Tories wanted to introduce further charges for services. Just as "only Nixon could go to China", so only Labour could be trusted to reform the public services—even if voters were not always impressed with the results.

Drawbridge Issues:
Crime, Immigration, Terrorism and Europe

Security issues have assumed a far greater importance to British voters since 9/11 (see Table 1.1 above). This proposition applies not just to terrorism but to other so-called drawbridge issues that incorporate a fear of some (internal or external) threat to personal or national security and a desire to take shelter from a dangerous world by pulling up the castle drawbridge. Crime, anti-social behaviour, immigration and asylum, and Europe are the other main drawbridge issues. In Britain, these issues, with the exception of Europe, are the responsibility of the Home Office. For most of Tony Blair's second term, the post of home secretary was filled by David Blunkett, a straight-talking Yorkshireman, who exemplified the working-class authoritarianism of his native Sheffield. His character was to be a profoundly important influence on the government's response to all these issues.

Crime and Anti-social Behaviour

One of the paradoxes of criminal-justice policy in Britain is that the fear of crime has run ahead of the reality on the ground. Between 1997 and 2004, overall crime fell by 30 per cent, with bigger falls in burglary (42 per cent) and vehicle theft (40 per cent). Violent crime fell by 26 per cent.[34] However, the authoritative British Crime Survey consistently found that most people *believed* that crime was increasing.[35] Much of the blame again appeared to lie with the media, which focused on exceptional cases and reinforced the impression that the country was in the grip of a crime wave.

Rather than try to alter these perceptions by educating voters about the real risks, the government felt that it was imperative to address these fears. The political debate over crime, therefore, often boiled down to which party could recruit more policemen and put them on the beat. In that respect Labour delivered: in 2004 police numbers in England and Wales stood at a record 139,200, an increase of 15,000 in four years.[36] That may have had some effect on crime rates, though the latter were falling before the extra recruitment. It is likely that the strong economy played a more important role in reducing crime. Higher levels of employment and greater wealth made the risky gains of property crime less attractive.[37]

Despite falling crime rates and rising police numbers people continued to feel threatened by lower-level disorder that made their lives a misery. Labour MPs representing inner-city and urban areas, such as Blunkett, had long been made familiar with this phenomenon by the stream of complaints about it from their constituents.[38] Graffiti, noisy neighbours, drunkenness in town centres, gangs of teenagers hanging around on the streets—many of these problems were not criminal offences but were sources of exasperation and anger. They were collectively termed "anti-social behaviour" and the government made the battle against them a priority.

The most controversial weapon created by the government to deal with the problem was the anti-social behaviour order or ASBO. ASBOs are civil orders issued by magistrates at the request of the police or local authorities. They are most famously served on "yobs", or what the media call "neighbours from hell", who cause trouble in their localities but against whom the police have insufficient evidence to bring charges of criminal offences. ASBOs can be specially tailored for individual offenders, such as excluding yobs from particular streets or forbidding them from congregating with certain people. Those caught breaking the terms of an order face up to five years in prison. Some ASBOs have been served on children as young as 10. Despite criticisms from civil-liberties campaigners, ASBOs proved popular in deprived areas. Between 1999 and December 2004, 4,649 ASBOs were served in England and Wales.

Immigration and Asylum

On the broad issue of immigration, Labour's policy was fairly liberal, as dictated by the needs of the economy. Companies that could not fill vacancies, particularly skilled ones, from domestic or European Union (EU) applicants (who have the right to work in Britain), could apply for work permits for non-EU nationals. Such applications were increasingly waived through by a government concerned about shortages in certain sectors. In 1997 63,000 economic migrants and their dependents legally entered the United Kingdom. In 2003 there were 119,000 new entrants.

Another burst of immigration came following the accession to the EU of eight East European countries (plus Cyprus and Malta) on May 1, 2004. The government had initially said that no more than 13,000 migrants per year were expected to come to the United Kingdom, but by mid-2005 about 120,000 East Europeans had arrived. Their access to welfare benefits was severely restricted and they had to become self-supporting. Consequently, their presence became virtually a non-issue, and they filled important gaps in the service, construction and agricultural sectors, with about 80 per cent earning less than £6 per hour. Nevertheless, the government remained cautious about trumpeting the benefits of a liberal migration policy, and shortly before the election it responded to Conservative and media pressure by announcing that it would introduce a points system. The more highly-skilled applicants would gain more points and be more likely to have their applications accepted.

The attitude of British voters to economic migration appeared to be fairly relaxed, provided that migrants were self-supporting and not a burden on the state. In this respect, attitudes towards asylum-seekers were much tougher. The law prevents people seeking political asylum in Britain from undertaking paid employment until their claims have been processed, forcing them to rely on state benefits. Resentment of asylum-seekers grew, reinforced by suspicions that they were queue-jumpers for social housing and making large demands on public services. Wars, conflicts and political repression had greatly increased the number of asylum-seekers in the EU as a whole, but Britain was a particularly attractive destination. Tabloid newspapers such as the *Sun*, *Daily Mail* and *Daily Express* carried scare stories about asylum-seekers and there was a widespread feeling that Britain was seen as a "soft touch". Public anxiety was increased by the presence of a Red Cross refugee camp at Sangatte near Calais in northern France, which had been established because so many migrants used the town as a stop-over point on their way to Britain. Despite British pressure, the French government failed to close the camp. British anger came to a head on Christmas Day, 2001, when television news cameras showed hundreds of would-be asylum-seekers storming the Calais entrance to the Channel Tunnel. The French authorities were nowhere to be seen.

Such events, together with tabloid pressure, compelled the government to toughen its policy. Benefits for asylum-seekers were cut and would-be applicants were now required to apply for asylum as soon as was practicable—essentially, the moment they arrived in the United Kingdom—though the courts later ruled against the decision to deprive thousands of asylum-seekers of housing and benefits because they had not applied quickly enough. The government also reduced legal aid for asylum-seekers appealing against rejected claims and built new detention centres to hold rejected applicants before they were deported. Technology was developed to spot people entering the country while hiding in the back of lorries, British immigration officials began operating in northern France to check papers, and the French government eventually closed the Sangatte camp.

The influx peaked in the final three months of 2002, when nearly 23,000 people claimed asylum. In February 2003, Tony Blair pledged to halve the number of applications within six months. He hit this target and the numbers continued to fall; in the first quarter of 2005, there were 7,000 applications. Moreover, applications were dealt with much more quickly—80 per cent within two months—thus reducing a large backlog of cases that had built up. Finally, the proportion of applications being rejected rose significantly, from about 65 per cent in early 2002 to 85–90 per cent three years later. These measures helped Britain achieve the biggest fall in new asylum applications of any EU country.[39] The continued political salience of immigration, however, suggested that the public remained unconvinced.

Terrorism and Civil Liberties

Following the 9/11 attacks in the United States, the Blair government felt compelled to seek a new balance between individual liberties and national security. It introduced tough legislation to assist it in combating terrorism planned and/or carried out in Britain. Although the government had public opinion on its side it faced fierce opposition from civil-rights and Muslim lobby groups. It also encountered opposition from a group that had traditionally considered itself above politics, the judiciary.

The Anti-Terrorism, Crime and Security Act of 2001 gave the government the power to order the indefinite detention without trial of foreign nationals suspected of terrorist links, where the evidence would either be insufficiently strong to result in conviction, came from wire-tapping (inadmissible in British courts) or came from sources the government did not want to reveal. Deportation of such suspects was not possible if they were likely to face persecution in their home countries, but the security services had warned that some suspects posed such a risk to national security that they had to be detained. The provisions of the act made it necessary for the government to opt out of Article 5 of the European Convention on Human Rights (incorporated into law in Britain as the Human Rights Act 1998), guaranteeing the right to liberty. Fourteen men were promptly arrested and imprisoned in the Belmarsh maximum security prison.

In 2004 the House of Lords, the highest court in the land, ruled that such detentions were unlawful and that the government's measures were disproportionate. The law lords also found the act discriminatory, as it applied only to foreign nationals. In response, the government freed on bail the remaining detainees (some had been released earlier). It later passed a new Prevention of Terrorism Act, after a marathon battle in parliament, shortly before the 2005 election. This act enabled the home secretary to apply to judges for control orders on suspects, whether British or foreign. The new orders were immediately imposed on the men who had been detained under the old law.

The battle against Islamist terrorism created acute problems for the government. Most suspects arrested under the new legislation were released and there were few convictions, leading some critics to accuse the authorities of "Islamophobia". The police believed the tactic gave them an insight into terrorist networks and helped to disrupt their activities by sowing suspicion among them.[40] The government also faced demands to secure the release of a handful of British-born suspects held by the United States in the Guantanamo Bay detention camp. Eventually it did, and on their return to Britain they were released without charge.

Europe

European integration is a drawbridge issue because it concerns questions of national identity and the extent to which people are willing to permit non-British institutions to intervene in domestic politics. The government's room for manoeuvre was constrained by a Eurosceptic press, Conservative opposition and public opinion. The most important issue facing the government was the adoption of the single currency, the euro. The government was, in principle, in favour of monetary union, provided that a series of economic tests were passed. It had committed itself to making a judgement on the tests by June 2003. That month the chancellor announced that they had not been passed and Britain would not adopt the euro, though that could change if the tests were passed in the future.

Labour's long-standing position had been to hold a referendum before joining the euro zone. Polls regularly showed two-to-one majorities against joining, ensuring that the government would face an uphill task in a referendum. The promise of a referendum saved the government from political damage because Eurosceptic voters—and Labour-supporting Eurosceptic newspapers such as the *Sun*—knew that a vote for Labour was not a vote for the euro. Conservative attempts to claim otherwise during the 2001 general election went unheeded. Indeed, after 2001 the Conservatives talked about Europe less frequently, because voters were more concerned about other issues. Constantly raising the subject of Europe simply made them appear obsessive.

A second major development in European policy emerged in 2004 when Blair was forced to concede a referendum on the proposed European constitution. This constitution would incorporate existing EU treaties but would also advance integration. Blair initially claimed that it would merely "tidy up" existing treaties and, therefore, did not warrant a referendum. His resolve wilted amid tabloid attacks and a fear that the Conservatives could profit in the European Parliamentary elections in June 2004. As with the euro, the promise of a referendum helped to neutralize the threat in the short term. Polls showed majorities against the constitution and since the treaty had to be approved by 2006, the government was left with little time to reverse public opinion. Alone among the drawbridge issues, Europe declined in salience in Labour's second term (see Table 1.1). That was almost certainly a consequence of Labour's concession of referendums and the Conservatives' reluctance to campaign on the issue.

Raising the Drawbridge

Centre-left parties have often been associated with liberal policies on security issues, but Labour ministers believed they could pay an enormous electoral price if they were seen as "soft" on crime, immigration and terrorism. The tabloid press exerted pressure on the government in relation to crime and asylum. Since the government took newspapers such as the *Sun* and *Daily Mail* very seriously, it felt compelled to adopt authoritarian rhetoric. Crime and immigration were also virtually the only issues on which the Conservatives offered strong opposition to Labour. The government often found itself having to respond to Conservative announcements with its own "tough" measures. Yet even this strategy was not enough. By the end of Labour's second term, voters preferred the Tories on crime and immigration (see Figure 1.6). These issues posed a real threat to the government given their increasing salience (see Table 1.1).

The government's concern to sound tough was understandable in the face of sustained pressure from the Conservatives and the media, as well as the evidence of the polls. The same policies that appealed to the *Sun* and *Daily Mail*, however, worried other groups: these included parts of the judi-

Figure 1.6 Party Ratings on Eight Issues

Q. Which party would handle each of these problems best?

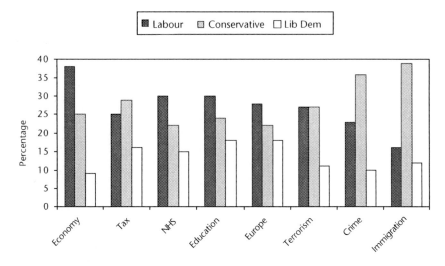

Source: YouGov, "Current Political Issues", poll for the *Daily Telegraph,* March 2005, http://www.yougov.com/archives/pdf/TEL050101010_1.pdf.
Note: The figure shows the percentage of respondents citing each party.

ciary, liberal lobby groups such as Liberty, the *Guardian* and *Independent* newspapers, broadcasters, the Liberal Democrats, many Labour back-benchers and Muslim organizations. Indeed, many of these forces were among those pressing the government to seek the repatriation of the Guantanamo detainees.

David Blunkett's response to such groups was typically direct and undiplomatic. He repeatedly criticized judges for frustrating efforts to deal with terrorism, crime, anti-social behaviour and asylum. The judiciary used their powers under the Human Rights Act (which Labour had itself introduced in 1998) to assess the lawfulness of ministerial actions and the compatibility of legislation with human rights. This judicial activism was most notable in the case of the Anti-Terrorism, Crime and Security Act. Fortunately for the government, its anti-terrorism strategy had left the Conservatives divided. Michael Howard favoured tougher measures than those advocated by Labour, whereas libertarians were worried about the erosion of civil liberties. These confused signals may have reduced the appeal of the opposition.

The government's main problem in relation to drawbridge issues was that it was caught between the liberal elite (which pressured it not to erode civil liberties) and the authoritarian right (which was never convinced that it could be "tough enough"). Hard-line measures on asylum and terrorism impressed most voters but were opposed by a significant minority. The result was that the government's credibility with voters was damaged because opposition from the courts and civil-liberties groups ensured that it could not always deliver on its tough promises.

Discord in the Government

Party Troubles

When Tony Blair became prime minister he warned his party that in government it faced hard choices. His warning was interpreted to mean that, just as a Labour government had done in the 1970s, his government would want to implement policies that Labour activists would find hard to stomach. In this earlier period, there was a breakdown in relations between the government and party, with activists regularly denouncing ministers at Labour's annual conference. In the event, however, there was no such breakdown in relations between the Blair government and the party. One reason was that the party after the mid-1990s was more tightly managed but, in addition, the party had become more disciplined after eighteen years in opposition.[41] The Iraq War caused enormous tensions in the Labour Party but it did not tear it apart. There was a large back-bench rebellion and the Labour Party's membership in the country fell, but there did not appear to be any serious threat to Blair's position.

Nevertheless, there were signs of a partial breakdown in discipline in the Parliamentary Labour Party. They were evident from the first session of the 2001–2005 parliament, when there were seventy-six back-bench rebellions, the highest ever for a Labour government's first parliamentary session after a general election. By 2003 that figure had risen to 141. Most consisted of fewer than ten MPs but 15 per cent consisted of thirty or more, on issues such as Iraq, foundation hospitals and asylum. The PLP often appeared to be a coalition of three separate parties: the payroll vote comprising ministers and private parliamentary secretaries (who had to vote for the government or resign), together with those who aspired to ministerial office, who were loyal to the government; a hard core of thirty to forty unreconstructed left-wingers who were inveterate rebels; and a middle group of MPs who were often ex-ministers and who normally supported the government but sometimes joined the rebels.[42]

A traditional source of difficulties for Labour governments has been Labour-affiliated trade unions. Before 1997, three of the previous five Labour governments were wrecked on the rock of party–union conflict. Blair's second-term programme for the public services also sparked disagreements with public-sector unions. From 2001 onwards most elected left-wing leaders who were increasingly prepared to criticize government policy on issues such as foundation hospitals and the PFI. Some unions, such as the GMB general workers' union, reduced their funding to the party in protest, a development virtually unique in Labour's history. Yet there was only one major schism between the government and any union: a strike by fire-fighters in 2002, when the government faced down a 40 per cent pay demand by the Labour-affiliated Fire Brigades Union (FBU) and insisted on modernization of the service to eliminate inefficient practices.[43]

Blair did not alter his rhetoric about the need to reform the public services. His speech at Labour's 2004 annual conference warned his opponents, "I've not got a reverse gear".[44] Nevertheless, the government moved to assuage union fears with a "concordat" at the July 2004 meeting of Labour's National Policy Forum in Warwick, where assurances were given on public-sector workers' rights. It was enough to persuade most unions to make large donations to Labour's 2005 election fund.

Trouble at the Top: Blair and Brown

The biggest challenge to the government's stability came from within itself. The relationship at the top of the government between Tony Blair and Gordon Brown is unique in the modern era. No other modern chancellor has enjoyed such power over domestic policy. No other modern prime minister has had to endure such a powerful rival often frustrating his plans and always waiting to take his job. Much of the tension could be put down to the two men's clash of ambitions but during Labour's second term policy differences came increasingly to the fore. Some of the prime minister's advisers suspected that the chancellor's allies on the back benches were trying to sabotage key policies on the public services. Blair's problem was that Brown could not be sacked or even deprived of any of his power. Brown would foment discord on the back benches and in the party at large, where he enjoyed a large following. The government's reputation for economic competence, moreover, was almost entirely associated with the person of the chancellor, and if he left the Treasury the financial markets might lose confidence in Labour's ability to manage the economy.[45]

These tensions threatened to undermine policy cohesion. That was most clearly evident in policy-making on the health and education, with Blair eager to push a markets-and-choice agenda whereas Brown preferred spending increases and central controls. Blairite ministers, fearing that their plans for market-based reforms would be unpicked by the Treasury, were careful not to give too much away too early. Consequently, they later ran into difficulties with MPs and activists because they had not prepared the ground. The result was that flagship policies such as tuition fees and foundation hospitals had to be diluted. In an attempt to claw back control over domestic policy from the Treasury, Blair instructed ministers in key public-service departments to draw up five-year plans for policy and delivery.[46] Ministers worked closely with Blair and the Treasury was not involved. The published plans were more in keeping with the Blairite choice agenda, particularly in health. Nevertheless, policy on the public services lacked clarity because the two men at the top disagreed over whether schools and hospitals should have more autonomy or be subjected to tight central control.

Blair and Brown also had disagreements on the single currency. Blair had long wanted Britain to adopt the euro but Brown wielded a veto because the issue fell within his economic-policy sphere. In 2002 some of Blair's advisers thought that a referendum on adopting the euro could be held in 2003 or 2004.[47] However, the Treasury was responsible for determining whether the economic tests had been satisfied. Brown was sceptical about the benefits of British membership and it was no surprise when he told parliament in 2003 that the tests had not been passed.

One of Blair's main weapons against the chancellor's influence over policy was his power of patronage. He sought to ensure that ministers he could trust were put in charge of key departments. In 2001 he appointed the Blairites, Alan Milburn and Stephen Byers, to health and transport respectively, while another ally, Estelle Morris, went to education. David Blunkett replaced Jack Straw at the Home Office. However, during the course of the parliament, Blair lost all of these allies.

Byers resigned as transport secretary in May 2002 following revelations about the activities of "spin doctors" in his department. He was replaced by Alistair Darling, who was close to the chancellor. The resignations of Morris and Milburn were stranger. Morris stood down in October 2002 because she had faced criticism that she lacked the skills to do the job. Milburn resigned as health secretary for personal reasons in June 2003. He was the driving force behind foundation hospitals and the *bête noir* of the chancellor because of his enthusiasm for market forces in the NHS. He returned briefly to the cabinet to head Labour's general-election campaign, much to Brown's irritation. Morris and Milburn were replaced by the Blair loyalists John Reid and Charles Clarke. Finally Blunkett was forced to resign as home secretary in December 2004 after allegations that he had instructed civil servants to speed-up the visa application of his lover's nanny. He was replaced by Clarke, whose old job at education was taken by another Blairite, Ruth Kelly. On top of these resignations, Blair also lost his trusted communications chief, Alastair Campbell, in 2004. With each ally that departed, Blair appeared more isolated.

Yet Brown was never confident enough to challenge Blair for the leadership, probably because he feared being blamed for any resulting damage to the party and the government. He contented himself with thinly-veiled attacks on Blair, most famously at Labour's 2003 annual conference when he told delegates, "We are best when we are Labour", ostentatiously omitting the word "New".[48] Such incidents were symptomatic of a general deterioration in Blair and Brown's relationship during Labour's second term. At one point, the deputy prime minister, John Prescott, felt compelled to arrange a dinner with the two men in order to thrash out differences. In the spring of 2004, Blair had a notorious "wobble" in which he allegedly considered resigning amid fears about his health and the emergence of pictures of American soldiers abusing

Iraqi prisoners in Abu Ghraib prison.[49] He recovered and to Brown's chagrin announced that he would lead Labour into the coming general election and, if re-elected, would serve a full third term—but then not fight a fourth election. Brown was widely quoted as telling the prime minister: "There is nothing that you could ever say to me now that I could ever believe".[50]

Voters were aware of the rows between the Blair and Brown camps but they were split over whether the government's performance was hindered as a result. A YouGov poll shortly before the 2005 election found that 49 per cent of respondents believed that the Blair–Brown feuding made little or no difference to the government's ability to take the right decision, though 44 per cent believed it did.[51] The same poll found that 49 per cent of respondents thought Brown was doing a better job as chancellor than Blair was as prime minister (just 19 per cent thought the opposite); Blair's asset rating (percentage believing he was an asset for Labour minus those who thought he was a liability) was -10 whereas Brown's was +46; and 39 per cent thought Brown would make a better prime minister, compared with 30 per cent who thought Blair would. Blair's only comfort was that Labour voters preferred Blair to Brown by 61 per cent to 28 per cent.

Brown's greater popularity among voters presented a threat to Blair's position. However, as the 2005 election approached, the two men put aside their differences and campaigned together. Each wanted Labour to win a third big majority—Blair to enable him to govern effectively during a third term, Brown to ensure that he inherited a strong position if he did finally take over from Blair. Their ensuing bonhomie elicited much mirth among watching journalists.

Conclusion

On 6 February 2005 Tony Blair became the longest-serving Labour prime minister ever, beating Harold Wilson's combined spells in office, and three months later he was the first Labour leader to win three consecutive general elections. Blair modernized his own party, beat the Conservatives into submission, and transformed the face of British politics. However, it is the events of 2003 for which he will probably be best remembered. The Iraq War tested his resilience to breaking point and in the process eroded public trust in him. If spin and exaggeration were perennial features of New Labour governance, Iraq's WMD marked its nadir in that respect.

The public's loss of trust in the government, which in truth occurred long before the invasion of Iraq, also coloured perceptions of Blair's efforts to improve security and public services in Britain. Money was lavished on health and education, and the government oversaw a fall in crime and, eventually, in asylum-seekers entering Britain. Blair also broke with Labour's past in introducing market forces into the public services, resulting in disputes with Brown. However, many of the government's achievements went unacknowledged by voters, a debilitating legacy of spin.

Yet despite being distrusted and unloved, the government rarely looked in serious electoral danger during its second term. It consistently led the Conservatives in the opinion polls. Apart from causing the government occasional discomfort over asylum, the Tories were largely out of the game and not seen as a government-in-waiting. The Liberal Democrats damaged Labour over Iraq but were never going to supplant it in office. Labour's strong electoral and parliamentary position may even have given left-wing and Brownite critics licence to attack the government more frequently than they would have had the Conservatives looked capable of winning a general election.

The result of Labour's dominance and the opposition's weakness was that most of the major debates on policy, especially domestic policy, were conducted *within* the governing party between Blairites and Brownites. Yet Blair's announcement that he would not contest a further election if re-elected in 2005 and his decision to campaign during the election alongside the chancellor signalled to voters that if they voted for Blair they would eventually get Brown as prime minister. It was a fitting reminder that despite internal disagreements over policy, New Labour was always first and foremost an *electoral* project. Blair and Brown were agreed on one thing at least: it was much better to argue in government than to flounder in opposition.

Notes

1. See Caroline Kennedy-Pipe and Rhiannon Vickers, "Britain in the International Arena", in Patrick Dunleavy, Andrew Gamble, Richard Heffernan and Gillian Peele, eds, *Developments in British Politics 7* (Basingstoke: Palgrave Macmillan, 2003), pp. 321–37. For more general reflections on foreign policy in the post-9/11 world, see the debate between Robert Cooper, *The Breaking of Nations: Order and Chaos in the Twenty-First Century* (London: Atlantic Books, 2003), and Robert Kagan, *Paradise and Power: America and Europe in the New World Order* (London: Atlantic Books, 2003).
2. Jim Buller, "Foreign and European Policy", in Steve Ludlam and Martin J. Smith, eds, *Governing as New Labour: Policy and Politics under Blair* (Basingstoke: Palgrave Macmillan, 2004), pp. 193–210, at p. 206.
3. Anthony Seldon, *Tony Blair* (London: Free Press, 2005), p. 597 and p. 682.
4. See "Hutton Report—'Sexing up' the Dossier—Not Guilty", and "Hutton and the BBC—Auntie Goes Down", *The Economist*, January 31, 2004.
5. "Intelligence Failures—The Weapons That Weren't", *The Economist*, July 17, 2005.
6. "Sincere Deceivers", *The Economist*, July 17, 2005.
7. I thank Ivor Crewe for providing the polling data in Figure 1.2.
8. Anthony King, ed., *British Political Opinion, 1937–2000: The Gallup Polls* (London: Politico's, 2001), pp. 197–8. Later data are from YouGov, "Political Trackers 2003–2005", for the *Daily Telegraph*, http://www.yougov.com/archives/pdf/TEL020101018_24.pdf.
9. See YouGov, "Political Trackers 2003–2005", for the *Daily Telegraph*.
10. See Labour's Web site at http://www.labour.org.uk/index.php?id=news&ux_news_id=ac04tb.
11. See Anthony King, "Britain's Constitutional Revolution", in Anthony King, ed., *Britain at the Polls, 2001* (Chatham, NJ: Chatham House, 2002), pp. 45–67.

12. For a critical review of the Blair government's second-term policies, see David Coates, *Prolonged Labour: The Slow Birth of New Labour Britain* (Basingstoke: Palgrave Macmillan, 2005).

13. NICs are paid by employees (and employers, as well as the self-employed) along with income tax. NICs are the remnants of a social-insurance system introduced in 1911 under which contributions entitled people to social-security benefits and state old-age pensions. Nowadays, NICs are, for most people, hardly distinguishable from income tax.

14. Anthony King, "Few are convinced that things will get better", *Daily Telegraph*, April 19, 2002.

15. The euro zone consists of the twelve countries that have adopted the single currency: Austria, Belgium, Finland, France, Germany, Greece, Ireland, Italy, Luxembourg, the Netherlands, Portugal and Spain.

16. House of Commons Library, Research Papers, Economic Indicators, 01/109, 02/70, 03/81, 04/87, 05/53.

17. Office of National Statistics, *Social Trends*, No 35 (2005), p. 181, p. 177.

18. Initially, the Treasure said the economic cycle had begun in 1999 and was due to end in 2006. However, two months after the 2005 general election, and following data revisions by the Office of National Statistics, the chancellor announced that the economic cycle had in fact started in 1997. The effect was to incorporate budgetary surpluses from 1997 to 1999 into the calculations, making it likely that the "golden rule" would be met. This move was greeted with derision from the opposition parties.

19. "Public Spending—The Firing Line", *The Economist*, July 17, 2004.

20. Martin J. Smith, "The Core Executive and the Modernization of Central Government", in Patrick Dunleavy, Andrew Gamble, Richard Heffernan and Gillian Peele, eds, *Developments in British Politics 7* (Basingstoke: Palgrave Macmillan, 2003), pp. 60–81, at pp. 68–9.

21. Rajiv Prabhakar, "New Labour and the Reform of Public Services", in Steve Ludlam and Martin J. Smith, eds, *Governing as New Labour: Policy and Politics under Blair* (Basingstoke: Palgrave Macmillan, 2004), pp. 161–76, at p.166.

22. Polly Toynbee and David Walker, *Better or Worse? Has Labour Delivered?* (London: Bloomsbury, 2005), p. 16.

23. Toynbee and Walker, *Better or Worse?* pp. 12, 45; House of Commons Library, Research Paper, Social Indicators, 05/44, p. 27.

24. "National Health Service—This May Hurt", *The Economist*, January 8, 2005; "Health—New Blood for the Health Service", and "Getting the NHS Right", *The Economist*, April 23, 2005.

25. Rajiv Prabhakar, "Do Public Interest Companies Form a Third Way within Public Services?" *British Journal of Politics and International Relations*, 6 (2004), 353–69.

26. Toynbee and Walker, *Better or Worse?* pp. 22–3.

27. Yougov, "Party Leadership and the NHS", poll for the *Sunday Times*, May 2004, http://www.yougov.com/archives/pdf/STI040101001_2.pdf.

28. "British Public Services—Has Tony Wasted Your Money?" *The Economist*, July 10, 2004.

29. Toynee and Walker, *Better or Worse?* pp. 90–2.

30. Department for Education and Skills, Autumn Performance Report 2004: Achievement against Public Service Agreement Targets, 2000–2004, p. 11.

31. Toynee and Walker, *Better or Worse?* pp. 97–100.

32. " 'Education—Much More to Do', British Election 2005: A Special Briefing", *The Economist*, April 9, 2005.

33. YouGov, "Taxes and the Public Services", poll for the *Daily Telegraph*, December 2003, http://www.yougov.com/archives/pdf/TEL020101041_1.pdf.

34. Home Office Statistical Bulletin 10/04, July 2004: Crime in England and Wales, 2003/2004, Table 2.01, p. 21.
35. Home Office Statistical Bulletin 10/04, pp. 16–17.
36. House of Commons Library, Social Indicators, Research Paper 05/44, pp. 3–4.
37. " 'Crime—Toughing It Out', British Election 2005: A Special Briefing", *The Economist,* April 9, 2005.
38. Toynee and Walker, *Better or Worse?* p. 224.
39. Toynee and Walker, *Better or Worse?* p. 209. Detailed statistics on asylum since 2001 can be found in Home Office, Asylum Statistics: 1st Quarter 2005, United Kingdom, 2nd edn, Table 1; and 1st Quarter 2004, Table 1.
40. "Domestic Terrorism—A Bigger Fish", *The Economist,* August 7, 2004.
41. See Thomas Quinn, *Modernising the Labour Party: Organisational Change since 1983* (Basingstoke: Palgrave Macmillan, 2004).
42. The data in this paragraph are from Philip Cowley and Mark Stuart, "When Sheep Bark: The Parliamentary Labour Party, 2001–2003", in Roger Scully, Justin Fisher, Paul Webb and David Broughton, eds, *British Elections and Parties Review 14* (London: Frank Cass, 2004), pp. 211–29.
43. The FBU eventually voted to disaffiliate from Labour in June 2004. Its exit was preceded by that of the Rail, Maritime and Transport (RMT) union, which was expelled for a breach of party rules in February 2004.
44. "Brimming certainty gives way to painful humility", *Guardian,* September 29, 2004.
45. Among the most important books on Blair and Brown are: Seldon, *Blair*; Andrew Rawnsley, *Servants of the People: The Inside Story of New Labour* (London: Penguin, 2001); and James Naughtie, *The Rivals: Blair and Brown—The Intimate Story of a Political Marriage* (London: Fourth Estate, 2002).
46. Andrew Rawnsley, "Whose lead will Labour follow?" *Observer,* March 21, 2004.
47. Seldon, *Blair,* p. 638.
48. Seldon, *Blair,* p. 684.
49. Seldon, *Blair,* pp. 627–55.
50. Toby Helm, "Allegations, deals and denials in the feud that never ends", *Daily Telegraph,* January 10, 2005.
51. YouGov, "Tony Blair and Gordon Brown", poll for the *Daily Telegraph,* January 2005, http://www.yougov.com/archives/pdf/TEL050101003_2.pdf.

2

The Conservative Party: The Politics of Panic

Philip Norton

Conservatives who stayed up beyond midnight on May 5, 2005, experienced something they had not seen for twenty-two years: a television screen that continued to flash "Conservative Gain" throughout the night. The gains included the iconic seat of Enfield Southgate—the seat memorably lost by Michael Portillo, then secretary of state for defence and torchbearer for the Thatcherite right, in 1997. When the results were in, the party had made a net gain of more than thirty seats. The party was moving forward.

However, the party was not moving that far forward. The outcome of the 2005 general election was the party's third worst election result for a century. Turnout was a mere 61.5 per cent, and only one in three electors who went to the polls voted Conservative: in other words, only one in five of those registered to vote actually voted for the Tories, as the Conservatives are familiarly known. The party, moreover, came third among voters aged under 35. Following the election, the party leader, Michael Howard, emulated his two predecessors and announced that he was standing down, though he deferred his retirement to allow consideration of possible new rules for electing the leader. His replacement would be the fifth person to lead the party in less than ten years. In the twentieth century, the party only had one leader (Austen Chamberlain) who had never become prime minister. In the first five years of the twenty-first century, three further leaders (William Hague, Iain Duncan Smith and Michael Howard) were added to that select club.

There are thus two questions to be addressed about the party's performance in the 2005 general election. First, what explains its "success"? Why was it able to make gains in the election? Second, what explains its "failure"? Why was it still in a worse position, in terms of seats, than the Labour Party in 1983?

The party's success in the twentieth century has been attributed to four factors specific to the party and one external to the party.[1] Those that were specific to the party contributed to its image as a party of governance. They comprised competence in handling the affairs of the nation (especially its public finances), unity, strong leadership and a sense of public service. The factor external to the party was the nature of its principal opponent party, which has often split at times opportune to the Conservatives.

The most important of these factors was the first: the key to the party's success has been in showing that it knows how to handle the affairs of the nation—that it was, in short, a "safe pair of hands". The other factors reinforced this perception. Voters consequently rewarded the party, engaging in prospective and not simply retrospective voting: that is, voting for what the party is expected to deliver rather than simply on the basis of what it has done in the past.[2] These factors combined to produce extended periods of success. Indeed, following the 1992 general election, Anthony King was able to draw attention to the extent to which the Tories' success had generated, in Giovanni Sartori's terminology, a "predominant-party system".[3]

The problem for the party in the twenty-first century has been that the tables have been turned. At the start of the new century, not only did New Labour stand accused of stealing the Tories' clothes in terms of policy, but it also acquired those features that had made the Conservative Party the "in" party for most of the previous century. It was Labour that appeared to be the party of governance. Completing the circle, it was the Labour Party that had strong leadership, was united and faced an opponent that split at a time opportune for the emergence, and electoral success, of New Labour.

This framework also provides the basis for explaining the Conservative performance in 2005. The principal reason for its success was to be found in the variable external to the party. Its relative position improved courtesy of Labour's unpopularity with its own supporters. Former Labour supporters either stayed at home or voted for Liberal Democrat candidates.[4] The Conservative Party's share of the vote increased by a mere 0.6 points. The decline in Labour's share of the poll in marginal seats where Conservatives were the principal challengers resulted in the Tory gains. The failure to achieve a significant increase in its share of the vote, however, meant that the gains represented only a minority of the party's declared target seats. The party appeared to benefit from the actions of the Labour government but not from its own efforts.

The Conservative appeal to the electorate was showing signs of diminishing in the late 1980s. There was an economic recession and the party was split badly on a number of key issues, including European integration. Fears that the party would lose the next election under its existing leader prompted Tory MPs to replace Margaret Thatcher in 1990 with a largely untried cabinet minister, John Major. The strategy succeeded. Electors blamed Thatcher for the country's economic problems, not her successor, and Major led the party to a narrow, and largely unexpected, election victory in 1992.[5] However, within five months of that election, the political landscape was transformed. Britain's ignominious withdrawal from the Exchange Rate Mechanism (ERM) in September of that year prompted a collapse of trust in the Tories as a safe pair of hands in handling the nation's finances. Labour established a massive lead in the opinion polls, which persisted until well into its second term in government.[6] The Conservative government's unpopularity was reinforced by internal divisions over European integration, a beleaguered leader, and accusations of "sleaze".[7] Labour had reinvented itself as a new and electable party and so the tables were turned. In 1997, the Tories suffered their worst election defeat in modern political history.

In the 1997 election, many voters cast a judgement on what the Tories had done in office. The challenge for the party since 1997 has been to get voters to think what a future Conservative government might achieve or be like. It has been noted that it is more rational for voters to rely more on past actions, which are more tangible than future promises.[8] The challenge for the party—as for Labour after its rejection following the Winter of Discontent of 1978—has thus been a formidable one. However, in trying to get voters interested in what it has to offer, it has tried too hard.

The essential dilemma for the party in the parliament of 1997 to 2001 was that, on the one hand, it was desperate to get back into government—it was not used to being in opposition—and, on the other, it had no clear strategy for achieving that goal. Voters were not inclined to trust the party. New Labour moreover, and crucially, had invaded the Tories' traditional territory. It too favoured market solutions to economic problems, as well as parental choice in education, and it too supported a tough stance on law and order. The Tories, then, had to decide whether to attempt to snatch back their clothes from New Labour or to fashion a new wardrobe. Should they accept the basic approach of the government and say that they could do better? Or should they seek to put "clear blue water" between the two? Complicating the debate was the extent to which, under Margaret Thatcher, the party had adopted a more ideological stance. Strands of thought within the parliamentary party were more clearly delineated, and adherents of these approaches more willing to push for their particular solutions to the nation's problems.

The party thus entered opposition unsure of how to respond to New Labour. Its problem since 1997 has been that it has never managed to overcome this uncertainty. Successive leaders have had to seek electoral victory without an agreed philosophical bedrock. There has been a reluctance, in the words of The Times columnist Peter Riddell to be bold; innovative proposals, he noted, were prone to be toned down in response to findings from focus groups.[9] Seeking clear blue water did not mean looking for new oceans. Instead, leaders have resorted to identifying particular policies that they think will prove popular; when these have failed to make an impact in the polls, they have tried others. The harder the party has tried to curry support, the less obvious it has been to electors what it stands for.

The party after 2001 repeated the mistakes it made after 1997. Under William Hague's leadership, the party tried to re-engage with the people, attracting their interest and offering a vision for the future. When initial attempts to generate policies that resonated with electors failed, a new set of policy documents was generated.[10] Former chancellor of the exchequer, Lord Howe of Aberavon, noted that the party needed fresh positions: "That certainly doesn't require another bible of detail on everything under the sun, such as the Common Sense Revolution document".[11] Attempts to re-launch the party contributed to the impression of failed attempt following failed attempt. Electors had no clear view of what the party stood for and where it was going; the generation of new policies itself contributed to the impression of opportunism, the party appeared to jump on passing bandwagons, by expressing support for Tony Martin (a farmer who was jailed for shooting and killing a burglar) and the fuel protestors in 2000.[12] When there was little change in the opinion polls and as the next election loomed, the strategy of the leadership was to fall back on what was assumed to be its "core support", comprising right-wing electors who could be mobilized on a number of key issues, such as Europe, immigration and "family values". The result was an election failure on a par with that of 1997. On the face of it, the 2001 election was a standstill election. For the Conservatives, it was worse than that. It suggested that former Tory voters had not only voted for Labour in 1997 but that they had done so again in 2001, further weakening their attachment to the Tory Party. It also suggested that a future Conservative victory would require three, rather than two, general elections, leaving the party in the wilderness for at least a dozen years.

In the 2001 to 2005 parliament, the party emulated what it had done in the previous parliament. When, under a new leader, the opinion polls continued to show the Tories making no headway, the party thrashed around for attractive policies. The parliamentary party showed even greater impatience than in the previous parliament and, in mid-parliament, replaced their leader. Expectations of the new leader were high, but the pattern under previous leaders was repeated. Just as William Hague had failed to generate "a big idea", so his successor failed to produce a clear vision for the future. When the opinion polls failed to deliver a Conservative lead, and the 2005 election neared, the leadership appealed again to the party's core vote. In so doing, it helped mobilize Tory voters but also had the effect of alienating those whom the party needed to deliver victory.[13] The consequence was to push back the prospect of victory by yet another general election.

Changing Leaders

The party, in short, proved prone to panic in the face of negative opinion polls. The most significant manifestation of the politics of panic was the party's change of leader halfway through the parliament. When policies failed to produce a shift in the opinion polls, Tory MPs opted to change the leader.

Winston Churchill once observed, "The loyalties which centre on number one are enormous. If he trips he must be sustained. If he makes mistakes they must be covered. If he sleeps he must not be wantonly disturbed. If he is no good, he must be pole axed".[14] Folklore has held that Tory leaders who were no good went after receiving a visit from "the men in grey suits", a reference to the members of the executive of the 1922 Committee, the body comprising all Tory MPs, other than the leader, when the party is in opposition (and all Tory MPs, other than ministers, when it is in government). In fact, no leader was ever despatched in this manner.[15] Indeed, it has only been since the introduction in 1975 of the provision for re-election—and in 1998 for a vote of no confidence—that Tory MPs have proved willing, publicly and definitively, to pole axe the leader. Edward Heath was ousted in 1975 after ten years as leader and Margaret Thatcher got the chop in 1990 after fifteen years. Iain Duncan Smith was dismissed after a mere twenty-five months.

In 2001, William Hague emulated his predecessor John Major by announcing his resignation as leader once it became clear that the party had suffered a stunning defeat. A consequence of the new rules for electing the leader, which he had introduced and which took effect in 1998, was that the party was plunged into a bitter and public three-month leadership election. Before the election could get under way, however, the 1922 Committee had to elect a new chairman and there was a danger that the parliamentary contest could, if several candidates stood, extend into the summer recess, with balloting taking place when party members were on holiday. To take account of this, the period for the return of ballot papers was extended.

Under the new rules, MPs eliminated contenders in successive ballots until two candidates remained. Party members then made the final choice in a national ballot.[16] Five candidates declared themselves in 2001. The contest itself reflected in many respects the ideological re-aligning that was taking place in the parliamentary party. Various philosophical strands were discernible in the parliamentary party in the 1980s and 1990s: these are shown in Table 2.1.[17] "Thatcherism" had begun to unravel in opposition, with a growing divide between its economic liberal and social conservative elements.[18] The "economic liberals" tended to represent the more intellectual and reflective element of Thatcherism; the "social conservatives" comprised the more instinctive element.[19] The scale of the defeat in 1997 caused the neo-liberals to reflect more deeply on the reasons for defeat than those who felt instinctively that people were still wedded to a socially conservative creed. Michael Portillo, who had lost his seat in 1997 and re-entered the House of Commons in 1999, was in the van of the liberal re-think. This widened his appeal to those who had previously formed the "damp" wing of the party, for whom social liberalism was always an element of their credo.

The former chancellor Ken Clarke also entered the contest and drew his support from the "wet" strand of the party, those committed to European integration and economic statism, and more socially conservative than the damps. The socially conservative wing of Thatcherism was represented by both David Davis and Iain Duncan Smith. Davis had been minister for Europe in the Major government but had spent the previous parliament as chairman of the Commons Public Accounts Committee. Duncan Smith had served in the shadow cabinet but, unlike Davis, had no ministerial experience. His core appeal was to the traditional Tory right and Thatcherite social conservatives. Both had a military background: Davis was a member of the elite Territorial Army Special Air Service and Duncan Smith a former Guards Officer. The fifth candidate was party chairman and former minister Michael

Table 2.1 Ideological Strands Within the Parliamentary Conservative Party

Category	Stance	Examples of MPs in this category
Neo-liberal	Economic liberal Social liberal Eurosceptic	Alan Duncan John Bercow
Thatcherite	Economic liberal Social conservative Eurosceptic	John Redwood Iain Duncan Smith David Davis
Tory right	Economic agnostic Social conservative Eurosceptic	Ann Widdecombe Julian Brazier
Populist	Economic statist Social conservative Anti-Europe	Sir Nicholas Winterton Ann Winterton
Party faithful	Put party interests ahead of ideological preferences	Michael Ancram
Damp	Moderately economic statist Social liberal Pro-Europe	Tim Yeo Peter Bottomley David Curry
Wet	Economic statist Social conservative Pro-Europe	John Gummer Tony Baldry

Source: Philip Norton, "The Conservative Party: Is There Anyone Out There?" in Anthony King, ed., *Britain at the Polls 2001* (Chatham, NJ: Chatham House, 2002), Table 3.3, p. 86.

Ancram, representative of the old strand of Tory aristocracy. (He was heir to the Marquess of Lothian and son-in-law of the Duke of Norfolk.) He stood as a compromise candidate, appealing essentially to the ranks of the party faithful. Another potential candidate, former shadow home secretary, Ann Widdecombe, decided not to stand after taking soundings among her parliamentary colleagues.

The results of the ballots are reproduced in Table 2.2. Portillo topped the poll in the first ballot, but attracted the support of less than a third of all Tory MPs. Duncan Smith polled more strongly than expected, coming second and establishing himself as the standard bearer of the right. Clarke came a close third. The rules stated that the candidate coming last was to drop out for subsequent rounds, but Davis and Ancram tied for last place, a situation for which the rules, embarrassingly, made no provision. The new chairman of the 1922 Committee, Sir Michael Spicer, announced that the contest would be re-run and that, in the event of another tie for last place, both candidates would be eliminated. In the second ballot, there was little change. Ancram came bottom of the poll and dropped out; after consultation with colleagues, Davis

Table 2.2 The Conservative Parliamentary Leadership Ballots

First Ballot		Second Ballot		Third Ballot	
Portillo	49	Portillo	50	Clarke	59
Duncan Smith	39	Duncan Smith	42	Duncan Smith	54
Clarke	36	Clarke	39	Portillo	53
Davis	21	Davis	18		
Ancram	21	Ancram	17		

Source: Philip Norton.

also announced his withdrawal. In the final ballot, the Ancram and Davis supporters opted disproportionately for Clarke and Duncan Smith, Ancram's supporters voting predominantly for Clarke (Ancram himself voted for Duncan Smith) and Davis' for Duncan Smith.[20] Portillo picked up only an additional three votes, putting him one vote behind Duncan Smith and eliminating him from the final contest.

The outcome of this first-stage of the contests was heavily influenced by those MPs who put aside their ideological preferences and voted for the candidate that they thought would be most likely to deliver electoral victory, a consideration that boosted Clarke. It was also heavily influenced by negative voting.[21] Portillo had not yet completed his perceived ideological odyssey; though it was not as radical as many portrayed it to be, he looked as if he could be venturing into uncharted, or at least "un-Conservative", territory. This, coupled with claims of previous disloyalty to party leaders and an admission of a homosexual past, contributed to a significant "stop Portillo" movement.[22] Some in this movement, such as Ann Widdecombe, opted for Clarke as a way to stop him, others—notably the Davis supporters in the final round—plumped for Duncan Smith. The voting was also complicated by a "stop Clarke" campaign, especially amongst those most opposed to further European integration. The person who benefited most from this negative voting was Duncan Smith. He narrowly beat Portillo into second place.

Party members were thus denied the opportunity to elect Portillo as leader. Had the choice been between Portillo and Clarke, then, whichever of the two won, the outcome would have been the election of a charismatic political heavyweight with high public visibility. To some extent, it would have been a "win, lose" contest, a Portillo victory having the potential to widen popular support for the party, a Clarke victory offering a similar potential but with the prospect of a potentially disastrous party split. In the event, party members were offered what appeared to be a "lose, lose" contest.

In the final stage of the contest Clarke and Duncan Smith toured the country addressing party gatherings. Their supporters argued their cause in the letters column of the *Daily Telegraph,* which was widely viewed as the Tory newsletter. The contest became bitter, not least because of a public squabble between two former Tory prime ministers. Baroness Thatcher declared her support for Duncan Smith (as did William Hague) and, in so doing, attacked Clarke. John Major then weighed in to support Clarke, describing Duncan Smith as "very right wing" and Clarke as "infinitely the most experienced candidate". Though some previous leadership contests had been bitterly fought, this one was in public and over an extended period of time: it dominated the traditional media "silly season" in the later summer and early autumn when parliament is in recess. Clarke played on his personal standing rather than the issues. His manifesto made essentially three points: he was popular, he had extensive experience in government, and he would deal effectively with the issue of Europe. Though opponents in the party may have conceded the first two points, they contested the third. Indeed, it was this that largely cost him the leadership.

However popular Clarke may have been in the country, he carried too much political baggage for most Conservative Party members. It was not simply that they disagreed with him on the issue of European integration, though they did, but also that they realized that his stance on the issue was bound to split the party, certainly badly and possibly catastrophically.[23] They were simply not prepared to take the risk. They voted for Duncan Smith. Shortly after 5.00 p.m. on Thursday, September 13, 2001, the results of the ballot were announced: Duncan Smith received 155,933 votes (61 per cent) and Clarke 100,864 (39 per cent). Clarke congratulated the new leader, somewhat half-heartedly, and Duncan Smith made a short statement. The new era got off to a subdued start, since the announcement of the results had been delayed by a day because of the attacks of September 11, 2001.

Duncan Smith's leadership of the party seemed to be doomed, or at least blighted, from the outset. As is apparent from Table 2.2, he enjoyed the support of less than one-third of Conservative MPs. He was elected less for who he was than for who he wasn't: he had reached the final ballot because he wasn't Michael Portillo and he won the ballot because he wasn't Ken Clarke. He took over the leadership with no previous ministerial experience. He was portrayed by opponents as largely unknown and offering little that William Hague did not offer. One Clarke supporter asked: "What can Duncan Smith bring to the party that Hague didn't bring, apart from the word 'never'?" (in relation to the euro).[24] It was also variously pointed out that Duncan Smith even looked like Hague (or, even less kindly, as if he could be Hague's father). In the event, he could be likened to a poor man's William Hague, lacking the intellect and debating skills.

Duncan Smith did not get into his stride as leader. He was never able to convey a clear view of where he wanted to go. Though he advocated a "Fair deal for everyone" and focused on the more "vulnerable" in society, his speeches failed to make a mark. He appeared inconsistent on issues. During the final election contest with Clarke, for example, he indicated a willingness to review Section 28 of the 1988 Local Government Act, which outlawed the "promotion" of homosexuality by local authorities.[25] When leader, however, he imposed—following an acrimonious meeting of the shadow cabinet—a three-line whip to oppose a clause in the Adoption and Children Bill permitting adoption by unmarried couples; a debate that inevitably focused on adoption by gay couples. In a vote in November 2002, when the issue came back from the Lords, eight Tory MPs voted for the provision, including Ken Clarke and Michael Portillo.[26] They were joined by John Bercow, who resigned from the shadow cabinet in opposition to the party's stance. Bercow was previously seen as a rising star in the party and he became a vocal critic of the leadership.

This decision was seen as a tactical blunder by Duncan Smith. However, rather than letting the issue fade, Duncan Smith read into it a wider agenda, one designed to destabilize his leadership. Following the vote in the Commons, he called a surprise press conference and announced that "for a few, last night's vote was not about adoption but an attempt to challenge my mandate to lead the party". The party, he declared, had "to unite or die".[27] It was a melodramatic call that undermined rather than bolstered his position. He was viewed by many MPs as being in a poor position to demand unity, when he himself—as a leading Maastricht rebel—had denied it to John Major.[28] It also suggested that he was prone to panic in response to a crisis, in this particular instance one of his creation. In response to the "unite or die" declaration, former Tory MP and *The Times* columnist Matthew Parris declared prophetically, "death is a distinct possibility".[29]

Duncan Smith not only clashed with social liberals in the party in the Commons, he clashed with the parliamentary party in the Lords. He sought early in 2002 to outflank the government by advocating a second chamber with 80 per cent of its members elected; a position at variance with that of Tory peers. He gave a defensive speech to a special meeting of the Association of Conservative Peers (the equivalent in the Lords of the 1922 Committee) that was not well received. In the Commons, support for the party line on the issue decreased rather than increased.[30] When various options for Lords reform were voted on in the Commons in February 2003, more Tory MPs voted against the 80 per cent option than voted for it.

Duncan Smith failed to convey the *gravitas* expected of a potential prime minister. His public performances never resonated with electors; despite an improvement in the polls in 2003, the party never came close to achieving a lead that would deliver victory in a general election (see Figure 1.2). His tendency to see conspiracies against him served only to turn the perception into reality. MPs did start to conspire against him.[31] Duncan Smith was not the only one prone to panic. Believing that the party stood no chance of success at the next election—indeed, that it was in danger of achieving another standstill election (or worse)—some members started agitating for another new leader. Complaints about Duncan Smith's leadership swelled after a botched front-bench re-shuffle in the summer of 2002 in which David Davis was removed as party chairman. They grew still further after the unceremonious removal of key staff from Conservative Central Office the following February, with Duncan Smith appointing former MP and close ally Barry Legg as chief executive and chief of staff, an appointment that, in the face of strong criticism, proved short lived.[32] Even those MPs who had previously supported Duncan Smith turned against him. In the words of one, "The poor man's just not up to it".[33]

Under the new rules introduced under William Hague, a leader could be removed if a majority of MPs voted against him in a vote of confidence; such a vote was triggered by 15 per cent of the parliamentary party writing to the chairman of the 1922 Committee requesting such a vote. With 166 MPs, the magic number was twenty-five. In early 2003, Michael Portillo made stinging criticisms of the botched changes at Central Office.[34] It was also reported that "Conservative MPs are already making plans to collect the twenty-five signatures".[35] One MP, Crispin Blunt, went public in May by resigning his frontbench post and calling for Duncan Smith to go.[36] Blunt's call, made on the day of the local elections, was somewhat undermined by better-than-expected results. The situation worsened in September, when the Liberal Democrats came from third place to win the supposedly safe Labour seat of Brent East in a by-election; the Tory candidate was pushed into third place. Duncan Smith was also mired in personal controversy the following month when claims surfaced that his wife had been paid out of his parliamentary office allowance without doing any work in return.[37] To add further to his woes, a leading party donor, Stuart Wheeler, said he would make no further donations to the party so long as Duncan Smith was leader.[38] The party's precarious financial position and reliance on large donors made this declaration particularly damaging.

Just before the party conference in October 2003, a YouGov poll found that 53 per cent of party members felt that the party made a mistake in electing Duncan Smith as leader.[39] Only 10 per cent felt that he was providing "strong and effective leadership". Duncan Smith hoped that his performance at the party conference that month would bolster his position; instead, his speech, which was notable for his stinging personal attack on the prime minister and his declaration that "the quiet man is here to stay and he is turning up the volume", served rather to undermine it.[40] One columnist not well disposed to Duncan Smith dismissed it as "snarling and puerile".[41] The last thing some MPs wanted was the volume turning up. Others were turned off by the seventeen standing ovations, likened by some to a sort of Nuremberg rally. When parliament returned, more letters demanding a vote of confidence were sent to Sir Michael Spicer. On the morning of Tuesday, 28 October, former shadow chancellor Francis Maude confirmed that he was one of those who had written. Later that morning, Spicer announced that he had received the necessary number to trigger a confidence vote and that a vote would take place the next day.

On the following day, the 1922 Committee met at 2.30 p.m. to hear a speech from Duncan Smith. Despite Geoffrey Wheatcroft, the *Daily Express* columnist, describing it as "another embarrassing flop", it was one of the best speeches of Duncan Smith's career.[42] He had made mistakes, he said, but had learned from them; he was proud of what he had achieved, but it was now up to MPs to decide.[43] It was not enough. In the laconic observation of one ex-minister at the end of the meeting: "Too late".[44] He characterized it as a dignified swan-song. When the results were announced four hours later, Duncan Smith had lost by ninety votes to seventy-five. For some, the wonder was not that he had lost, but that he had mustered as many as seventy-five votes: as is apparent from Table 2.2, it was more than he had ever received in the initial parliamentary leadership ballots.

The BBC journalist Michael Crick has made a plausible case that Duncan Smith's departure was engineered by the whips, led by the chief whip, David Maclean.[45] Recognizing that Duncan Smith's leadership was doomed, they acted to ensure that the confidence vote was not delayed. However, once Duncan Smith was toppled—under the rules, he could not stand again—the search was on for a successor. One thing that MPs were wary of precipitating was another drawn out, bitter and public leadership election. Support rapidly coalesced around the figure of Michael Howard. He had Cabinet experience, he was one of the few remaining political heavyweights on the front bench, and he had performed effectively as shadow chancellor. This contrasted not only with the performance of his predecessors, all of whom were seen off by Gordon Brown, but with that of other portfolio holders on the front bench. Aided by an effective campaign team, his candidature soon emerged not only as the leading one but potentially the only one.[46] A single nomination would obviate the need for ballots among MPs and, more importantly, a ballot of party members. Pressure thus built up on other potential candidates not to stand.

By the time that Howard declared his candidature he had already gathered the support of more than half the parliamentary party.[47] Michael Portillo had decided following the 2001 contest not to seek the leadership again and was increasingly interested in a career outside politics anyway. After two days of speculation, Ken Clarke let it be known that he was not interested in repeating the experience of coming second.[48] To stand against Howard would do other candidates no particular favours. Recognizing this, none did; though it was rumoured that Eric Forth, shadow leader of the House under Duncan Smith, was so annoyed that his favoured candidate, David Davis, was not standing that he was considering standing to force a contest. In the event, he decided against it and the only nomination Sir Michael Spicer received was that of Michael Howard. When Howard appeared in a packed Committee Room 14 in the Commons on Thursday, 6 November, to accept the leadership, the change in mood amongst MPs and peers present was palpable. They sensed they had a potential prime minister before them, someone who could—at last—lead them to victory. The mood in the party changed from one of pessimism, or despair, to one of optimism. Even if victory was not certain in the next election, it would be the next election but one.

In the event, it was not to be. Michael Howard, despite generating an initial increase in party support in the polls, mirrored the leadership of his predecessor. Although announcing his credo, he failed to present a clear vision

for the future. He declared what his beliefs were (including in full-page newspaper advertisements), but never managed to show where he was going. Like
Duncan Smith, there were inconsistencies. He tried to break with his past but
never quite managed it, to the despair of both sides in the party.

Although he was widely viewed as the architect of Section 28, Howard
appointed gays to leading positions in the leader's office and announced his
support for civil partnerships. When the Civil Partnerships Bill came before
parliament, it split the party. Howard failed to carry a large portion of his
MPs with him in supporting the proposal.[49] However, he avoided repeating
the mistake of Duncan Smith: the votes were *not* whipped. His approach contrasted with his actions as shadow chancellor, when he had voted to retain
Section 28 and was reported to be one of those (another was David Davis)
who had pressed Duncan Smith to issue the three-line whip on gay adoption.

Howard led the party in opposition to university top-up fees, despite the
policy having its roots both in Conservative principles and in the policies of
the previous Tory government. He sought to make political capital out the
absence of weapons of mass destruction in Iraq, while arguing he would still
have voted for the war. In Wheatcroft's observation, "the shift looked not
only intellectually unconvincing but slippery, with a touch of Macmillan's
'first in, first out' over Suez".[50] He also ran into trouble over the issue of
national identity cards. When the government brought forward a bill to
enable cards to be introduced, he decided that the party should support it.
Despite the opposition of a large number of Tory MPs, Howard recognized
that the policy was popular in the country. He argued his case at a meeting of
the 1922 Committee and in an article in the *Daily Telegraph*, but failed to
persuade many of his MPs.[51] In the event, only half of the parliamentary party
subsequently turned up to vote with him in favour of the bill.[52]

Like William Hague, Howard was an effective debater; he had honed his
skills as a minister. He used the dispatch box to attack the government, in a
manner that was effective as a debating technique but did not necessarily play
well outside the Commons. Yet, as with his predecessor, his inconsistencies
meant that it was difficult to convey a clear picture of where he stood. A
YouGov poll in September 2004 found that 68 per cent of those questioned
thought that it was "hard to know what the Conservatives stand for at the
moment".[53] This represented an increase on those giving a similar answer a
year before at the close of Duncan Smith's leadership.[54] It also left him open
to accusations of opportunism, accusations that Labour politicians were only
too ready to make.[55] Tony Blair had a ready list of quotes from speeches that
Howard had made in his previous ministerial incarnations.

As Kieron O'Hara has noted, drawing on a quote from one of Michael
Howard's speeches, Howard's actions "implies that Mr Howard may have
grasped intellectually the importance of differing 'with measured thought and
reflection', but isn't quite able to put it into practice. He can talk the talk, but
is having some difficulty walking the walk".[56]

The Conservative parliamentary party under Michael Howard was not necessarily more adversarial than in the past. Indeed, in terms of the number of bills it voted against, it was *less* adversarial than in the past. The perception was, however, more important than the reality.[57] In a Populus poll in September 2004, 70 per cent of respondents agreed that "the Conservatives just attack the government over whatever happens to be in the news, but never say anything positive".[58]

Howard even had a by-election disaster to match that of Brent East. The party performed poorly in by-elections in Birmingham Hodge Hill and Leicester South, being pushed into third place in both these seats. It also witnessed its share of the vote fall in the European Parliament elections in June 2004, in which the United Kingdom Independence Party (UKIP) did unexpectedly well, picking up twelve seats under the proportional electoral system. However, worse was to come in the form of the Hartlepool by-election in October. The party, previously the main challenger in the Labour-held seat, was pushed into fourth place, behind the UKIP candidate. Compounding the party's difficulties, Howard emulated William Hague in having a Tory MP defect to the opposition, something that did not even happen during Duncan Smith's tenure.[59] Former education minister, Robert Jackson, who had already announced his intention to retire from the House of Commons, defected to Labour in January 2005. He was scathing about the party's stance, accusing it of "incoherent" policies on the public services and declaring the party "deserved better leadership".[60]

As the 2005 election loomed, and the party's position in the polls suggested that it was heading for defeat, Howard emulated his predecessors and adopted a defensive strategy. He retreated to an appeal to a core Tory vote. Hague had gone for the issue of Europe; Howard, recognizing that opposition to European integration did not deliver votes for the party (see Chapter 4), opted for the issue of immigration. This became a central feature of the general election campaign. It was one of the few issues on which the party enjoyed a clear advantage over Labour and that impacted on the voters' consciousness.[61] However, it was not enough to sway votes, and certainly not enough to win the election. Early in the campaign Howard Flight, a party deputy chairman, made injudicious comments about the party's public spending plans in which he appeared to suggest that there would be more tax and spending cuts than were set out in the Conservatives' manifesto. Howard immediately sacked Flight and insisted on his de-selection as a Tory candidate; something that was widely seen as an over-reaction. Attacks on the government, masterminded by Lynton Crosby, a campaign manager imported from Australia, failed to reverse the party's fortunes. The party went down to another major defeat. By the standards of the twenty-first century, the party had not done too badly. By the standards of the twentieth century, it was a disaster.

The Consequences of Panic

The conclusions to be drawn from this narrative can be marshalled under the variables that previously have delivered Tory success.

A Safe Pair of Hands

The party's electoral disaster derived primarily—as with the two preceding general elections—from the fact that it was unable to persuade electors that the nation's finances and public services were safe in its hands. Throughout the parliament, Labour led consistently as the party electors thought it had the better policies for managing the economy.[62] The Tories managed to narrow the gap, but never to close it, in the first year of Michael Howard's leadership. The gap then widened as the 2005 election campaign approached. Labour's lead on the economy, which reached 30 points at the start of the campaign, was greater throughout the election than the Conservative lead on immigration. A YouGov poll carried out in September 2004 found that only 34 per cent of those questioned thought that the Conservatives "know how to run a successful low tax economy".[63] The dilemma was neatly encapsulated by former party treasurer, Lord Ashcroft, who said, 'Conservative efforts to convince voters that their economic policies were more credible than Labour's . . . came up against an apparently insurmountable obstacle: people thought the economy was on the right track, benefiting them personally'.[64] According to Lord Saatchi, the party co-chairman during the election, the party's answer to this conundrum was to run "a Basil Fawlty election— don't mention the economy".[65]

The party was prepared to discuss public services, but its attempts to do so hardly registered with the electors, and Labour maintained a clear lead on health and education.[66] Indeed, in the election campaign, ICM tracking polls found that these issues, along with the economy, increased in salience, Labour's lead extending during the campaign.[67] The Tories were thus damned if they mentioned an issue (health, education) and damned if they did not (economy). People did not particularly trust Tony Blair, but they trusted the Labour government to run the economy, the health service and education more than they trusted the Tories. These were the issues that they regarded as important. They favoured the Tories on immigration, but only 9 per cent of voters regarded this as the most important issue. On the issues that really mattered to most voters, Labour had the edge, usually by decisive majorities.[68] That determined the outcome.

Unity

Voters do not reward a divided party. Splits within a party may not be the cause of an election defeat but they can help reinforce or exacerbate the scale of the defeat. The Tories suffered from being badly divided during the premiership of John Major. The problem was not the number of issues on which they were divided; Tory MPs actually split on fewer issues than Labour MPs.[69] The problem related to one particular issue and the persistence of the divisions. European integration has been the fault-line of British politics for more than half a century and the divisions within Tory ranks again came to the fore during the 1992–97 parliament. The issue persisted in opposition under William Hague's leadership, and was compounded by divisions over social policy.[70]

In many respects, the party could claim to be in a stronger position in the 2001–2005 parliament. It was a parliament notable for the extent to which Tory MPs voted loyally with their party.[71] The problem was that the few occasions on which they did split were high-profile ones, attracting negative publicity and raising questions about the leader's relationship with his MPs. As Andrew Lansley MP noted of the splits in the previous parliament, "what they demonstrated was that in a matter of moments, resurrected negative images of our party can undo the work of months of positive policy formulation".[72] And, as in the previous parliament, the problem areas were principally but not exclusively those of European integration and social policy.

Although Duncan Smith managed initially to sideline the issue of European integration, the position changed after the May 2003 elections. He began appealing to what he assumed was his core vote in attacking the proposed new structure for the European Union. As one pro-European Tory MP noted, "the sense of déja vu in the Tory party was palpable ... He made no attempt to bridge the philosophical divide between the essentially Atlanticist anti-Europeans and the rest of us".[73] Duncan Smith's strident support of the government in going to war in Iraq did not win universal applause. Though media attention had focused on the major split in Labour's ranks, not all Tory MPs were united in backing the government. Some of the most powerful speeches against the war came from Tory MPs, notably Ken Clarke, Douglas Hogg and Edward Leigh. Some leading figures in the Lords, such as former foreign secretary Lord Hurd, were also among the critics.

However, the issue that attracted even more persistent media attention was the divide between those who were portrayed as "modernizers" and "traditionalists", a continuation of a division identified in the previous parliament. It represented, as we have already argued, a separation of the neo-liberal element from the social authoritarian element of Thatcherism. The problem for Duncan Smith and Howard was to bridge the gap between the two. In this, they failed. Both recognized the need for the party to come to terms with a society that was changing; the party, if it was to succeed, had to change with it. However, both were instinctive social conservatives and prone to heed the call of traditionalists, some of whom—notably former cabinet minister, Lord Tebbit—argued that moving to the right was necessary to see off a challenge from UKIP.[74]

Duncan Smith, as we have seen, initially indicated a willingness to review Section 28. However, on the issue of gay adoption, he led the party in opposition (or was pushed by some advisers to do so). The split was bad enough—not so much quantitatively as qualitatively, given the standing of the MPs voting against the party line—but what compounded the unwelcome media attention was Duncan Smith's elevation of the vote to an attack on his leadership. This raised questions about the leader's capacity to cope in a crisis. The crisis was largely self-induced. The issue was whether a gay couple could adopt. Single gays could *already* adopt, and the issue could have been made a free vote, as indeed it was by the party in the Lords. The party split that came to attract enduring media attention was not over that particular policy but over the leadership of the party. Headlines such as "Now it turns really nasty" reflected what was going on in the party and persisted until Duncan Smith's removal.[75]

Howard faced less criticism of his leadership, as MPs realized that he would lead them into the next election, but he faced splits that not only encompassed but also extended beyond the social inclusiveness the party was prepared to tolerate. By allowing free votes on moral issues, he reduced the political temperature; however, the perception of a party that was divided and old-fashioned lingered. By supporting change, Tory leaders were in line with the views of most voters. By opposing it, they were appealing to their core supporters. In a poll of voters commissioned by Lord Ashcroft, 65 per cent of those questioned thought that gay couples should have exactly the same rights as heterosexual couples; 70 per cent thought that it was not a matter for political parties to express a preference between marriage and couples living together outside marriage.[76] Modernizers could thus claim to be appealing to the voters, especially the young voters and women. Traditionalists could claim to be speaking to Tory activists, but only to a minority of Tory voters.[77] The party thus came across as both divided and out of touch; a poll of voters in 130 battleground seats found that the phrase most widely chosen to describe how the Conservatives had come across in the campaign was "old fashioned".[78]

The Iraq War also continued to divide Tory MPs. Criticism of the government intensified when no weapons of mass destruction were found and as it became apparent—as John Major and others had warned in advance of the conflict—that the real problem was not winning the war but winning the peace. Howard sought to exploit the government's position but then compromised the party by saying he would have supported the toppling of Saddam Hussein regardless (labelled by some, "regime change plus"). The party, as we have seen, was also not united on the issue of identity cards. The way in which the leader handled the issue, as with war in Iraq, became as much the story as the extent to which Tory politicians were split. Adding to the sense of déja vu was the apparent opportunism and the fact that, after Howard had taken his stance on the issue of identity cards, popular support for the cards declined. Like Duncan Smith, he appeared to have misjudged public opinion.

Looked at purely in terms of parliamentary voting behaviour, Duncan Smith and then Howard led one of the most united parliamentary parties of recent decades. However, that was not what the voters noticed. What they saw, as portrayed in the media, was the exceptions. And the exceptions suggested that the party had not really changed all that much, if at all, from the one they had voted against in the preceding two elections.

Leadership

Parties can win elections despite their leaders and not necessarily because of them.[79] Nonetheless, leaders can make a difference in "giving the party the cohesion and self-confidence which translate into a sense of purpose".[80] The problem for the Conservative Party has been that no leader has managed that since the heady days of Margaret Thatcher and even she was not able to deliver it in the later years of her premiership. John Major led a badly divided party which lost any sense of direction. Electors have not been impressed with Conservative leaders in opposition, which has reinforced their opinion in voting to keep them there. Duncan Smith followed Hague in not being seen as an alternative prime minister. Howard apparently did not have quite the same appeal to electors as he did to the parliamentary party.

The problem was not one simply of the *leader* but of the *leadership* of the party. There was the danger of it being seen as a one-man show, with voters having little awareness of who else occupied the opposition front bench. Some spokespersons occasionally proved effective, such as Oliver Letwin as shadow home secretary, but there was no consistent performer who maintained popular attention, and some attracted attention that was not always helpful. Party chairman Theresa May noted at the 2002 party conference that others had seen the party as the "nasty party", a phrase that many then attributed to her. The eccentric MP for Henley, Boris Johnson, had a short-lived tenure as a junior arts spokesman; reaction against criticism of the people of Liverpool in the *Spectator* magazine, which he continued to edit following his election to parliament, and allegations of his involvement in an extra-marital affair led to his return to the back benches, but ensured a media profile that most Tory politicians would die for.

Despite high expectations of Michael Howard, and an initial fillip in the opinion polls following his election as leader, he failed to resonate with electors. Although voters disliked Blair, they tended to prefer him to Howard.[81] A YouGov poll in September 2004 found that only 26 per cent of those questioned thought Michael Howard was providing strong leadership.[82] In a poll of voters in a dozen marginal seats early in 2005, most of those questioned disagreed with the statement that "Michael Howard has the personality and leadership qualities needed in a prime minister".[83] And a poll of potential Tory voters also found that, by a margin of more than two to one, they believed that the party had "no strong leaders".[84] This merely confirmed earlier poll findings.[85] The only redeeming feature for Howard was that focus groups regarded him as more effective than his recent predecessors; the problem was that, compared to Blair, he was regarded as insubstantial and lacking authority.[86] An ICM poll for the *Sunday Telegraph* in October 2004 found that 40 per cent trusted Blair more than Howard; only 29 per cent trusted Howard more than Blair.[87]

Sleaze

The Major government had been hit by accusations of a self-serving approach to politics; politicians, especially Tory politicians, were seen as being in politics in order to help themselves rather than help the people who elected them. However unfair the perception was of most MPs, it had gained currency as a result of the "cash for questions" scandal in 1994, when two MPs initially accepted offers of cash from an undercover reporter to ask parliamentary questions. Two others were later accused of having accepted money from a well-known businessman in return for asking questions. Parliament introduced new regulations governing MPs' conduct. William Hague instituted a new procedure to investigate complaints against party members. However, problems remained, particularly in the form of Jeffrey Archer, the author and former Tory MP, who had to abandon his bid to be Mayor of London when charged with attempting to pervert the course of justice (Archer was found guilty and sent to jail in July 2001). The issue was less to the fore during the 2001–2005 parliament, but nonetheless popular perceptions of politicians being in politics for their own good persisted. It hit the headlines during Duncan Smith's tenure when allegations were made that he was paying his wife, Betsy, out of parliamentary funds for secretarial work that she never performed. "Betsygate" ran in the media and was referred for investigation by the parliamentary commissioner for standards. It undermined Duncan Smith's leadership; by the time the commissioner decided that Duncan Smith had *not* improperly employed his wife, he had been voted out.[88] Others also attracted negative publicity. One Tory MP announced he would not be seeking re-election after having to pay back over £90,000 he had incorrectly claimed in allowances; another had the whip withdrawn, and then announced his retirement, after it was found he had been involved with a firm offering paid tours and dinners in the Palace of Westminster. Although sleaze was no longer the issue it had been a decade ago, the party had not managed to convey that it was now a standard bearer of high political standards. A Populus poll for *The Times* at the beginning of 2005 found that most of those asked did not believe that a Conservative government would "restore integrity to government".[89]

Conclusion

At the 2005 Channel 4 Parliamentary Awards ceremony, John Bercow won the award for opposition politician of the year. In accepting the prize, he said that MPs who fell out with their party often claimed that they had stayed the same but that the party had changed. In his case, he said, it was the other way round. He had changed but his party had not.[90] In so doing, he identified what has proved to be at the heart of the party's dilemma. Whereas Bercow appeared to embrace stances that resonated with electors, the party no longer did so. The party kept thrashing about for new policies, but without creating a clear, consistent and innovative vision for the future. Stuart Ball encapsulated this challenge well in his study of previous periods of Conservative opposition:

> A conclusion which can be drawn is that before there can be a Conservative return to power, rather than just a limited ebbing of the tide in the style of 1910, the party will need to find a new message rather than just recycling the old. It will need a distinctive voice, and one which can reach beyond the core vote and encourage the return of the members and votes lost since 1992. This is the crucial difference between the periods after the last two major defeats of this century, and without it the party is likely to repeat the sterility of 1906–14 rather than the recovery of 1945–51.[91]

The problem for the party was that it failed to find a new message. It failed to put in place the mechanisms which would allow it to do so. When one set of proposals failed to find favour with electors, it tried another set. It was a self-defeating exercise. People were not that interested and, faced with policy proposals after policy proposal, they became less rather than more interested. The extent to which electors were not interested was neatly encapsulated by a headline employed in a *Sunday Telegraph* story on the party's 2004 conference: "Didn't they do well? Shame nobody noticed".[92] People could not see what the party stood for. The more trees the party planted and felled, the less obvious was the wood. Where a long view was called for, leaders—desperate for success—resorted to the politics of panic. Instead of following the dictum of Corporal Jones in the long-running BBC sit-com *Dad's Army*—"don't panic, don't panic"— they fulfilled the prognosis of the gloomy Scot Private Fraser: "we're doomed, we're doomed".

Notes

1. Philip Norton, "The Conservative Party: 'In Office But Not In Power'", in Anthony King (ed.), *New Labour Triumphs* (Chatham, N.J.: Chatham House Publishers, 1998), pp. 75–122; Philip Norton, "The Conservative Party: Is There Anyone Out There?" in Anthony King, ed., *Britain at the Polls 2001* (New York: Chatham House, 2002), pp. 68–94.
2. Morris Fiorina, *Retrospective Voting in American National Elections* (New Haven, Conn.: Yale University Press, 1981).
3. Anthony King, "The Implications of One-Party Government", in Anthony King, ed., *Britain at the Polls 1992* (Chatham, NJ: Chatham House, 1993), pp. 224–5.
4. See Michael Ashcroft, *Smell the Coffee: A Wake-up Call for the Conservative Party* (London: n.p., 2005), pp. 98–9.
5. See Philip Norton, "The Conservative Party from Thatcher to Major", in King, ed., *Britain at the Polls 1992*, pp. 29–69.

6. See Ivor Crewe, "Electoral Behaviour", in Dennis Kavanagh and Anthony Seldon, eds, *The Major Effect* (London: Macmillan, 1994), p. 109.
7. Norton, "In Office But Not In Power", and Norton, "Is There Anyone Out There?"
8. Paul Whiteley, *The Labour Party in Crisis* (London: Methuen, 1983), pp. 92–3; and Anthony Downs, *An Economic Theory of Democracy* (New York: Harper and Row, 1957), p. 40.
9. Peter Riddell, "Who do you think you are kidding, Mr Hague?" *The Times*, February 19, 2001.
10. Norton, "Is There Anyone Out There?" p. 80; Philip Lynch and Mark Garnett, "Conclusions: The Conservatives in Crisis", in Mark Garnett and Philip Lynch, eds, *The Conservatives in Crisis* (Manchester: Manchester University Press, 2003), p. 251.
11. Lord Howe of Aberavon, *Independent,* January 4, 2000.
12. So much so that Hague was dubbed by some as "Billy Bandwagon". See Mark Garnett, "Win or Bust: The Leadership Gamble of William Hague", in Garnett and Lynch, *The Conservatives in Crisis*, p. 56. See also Ian Taylor, "The Conservatives, 1997–2001: A Party in Crisis", ibid., p. 239.
13. See Ashcroft, *Smell the Coffee*, pp. 41–2, 73.
14. Winston S. Churchill, *The Second World War,* vol. 2, quoted in Nigel Fisher, *The Tory Leaders* (London: Weidenfeld and Nicolson, 1977), p. 3.
15. Philip Norton, "The Party in Parliament", in Philip Norton, ed., *The Conservative Party* (London: Prentice Hall/Harvester Wheatsheaf, 1996), p. 131.
16. Constitution of the Conservative Party, February 1998.
17. The various groupings were first identified and analysed in Philip Norton, "'The Lady's Not for Turning': But What about the Rest of the Party? Margaret Thatcher and the Conservative Party, 1979–89", *Parliamentary Affairs,* 43 (1990).
18. Norton, "Is There Anyone Out There?" pp. 86–7. On the extent to which Thatcherism managed to blend these two not obviously compatible elements, see Andrew Gamble, *The Free Economy and the Strong State,* 2nd edn (London: Macmillan, 1994).
19. The economic liberals are drawn from the Whig strand in Conservative thought, the social conservatives from the Tory strand. The former tends to seek the rational and the latter to adopt a sceptical approach to human endeavour. See Philip Norton and Arthur Aughey, *Conservatives and Conservatism* (London: Temple Smith, 1981).
20. Philip Norton, "The Conservative Leadership Election", *British Politics Group Newsletter* (USA), Fall 2001, 11–16.
21. Norton, "The Conservative Leadership Election", pp. 11–16.
22. See Simon Walters, *Tory Wars* (London: Politico's, 2001), pp. 207–12; and Philip Cowley and Mark Stuart, "The Conservative Parliamentary Party", in Garnett and Lynch, *The Conservatives in Crisis*, pp. 77–8.
23. See David Cracknell, "Poll shows Europe is the main issue for Conservatives", *Sunday Telegraph,* August 26, 2001.
24. Tory MP to author.
25. Gyles Brandreth, "Your strengths are like Hague's and you're bald—why should you do any better?" *Sunday Telegraph,* September 2, 2001.
26. In addition to the eight voting with the government, another thirty-five were absent (not all of them necessarily abstaining), including some members of the shadow cabinet. See Philip Cowley and Mark Stuart, "Conservatives in Unity Shocker: Conservative Voting in the House of Commons, 2001–05", http://www.revolts.co.uk/Conservatives%20in%20Unity%20Shocker.pdf, pp.

2–3; Rosemary Bennett and Greg Hurst, "MPs who triggered Tory troubles", *The Times*, November 6, 2002.

27. Andrew Grice and Paul Waugh, "Duncan Smith fighting for his life", *Independent*, November 6, 2002.

28. Duncan Smith had been one of the party's most rebellious MPs during the passage of the Maastricht Bill in the 1992–93 session. He voted against the Major government on forty occasions.

29. "Can Duncan Smith Survive?" *BBC News Online*, November 6, 2002.

30. Of 303 MPs who had signed an Early Day Motion in the 2001–2002 session favouring elections to the second chamber, fifty voted for an all-appointed chamber in the votes in February 2003. Of these, thirty-two were Conservative. See Philip Norton, "Reforming the House of Lords: A View from the Parapets", *Representation*, 40 (2004), p. 193.

31. Philip Webster and Tom Baldwin, "Estelle has shown the way, says conspirators", *The Times*, October 31, 2002.

32. See especially Michael Gove, "How two Tory nobodies sparked fratricidal spree", *The Times*, February 22, 2003.

33. Rosemary Bennett, "Duncan Smith calls for truce before war", *The Times*, February 25, 2003.

34. See Colin Brown and Francis Elliott, "Who will have the last laugh?" *Sunday Telegraph*, February 23, 2003.

35. Eben Black, "Spoiling for a fight", *Sunday Times*, February 23, 2003. See also Rosemary Bennett, "Tory MPs seek support for challenge to leadership", *The Times*, January 17, 2003; and Colin Brown and Francis Elliot, "Duncan Smith's astonishing fightback: 'Portillo is mad', he says", *Sunday Telegraph*, February 23, 2003.

36. Philip Webster and Melissa Kite, "Tory resigns and tells his leader to go", *The Times*, May 2, 2003.

37. The story broke at the beginning of October when the BBC *Newsnight* programme decided not to broadcast claims by reporter Michael Crick about Mrs Duncan Smith's employment. See Michael Crick, *In Search of Michael Howard* (London: Simon and Schuster, 2005), pp. 418–20; Andrew Alderson, "Dossier poses testing questions for IDS over salary paid to his wife", *Sunday Telegraph*, October 12, 2003; and Philip Webster, Tom Baldwin and Melissa Kite, "The leader, his wife and the plotter", *The Times*, October 14, 2003.

38. Philip Webster and Tom Baldwin, "Tory leader on the ropes but refuses to quit", *The Times*, October 23, 2003.

39. Anthony King, "Adequate at best, and weak at worst: members' verdict on Duncan Smith", *Daily Telegraph*, October 9, 2003.

40. Philip Webster, "Is this loud enough to save him?" *The Times*, October 10, 2003.

41. Bruce Anderson, "It should be between Letwin and Howard", *Sunday Telegraph*, October 12, 2003.

42. Geoffrey Wheatcroft, *The Strange Death of Tory England* (London: Allen Lane, 2005), p. 265. Wheatcroft also incorrectly dates the meeting to the Tuesday rather than the Wednesday.

43. See also Iain Duncan Smith, "Back me: I'm ready to address my leadership's shortcomings", *The Times*, October 29, 2003.

44. Tory MP to author at the conclusion of the speech.

45. Crick, *In Search of Michael Howard*, pp. 422–6. See also Richard Woods and Eben Black, "Howzat!" *Sunday Times*, October 26, 2003.

46. See Crick, *In Search of Michael Howard*, pp. 420–34.

47. George Jones, "More than half of MPs swing behind leadership bid", *Daily Telegraph*, October 31, 2003.

48. Benedict Brogan, "It's Howard unopposed as Clarke stands aside", *Daily Telegraph*, November 1, 2003.
49. See Cowley and Stuart, "Conservatives in Unity Shocker", pp. 2–3.
50. Wheatcroft, *The Strange Death of Tory England*, p. 268.
51. He faced a sceptical audience when he addressed the 1922 Committee on December 15, 2004. See also George Jones, "Howard fights to head off Tory revolt over ID cards", *Daily Telegraph*, December 20, 2004.
52. Eighty-two Conservatives voted for the bill's second reading; ten voted against. During the passage of the bill, a total of twenty-one Conservatives voted against front-bench advice. Cowley and Stuart, "Conservatives in Unity Shocker", p. 5.
53. Anthony King, "Can Howard rally his party and steer it out of the doldrums?" *Daily Telegraph*, October 4, 2004.
54. "His big problem: the voters are confused", *Sunday Times*, October 5, 2003.
55. See Ashcroft, *Smell the Coffee*, pp. 21, 92.
56. Kieron O'Hara, *After Blair: Conservatism Beyond Thatcher* (Cambridge: Icon Books, 2005), pp. 322–3.
57. The party voted against approximately one-third of government bills on second and/or third reading, a slightly lower proportion than in preceding parliaments. See Cowley and Stuart, "Conservatives in Unity Shocker", pp. 10–11.
58. Ashcroft, *Smell the Coffee*, p. 7 (see also p. 64); Andrew Cooper, "Pass the Coca-Cola test and enter No. 10", *The Times*, August 2, 2005.
59. Under Duncan Smith, at least one ex-MP defected; Harold Elletson, former MP for Blackpool North, defected to the Liberal Democrats in November 2002.
60. Melissa Kite, "Tory ex-minister joins Labour benches and warns: 'Howard will harm Britain'", *Sunday Telegraph*, January 16, 2005.
61. Ashcroft, *Smell the Coffee*, pp. 33–5.
62. MORI polls: http://www.mori.com/polls/trends/bpoki-economy.shtml.
63. King, "Can Howard rally his party?"
64. Ashcroft, *Smell the Coffee*, p. 66.
65. Maurice Saatchi, *If This Is Conservatism, I Am a Conservative* (London: Centre for Policy Studies, 2005), p. 2.
66. See Ashcroft, *Smell the Coffee*, p. 70.
67. Ashcroft, *Smell the Coffee*, pp. 72–3, 92.
68. Ashcroft, *Smell the Coffee*, p. 72. On crime, traditionally seen as a Tory issue, neither party had the lead.
69. Philip Cowley and Philip Norton, with Mark Stuart and Matthew Bailey, *Blair's Bastards: Discontent within the Parliamentary Labour Party*, Research Papers in Legislative Studies 1/96 (Hull: Hull University Centre for Legislative Studies, 1996), pp. 17–19.
70. Norton, "Is There Anyone Out There?" pp. 81–8.
71. Cowley and Stuart, "Conservatives in Unity Shocker".
72. Andrew Lansley, "From Values to Policy: The Conservative Challenge', in Garnett and Lynch, *The Conservatives in Crisis*, p. 223.
73. Taylor, "The Conservatives, 1997–2001", p. 245.
74. Helen Rumbelow, "Wounded Howard gets summertime blues", *The Times*, July 26, 2004.
75. Gaby Hinsliff, "Now it turns really nasty", *Observer*, November 3, 2002.
76. Ashcroft, *Smell the Coffee*, pp. 26–7.
77. Fifty-seven per cent of Tory voters supported the proposition that gay couples should have exactly the same rights as heterosexual couples. Ashcroft, *Smell the Coffee*, p. 26.
78. Ashcroft, *Smell the Coffee*, pp. 102–3.
79. Anthony King, ed., *Leaders' Personalities and the Outcomes of Democratic Elections* (Oxford: Oxford University Press, 2002).

80. Stuart Ball, "The Conservatives in Opposition, 1906–1979: A Comparative Analysis", in Garnett and Lynch, *The Conservatives in Crisis*, p. 15.
81. Ashcroft, *Smell the Coffee*, pp. 48–9.
82. King, "Can Howard rally his party?"
83. Ashcroft, *Smell the Coffee*, pp. 46–7.
84. Ashcroft, *Smell the Coffee*, pp. 21–2.
85. See Peter Riddell, "Tories are out of touch and incompetent, poll says", *The Times*, October 4, 2003.
86. Ashcroft, *Smell the Coffee*, p. 55. See also Peter Riddell and Philip Webster, "Tory leader leaves voters unmoved", *The Times*, February 10, 2004.
87. Patrick Hennessy and Melissa Kite, "ICM poll shows Tories 9 points behind Labour", *Sunday Telegraph*, October 10, 2004.
88. See Select Committee on Standards and Privileges, *Conduct of Mr Iain Duncan Smith*, Fourth Report, Session 2003–2004, HC 476-I; Tom Baldwin and David Charter, "Clampdown on MPs' cash after IDS cleared", *The Times*, March 30, 2004.
89. Peter Riddell, "Manifesto launched, but no Tory lift off", *The Times*, January 13, 2005.
90. Channel 4 Parliamentary Awards Ceremony, held at Channel 4 Headquarters, London, on Tuesday, February 8, 2005.
91. Ball, "The Conservatives in Opposition, 1906–1979", in Garnett and Lynch, *The Conservatives in Crisis*, p. 26.
92. Patrick Hennessy and Melissa Kite, "Didn't they do well? Shame nobody noticed", *Sunday Telegraph*, October 10, 2004.

3

A Restless Electorate:
Stirrings in the Political System

Nicholas Allen

A mood of discontent permeated British politics before the 2005 election at both the elite and the mass level. At Westminster, Labour and Conservative members of parliament (MPs) alike were increasingly rebellious. Labour MPs revolted over issues as diverse as foundation hospitals, university top-up fees and the Iraq War. Their Conservative opposite numbers deposed a leader who had been elected by the entire party membership only two years earlier. In the national media, commentators found fault not just with the government of the day but with virtually every political institution, process and policy. The growing sense of unease even reached "establishment" figures such as Lord Butler, who produced a devastating critique of Tony Blair's "sofa style" of government.[1] At the mass level, there were signs that much of the electorate was becoming restless. Support for the Blair government in the polls fell, fringe and protest parties performed well in secondary elections, and millions took to the streets. Voters' discontent often focused on the person of one individual, Tony Blair, but other politicians were not immune. Indeed, one commentator wrote during the 2005 campaign: "I have never witnessed an election where there was so much disillusion and contempt shown for the people we are about to elect to govern us".[2] To some extent, the electorate's mood reflected the usual short-term political dissatisfaction with the government of the day and the impact of intense, but essentially ephemeral, events. To an unknown extent, however, it also appeared to reflect a growing discontent with the political class, traditional institutions and possibly even democracy itself.

The electorate's disgruntled mood had obvious implications for the outcome of the 2005 election, which Anthony King explores in Chapter 7. The aim of this present chapter is to examine evidence of discontent, paying particular attention to voters' changing relationships with the major parties. Since 1945, British general elections have usually been thought of as contests between Labour and the Conservatives.[3] For three generations, these two parties have played a central role in British politics and fulfilled important systemic functions. They have defined the major political issues, recruited political leaders, integrated the public into the democratic process and, most importantly, framed the choice of governments.[4] In this last respect, British politics has been largely a matter of choosing sides: Conservatives to the right and Labour to the left. Though neither party has ever won an absolute majority of the popular vote in the postwar era, Britain's "first-past-the-post" plurality (FPTP) electoral system converted a plurality of votes into a parliamentary majority on all but one occasion. In the 1970s the revitalized Liberals (now the Liberal Democrats) and nationalist parties in Scotland and Wales eroded the old duopoly, but the electoral system continued to ensure that Labour and the Conservatives dominated parliament, even though they no longer dominated elections to the same extent. More recently, voters have proven markedly less willing to vote Labour or Conservative or to vote at all. These developments, together with other changes in political behaviour, have led some commentators to question whether the major parties play the central role that they once played in British politics.[5]

This chapter assesses whether voters' current unhappiness with politics is general and enduring or specific and transient. One caveat needs to be noted. The chapter provides an analysis of the electorate as a whole, not of individuals: it is not suggested either that every voter was discontented or that every voter was equally discontented. The first section will use a variety of indicators to establish what exactly voters were dissatisfied with and why. The second will then establish how the electorate's discontent was manifested in terms of some modes of political behaviour. The third will explore how and why the discontent appeared to influence voting behaviour. The final section will discuss the implications of a restless electorate, both at the 2005 election and for the political system more widely.

Unhappy with Labour?

Studies of popular support for democracy have invariably distinguished between three political objects: authorities, regime and community.[6] These refer, respectively, to the holders of (and candidates for) political office, the institutions and offices of government, and the wider nation and political system. The electorate's mood in recent years can similarly be said to involve both short-term dissatisfaction with political authorities and a deeper unhappiness with aspects of the regime and possibly the political system itself.

Dissatisfaction with the Labour government was a major element of the first component of the electorate's mood. MORI polls conducted between the 2001 and 2005 general elections suggested that, on average, a mere 32 per cent of respondents were satisfied with Labour's record, with 58 per cent dissatisfied (a net satisfaction rating of -26). The significance of this statistic must be qualified: the electorate is almost always dissatisfied with the government of the day (see Table 3.1). Indeed, compared with evaluations of Tory governments between 1979 and 1997, Labour's low approval ratings represented something of an endorsement. Dissatisfaction with Labour since 2001 was, however, noticeably higher than it had been in the previous parliament, when 43 per cent of voters had, on average, been satisfied and just 42 per cent dis-

Table 3.1 Satisfaction with How the Government Is Running the Country, 1979–2005

Government		Average satisfaction	Average dissatisfaction	Net satisfaction
1979–83	(Conservative)	31	59	-28
1983–87	(Conservative)	32	59	-27
1987–92	(Conservative)	32	60	-28
1992–97	(Conservative)	15	77	-62
1997–2001	(Labour)	43	42	+1
2001–2005	(Labour)	32	58	-26

Source: MORI Political Monitor: Satisfaction Ratings, 1979–present, http://www.mori.com/polls/trends/satisfac.shtml.

satisfied (a net score of +1). Further evidence of the change in public mood was provided by the responses to a survey question that asked voters to describe their feelings about Tony Blair and the Labour government. In October 1999, 53 per cent of respondents were "reasonably well satisfied" and only 11 per cent were "very unhappy" with the government's performance. Exactly four years later, just 22 per cent were "reasonably well satisfied" and 39 per cent were "very unhappy".[7]

There was also evidence that voters were increasingly dissatisfied with Blair personally. Between his election as Labour leader in July 1994 and his assumption of the premiership in 1997, 47 per cent of respondents in regular MORI polls were on average satisfied with how Blair was doing his job as leader of the opposition, with 26 per cent dissatisfied (a net rating of +21).[8] During Labour's first term, 56 per cent expressed themselves satisfied with how Blair was doing his job as prime minister, with 33 per cent dissatisfied (a net rating of +23). Between the 2001 and 2005 elections, however, approval of Blair fell markedly, with just 39 per cent of voters reporting themselves satisfied and 53 per cent dissatisfied (a net rating of -14). A shift in the public mood was further suggested by a change in the attribute that voters most associated with the prime minister. In October 1997, the quality most commonly associated with Blair was that he was "a capable leader". By the end of 2004, the relevant quality had become "out of touch with ordinary people", a trait that had been associated with Margaret Thatcher before her fall.[9]

In part, voters' dissatisfaction with Blair and Labour was a simple product of incumbency. There is good evidence to suggest that governing parties lose public support as a result of a simple "cost of ruling".[10] Governments are blamed more for bad times than they are praised for good. Equally, voters' dissatisfaction probably reflected the partial erosion of the conditional support that Labour had enjoyed since the mid-1990s when New Labour emerged as a broad-based coalition offering something to just about everybody. Its second victory in 2001 had been accompanied by a sense that the party had failed to deliver on its pledges, especially in relation to the public services.[11] Several years on, there was still a feeling that Labour had failed to deliver on the public services, to tackle violent crime, to improve housing and to deal effectively with immigration. These feelings were common to all sections of society but appeared to be felt most keenly in Labour's heartlands. There was a higher than average swing away from Labour in 2005 among blue-collar workers, traditionally core supporters who might have expected to gain most from a Labour government.[12]

A significant part of voters' unhappiness with Labour, however, almost certainly resulted from the Iraq War and Blair's perceived closeness to President Bush. The failure to secure UN backing for the invasion of Iraq cost the government some support, while the failure to find Iraqi weapons of mass destruction (WMD), the suicide of Dr David Kelly and the Gilligan affair, did Labour further harm. Although only a minority of voters believed that Blair had deliberately lied over his claims about WMD, the government's reputation for honesty was severely damaged. At the 2001 election, 51 per cent of voters thought the government was "honest and trustworthy". By October 2004, only 26 per cent of the electorate thought the same.[13] Some voters did think Blair had lied. For a small but vocal minority, expressing their opposition to Blair, Bush and the Iraq War became a central part of their lives.

However, uniquely in postwar British history, dissatisfaction with the government of the day was matched by dissatisfaction with the opposition. A 2004 survey conducted for *The Economist* suggested that 58 per cent of respondents felt the Conservatives were "out of touch with modern Britain", and 60 per cent felt the party did not "understand their needs".[14] The Tories did little to improve their standing between 2001 and 2005 (see Philip Norton in Chapter 2). In contrast, the public did not appear nearly so dissatisfied with the Liberal Democrats. Their leader, Charles Kennedy, consistently enjoyed a positive approval rating. It may be, however, that voters were simply less critical of Kennedy because the Liberal Democrats were not regarded as serious contenders for office. British politics continued to be structured around the traditional dichotomous choice of Labour or Conservative. The Liberal Democrats were probably in part a vehicle for expressing discontent with that choice.

Unhappy with Politics?

Discontent with some aspects of the wider political structure provided the second component of the electorate's mood. It appeared to comprise a mixture of sentiments, some of which had been bubbling just beneath the surface for some time.

One ingredient of this deeper discontent related to political parties in general. As already indicated, voters appeared to be increasingly unhappy with the choices on offer. For example, a 2001 YouGov survey asked voters whether they would vote for "none of the above" if their ballot paper gave them that option: 17 per cent answered that, yes, they would. Four years later, that proportion had risen to 24 per cent, becoming the third most popular choice after Labour and the Conservatives.[15] An earlier snapshot of public attitudes at the 2001 election found that a large majority felt the parties spent "too much time bickering with each other" (83 per cent). A majority also felt that parties were "more interested in winning elections than in governing afterwards" (60 per cent) and were not telling people "about the really important problems facing the country" (60 per cent).[16] A growing number of voters, moreover, appeared to feel the parties were not listening to them. At the 1987 election, 15 per cent strongly agreed with the view that parties were "only interested in peoples' votes rather than their opinions". This increased to 27 per cent in 2001.[17]

To be sure, the parties' psychological grip on the electorate has been declining for a long time. This is evidenced by responses to the questions that seek to establish whether voters usually think of themselves as being Conservative, Labour or whatever (see Table 3.2). This sense of "party identification" has been thought to provide individuals with a framework with which they could understand and evaluate political events. It helps to mobilize voters, providing a reason to vote even when there are few real policy differences between parties.[18] In 1964, just 5 per cent of voters did not think of themselves as Conservative, Labour, Liberal or the like, whereas fully 44 per cent had a "very strong" attachment to a party. Since that time, the percentage of those with no identification has gradually increased. In 1997, 12 per cent of voters did not "identify", and in 2001 16 per cent did not. In 2005 18 per cent expressed no identification. At the same time, the proportion of those who identify "very strongly" with a party has declined even more, from a high of 46 per cent in 1966 to 13 per cent in 2001. The trend continued in 2005, with the British Election Study (BES) pre-election survey finding that just 8 per cent of voters "very strongly" identified with a party. Such changes suggest that parties are increasingly unable to rely on purely tribal or habitual loyalties as they did in the past. Successive generations of new voters have been less partisan, more conditional and more easily swayed by political messages.[19]

Table 3.2 Percentage Partisan Identification among British Voters, 1964–2005

	1964	1966	1970	Feb 1974	Oct 1974	1979	1983	1987	1992	1997	2001	2005
Very strong identifiers	44	46	43	30	26	21	22	19	18	16	13	8
Fairly strong identifiers	40	39	37	43	47	46	41	42	45	41	40	37
Not very strong identifiers	11	9	31	18	17	20	24	25	27	31	31	36
Total expressing some identification	95	94	91	91	90	87	87	86	90	88	84	81
Expressing no partisan identification	5	7	9	10	10	13	14	14	10	12	16	18

Source: British Election Studies Information Site, http://www.besis.org/MainMenu.aspx.

Note: Those expressing no sense of identification include "Don't knows".

A second ingredient of voters' mood was a sense of discontent with politicians. In 1995, Andrew Marr, a former BBC political editor, wrote: "Most people don't feel oppressed by their politicians, merely a bit contemptuous of them".[20] This depiction still applied ten years on. Voters appeared to feel that politicians were out of touch with their concerns. They also thought that most politicians were, at best, less than truthful, at worst, outright dishonest. Such sentiments were hardly new. Public opinion on politicians has rarely been flattering. A 1985 survey found that 79 per cent of voters felt MPs would tell lies if the truth would hurt them politically. This perception had increased to 84 per cent by 2004. However, an additional concern with institutional honesty appears to have developed recently, possibly a result of New Labour's tendency to overclaim successes. A survey in 2004 found that 80 per cent of voters felt governments frequently or sometimes fiddled the figures in an effort to meet their own targets.[21] Such measures hint at the public's unease with "spin" (see John Bartle in Chapter 6).

Recent years have also witnessed a growing concern with politicians' probity. The mood was particularly apparent in the 1990s during the era of Conservative sleaze. Yet, despite improvements over the last decade in the institutional arrangements for maintaining standards in public life, only 16 per cent of voters in 2004 felt such standards had improved. At the same time, scepticism about individual politicians' probity increased. In 1985, 42 per cent of voters thought that most MPs had a "high moral code". Nineteen years later just 17 per cent felt the same.[22] A majority of the public also believed that MPs made a lot of money by using public office improperly. Such attitudes indicate at least two things: the public's receptiveness to the drip-drip media coverage of scandal, and possibly also voters' ongoing detachment from politics at the elite level. These sorts of survey findings are as likely to reflect a general cynicism and contempt for politicians as they are to reflect a deep-seated belief among voters that politicians are corrupt.

A third ingredient of the electorate's discontent was a sense of dissatisfaction with democratic institutions. It is worth drawing particular attention to the low standing of parliament, the institution that lies at the constitutional heart of British politics. In a 2000 survey, the House of Commons was less trusted than other institutions such as the courts, the police, the banks and the civil service.[23] Local government was more trusted than the Commons, but only just. It seems that elected institutions were less well regarded than non-elected institutions, standing the usual assumption about the legitimizing effect of democracy on its head. Again, such opinions were not entirely new. In the early 1960s, the public appeared lukewarm about its MPs. Some 47 per cent thought that MPs could do a better job and only 21 per cent thought that they were actually doing a good job.[24] It should also be noted that survey data—and MPs' own experience—suggests people have become more willing than in the past to contact their MPs, thus confusing the picture.[25] However, many indicators suggest that overall dissatisfaction with the institutions of government has grown. After the 1987 election, 48 per cent felt that they had no say in what the government does. In 2001, 56 per cent felt this way.[26]

Public attitudes towards democratic institutions also point to a national variation in levels of discontent. Ten years ago, large proportions of the Scots and Welsh were unhappy with the United Kingdom's constitutional settlement. The sentiment could be summarized as "London is too far away; we want decisions affecting Scotland or Wales to be taken in Edinburgh or Cardiff". Many wanted their own parliament, but some wanted formal independence. Since 1999, however, the debate has changed. Scotland has a parliament and Wales has a national assembly (see Iain McLean in Chapter 5). Demand for independence has not increased, and most discontent is now focused on these new institutions. A survey in April 2003 found that roughly half of Scots, 49 per cent, disapproved of the record of the Scottish Parliament as a whole.[27] In Wales there is similar discontent. Labour's programme of devolution has merely shifted the focus of discontent.

Dissatisfaction with the practice and institutions of democratic politics can, however, be contrasted with the public's interest in politics. A survey undertaken for the Electoral Commission in December 2004 found that 53 per cent of the public were "very" or "fairly" interested in politics. A distinction should also be made between voters' attitudes towards "public affairs" and their views about party politics. A survey of first-time voters in early 2005 found that, although a large majority (74 per cent) claimed an interest in public affairs, defined in terms of how leaders handled such issues as global warming, poverty, crime, education and immigration, only a minority (42 per cent) expressed interest in politics, defined as the way in which Britain's politicians competed with each other and debated issues.[28] Although these findings related only to first-time voters, they appeared indicative of a wider mood: many people are simply turned off by party political competition.

The survey evidence was mixed as to whether voters were becoming more dissatisfied with democracy. The Electoral Commission found that the proportion who felt the system worked well had declined from 41 to 34 per cent between 1998 and December 2004, while those who thought it needed improving increased from 54 to 63 per cent.[29] However, these measures tended to correlate with support or lack of it for the governing party. The 2000 Citizen Audit found that just 35 per cent of the British public was very satisfied or satisfied with the way democracy works, with 33 per cent dissatisfied or very dissatisfied.[30] A large part of the electorate thus felt that British democracy was far from perfect. Weighing the range of evidence, it seems fair to conclude that voters' discontent in recent years has been both broad based and far reaching.

Explaining the Electorate's Mood

There are many potential explanations for the electorate's increasing discontent. What follows is a tentative rather than exhaustive list of factors.

One potential cause was the media's coverage of politics. In recent years it has become ever more critical and cynical, leading one commentator to describe the current era of political reporting as "the age of contempt".[31] Commentators of all political persuasions could be found expressing their dissatisfaction with one thing or another. Some even adopted a self-consciously anti-establishment bias in their writing and commentary.[32]

We cannot be certain whether the media was reflecting or leading public opinion. Media affects are extremely difficult to measure. That does not mean, however, that the media do not exert influence. A "culture of cynicism" in political coverage may well have contributed to the public mood in several ways. At its simplest, criticism may directly have caused public dissatisfaction. Typically, when the House of Commons published details of MPs' parliamentary allowances for the first time in October 2004, the *Sun* newspaper headlined the story as: "Trough at the top".[33] Its coverage implied, unfairly, that the allowances paid to MPs for hiring staff and facilities were being pocketed by the MPs themselves. Some readers may have dismissed such stories, while others may have found their cynicism about politicians reinforced. Others, however, may have discovered a newly minted cynicism. The media's adversarial relationship with politicians may also have contributed towards voters' feeling they wanted to turn their backs on the whole business. Inquisitorial interviews, such as those conducted by the BBC's Jeremy Paxman and John Humphrys, may have served to persuade some that politicians were to be ridiculed and scorned.

The media may also have influenced voters' attitudes in more indirect ways. Apart from the adversarial tone that they adopt with politicians, the media have also probably encouraged adversarialism among politicians. The decline in newspaper coverage of parliament and the demands for punchy soundbites have promoted the kind of partisan bickering that switches voters off politics. At the same time, greater scrutiny of politics has had the effect of shining a harsh light on the whole governmental process. The inevitable problems of government—delays, mistakes and false promises—are constantly highlighted by an ever-critical media.[34] These problems grate with the major parties' insistence that, if you vote for them, everything will come up roses. By promising the world, politicians contribute to their own poor reputations.

Another possible explanation for voters' aversion to politics has almost certainly been changes in the nature of party competition. Parties have become more centralized in recent years, partly through necessity because of their declining memberships, but also because of greater professionalism in campaigning. Furthermore, parties increasingly focus their dwindling resources on "golden voters"—undecided voters in marginal seats. As a result, the vast majority of voters have less personal interaction with politicians and party activists. Leading politicians have become, quite literally, more distant from voters. Long gone are the days when an incumbent prime minister would be driven around the country by his wife to speak to voters as Clement Attlee was in the 1950s. John Major's rediscovery of "soapbox politics" in 1992 stood out as an attempt to reconnect with the public. Although much was made of Blair's efforts to re-engage with "real voters" in 2005, most of his events were carefully choreographed for television, with Labour supporters bussed in for the occasion.[35] Equally, the rise of the career politician has perhaps made the political class more distant from the society they represent: fewer politicians know about anything other than full-time politics.[36]

Voters may also have been affected by a perceived ideological convergence in the party system. As recently as 1987, 83.5 per cent of voters agreed that there were "substantial differences" between the two major parties. In 1997 just 32.5 per cent felt the same way and in 2001 a mere 26.7 per cent did. There were signs before the 2005 election, however, that voters were swinging to some extent the other way. In July 2004, 32 per cent of voters felt that the Labour and Conservative policies were "very different", a figure that increased to 41 per cent in March 2005.[37] It is natural to interpret such responses as relating to ideological differences, but they may refer to other facets of party competition, such as those relating to competence and honesty. Importantly, convergence, together with the nature of contemporary campaigning, may also constrain political debate, with parties focusing on just a few key issues. Certainly, polls suggested that more than half of the electorate thought the 2005 campaign did not focus enough on the long-term future of pensions, Council Tax, global warming and law and order.[38]

The weakness of the Conservative opposition may also have contributed to voters' restlessness with established politics. Since 1997, when the Conservatives lost office, most voters have not viewed the party as a viable government in waiting. The result has been a perceived lack of choice. Moreover, whether there is ideological consensus or not, Westminster politics remains unremittingly partisan. "Ya-boo" politics, which seems incongruent with relatively small substantive differences between the parties, may simply switch voters off. In recent years, the emergence of the permanent campaign may have also heightened the adversarialism.[39] The Conservatives, being unaccustomed to opposition, have also tended to magnify partisan disagreements, alienating voters further from the political process.

The causes examined so far largely neglect changes within the electorate itself. In the past, voters thought of themselves as either Labour or Conservative, with those feelings often reinforced by class loyalties. Support for a party was exclusive. Those around you were either with you or against you. Many middle-class Conservatives were scared by the thought of a Labour government, and many working-class Labour voters feared Tory governments: Since the 1970s these fears have weakened. Voters have almost certainly become less inclined to believe that their party necessarily has the best policies and therefore have become more open to other parties' appeals. To be sure, the major parties' policies never "mapped" exactly on to the political views of the people who voted for them, as was noted in the 1960s, but the fit appears to be even looser now.[40] A large proportion of the electorate has evidently become "multi-party" at heart, supporting ideas and policies from different parties.[41] A survey conducted during the 2005 campaign, for example, found that only 45 per cent of respondents felt one political party adequately represented their views. These figures may reflect that it is no longer "socially desirable" to claim that a party represents oneself. However, such figures also point to the difficulties that parties encounter in the face of growing pluralism. It is far harder to reflect this pluralism and to produce consistent messages. It is also far harder to fashion a political programme that attracts broad support in an increasingly atomized society.[42]

Two general theories of social change may also have a bearing on the contemporary British electorate's somewhat sullen mood. The first originates from Robert Putnam's work on social capital, and focuses on the erosion of civic institutions.[43] In Britain, two institutions that once fostered social interaction—trade unions and the Church of England—have both experienced declining memberships. The significance of this decline has been even greater because of the unions' and the Church's association with the Labour and Conservative parties respectively. Unions once inculcated "Labour values" into their members, which sustained their loyalty to the Labour party. The Church, although less formally and overtly, similarly helped to sustain its members' conservative—and Conservative—values. Now they no longer do, at least not to anything like the same extent. The kinds of social interactions that once buttressed loyalty to the two major parties—and, by extension, to the political system as a whole—now, if they take place at all, take place elsewhere and no longer have the same system-reinforcing effects.

The second theory, cognitive mobilization, offers another possible explanation of voters' dissatisfaction with traditional politics. Since 1945, advanced democracies have experienced common structural changes. Access to education has greatly increased, while exposure to the media has grown massively.[44] In 2005 there were more graduates in Britain than ever before and many more sources of political information, including the internet and a vast range of television channels. It may be that voters are now both better informed and better able to process political information. It may also be that they are more sophisticated and their support for parties more conditional. The public is, moreover, confronted with stories of government failure almost every day. Better-educated voters may be more conscious of the limited influence that they, as individuals, can exert on the governmental process. If ignorance is bliss, knowledge may be both frustrating and disturbing. Meanwhile, education and growing affluence have contributed towards a shift in societal values.[45] "Quality-of-life" issues increasingly concern voters, so that a growing proportion of the electorate has a "post-material" outlook. More voters are willing to question existing political processes and values, and the traditional left–right dimension of political competition is sometimes unable to accommodate new issues, such as environmentalism or Europe. As a result, the dichotomous choice between Labour and the Conservatives is less likely to satisfy politically sophisticated voters.

Some commentators have also cited the rise of a consumer citizenry as an underlying cause of the electorate's moodiness.[46] Voters have become accustomed in everyday life to achieving instant results. Consumer credit enables most individuals to get what they want even before they can afford it, contributing to a "get now, pay later" mentality. This stands in marked contrast to the hard grind of government and politics. As Alastair Campbell notes: "Viewers can take part in a *Sky News* phone poll as to whether some new proposal is a good idea or a bad idea, and it gives a sense that it can be dealt with now, straightaway, easily. . . . But real solutions to real problems take time. And that can lead to a feeling of disempowerment, which adds to disillusion".[47] The inevitable failure of parties, politicians and the system to satisfy instant demands may thus cause some voters to feel grumpy.

Restless Behaviour: Bypassing the System

The behavioural consequences of the electorate's disenchantment with politics were united by a common theme: an increased willingness to bypass traditional institutions and processes. The most significant indicator in this respect has been the decline in turnout. Voting is, according to some accounts, an irrational act: the expected cost of voting (other opportunities forgone and shoe leather) almost always outweighs the expected benefit, since the voter is unlikely to be decisive.[48] In the past, however, very large proportions of the electorate *did* vote. In ten of the seventeen postwar general elections, over three-quarters of eligible voters—those officially registered on the electoral roll—voted (see Table 3.3). In both 1950 and 1951 turnout exceeded 80 per cent. Such levels of participation stand in marked contrast to the electorate's behaviour at recent general elections. The 1997 election established a new low for turnout at any postwar election, but the record was again smashed in 2001 when just 59.4 per cent went to the polls. A slightly larger proportion voted in 2005, when turnout rose to 61.5 per cent. Given the greater availability of postal ballots, however, that election only confirmed a downwards step-shift.

Several explanations were offered for the 2001 drop in turnout, many of them still applicable in 2005. The result of the 2001 election was a forgone conclusion and a contest between similar

Table 3.3 Turnout in General Elections, 1945–2005

General election	Turnout
1945	72.8
1950	83.9
1951	82.6
1955	76.8
1959	78.7
1964	77.1
1966	75.8
1970	72.0
1974 (Feb)	78.8
1974 (Oct)	72.8
1979	76.0
1983	72.7
1987	75.3
1992	77.7
1997	71.4
2001	59.4
2005	61.5

Sources: House of Commons Library, Research Papers, 04/61 and 05/33.

Note: Turnout is defined as the percentage of registered electors voting.

parties. The Conservatives never looked like winning, so voters stayed away: voting would make no difference. Labour was also expected to win in 2005, so the same effect may have been at work again. When voters think an election is close, turnout tends to be higher, as it was in 1992. However, runaway victories and ideological convergence have sometimes coincided with high turnouts, suggesting that deeper changes have occurred in the electorate's attitudes towards voting.

This suggestion is reinforced by falling turnouts in other kinds of elections. With the exception of the short gap between the two general elections of 1974, when only one by-election was held, the average turnout in the by-elections held between the 2001 and 2005 elections of 37.9 per cent was the lowest of any parliament in the postwar era.[49] It was also the first full-length parliament since 1945 during which turnout failed to reach 50 per cent in at least one by-election. Similarly, there appears to have been a downwards step-change in turnout at local elections since the 1997 general election.[50] Turnout did increase in the 2004 local elections, but these took place on the same day as European Parliament elections—a British "super Thursday"—and the greater availability of postal ballots almost certainly increased participation. Indeed, this election recorded the highest turnout, 39 per cent, in any British election to the parliament sitting in Strasbourg.[51] But these elections were the exception to the general rule that voters have become progressively more reluctant to vote.

The failure to register to vote also suggested that turnout amongst all eligible voters—as distinct from amongst registered voters—is actually lower than the official figures suggest. A report published by MPs just before the 2005 election found that the problem of non-registration was growing and estimated that the registration level among potential voters was only 93 per cent.[52] The report also noted that certain groups were less likely to register, including "those living in urban areas and areas of economic deprivation; those aged seventeen to twenty-four; those in privately rented accommodation; and those from black and minority ethnic communities". In short, MPs found evidence that the socially excluded were also excluding themselves politically, not necessarily as a deliberate act but more as a result of their "disengagement from the political process and politics generally".[53]

There has been an even longer-term decline in another traditional mode of political participation: membership of parties. In 1953 the Conservatives claimed over 2.8 million and Labour just over one million individual members (excluding affiliated trade unionists).[54] By 1975 these figures had fallen to 1.12 million and 675,000 respectively. Such figures must be treated with caution. Accurate data are impossible to obtain before the 1990s.[55] Nevertheless, it appears that the pattern of the last few decades has been one of further decline (see Table 3.4 below), with the exception of the mid-1990s when Labour temporarily increased its membership.[56]

Part of the story of this long-term decline was almost certainly a growing detachment of voters from parties. The weakening of voters' partisanship has

Table 3.4 Approximate Individual Party Membership, 1983–2005

	Labour	Conservatives	Liberal Democrats
1983	295,000	1,200,000	145,000
1987	289,000	1,000,000	138,000
1992	280,000	500,000	100,000
1997	405,000	400,000	100,000
2001	311,000	350,000	90,000
2005	215,000	320,000	73,000

Sources: Patrick Seyd and Paul Whiteley, "British Party Members: An Overview", *Party Politics*, 10 (2004), 357; and Andrew Russell, "The Party System: Deep Frozen or Gentle Thawing?" *Parliamentary Affairs*, 58 (2005), 353.

shrunk the pool of potential members, while the decline in trade union and church membership has acted as a non-political catalyst to the decline. People now have many other things to do, making them less likely to join a party.[57] However, membership levels before the 2005 election were probably also affected by short-term dissatisfaction with both the major parties. Some Tories, for instance, almost certainly let their membership lapse as a result of the party's internal strife. Meanwhile, dissatisfaction with the government, especially over the war in Iraq, undoubtedly led many Labour members to leave.[58]

There also appears to have been a qualitative shift in the nature of membership, affecting all the major parties. Surveys of Labour, Conservative and Liberal Democrat party members conducted during the 1990s all reported a decline in the members' reported activism.[59] As *The Economist* noted in July 1999: "today, belonging to a British political party is more like being a supporter of some charity: you may pay a membership fee, but will not necessarily attend meetings or help to turn out the vote at election time".[60] Whether changes in membership have been a cause or a consequence of greater professionalism in party campaigns, the outcome is the same: parties have a smaller core of activists on which to draw. At the same time, many fewer people are now willing to display party posters. In 1992 it was easy to spot houses festooned with signs inviting passers-by to vote for one party or another. In 2005 looking for posters was like trying to find a non-black Model T. Party members, like voters more generally, seem less ready to make a display of their partisan loyalties. Indeed, party membership is almost akin to membership of a secret society.

If membership of parties has been declining, other modes of political participation have been increasing. Activities such as signing petitions, taking part in demonstrations or joining boycotts have become more common in Britain, as they have in many other advanced industrial nations.[61] Such behaviour perhaps reflects a general dissatisfaction, at least among the politically engaged, with political parties as vehicles for achieving their objectives. They now want to engage with narrow-based single-issue groups instead of with more broad-based parties. Parties require politically active individuals either to agree with or at least consent to a whole package of policies and values. Single-issue campaigns do not.

The public's recent restlessness with conventional political channels was manifested most clearly in protest activity. On the one hand, recent surveys found a marked increase both in the willingness of individuals to protest or demonstrate and in their reported participation in such actions.[62] On the other hand, available survey data also suggested that levels of protest in 2001 were no greater than in the 1970s.[63] Nevertheless, a series of demonstrations and actions—principally but not entirely after the 2001 election—contributed greatly to a Zeitgeist of protest. Notable protests leading up to the 2005 election included the following:

- Fuel protests—In September 2000, a well-organized group of hauliers and farmers blockaded oil refineries in protest about high fuel taxes. Britain's petrol pumps ran dry and the country ground to a halt, if only for a couple of days.

- May Day protests—Thousands of "anti-capitalist" protestors took to the streets of London in May 2001, defacing monuments and vandalizing "symbols of globalization" such as McDonald's and Starbucks.

- Animal rights protests—There was a spate of attacks on individuals and companies involved in animal research.

- GM protests—Campaigners against genetically modified crops donned white overalls and destroyed the offending crops.

- Iraq War protests—Nearly a million people took to the streets of London in February 2003 to protest at preparations for the invasion of Iraq. Organizers of the "Stop the War" march estimated that some two million individuals took part, although the police put the figure at 750,000.

- Hunting/Countryside Alliance protests—Before the "Stop the War" march, Britain's largest mass protest was the September 2002 "Liberty and Livelihood" march. An estimated 400,000 protested for rural rights and against a proposed ban on fox-hunting. Eighteen months later, as MPs debated the ban, a small group of campaigners infiltrated the House of Commons and protested in the chamber.

- Fathers4Justice—Activists campaigning to improve fathers' rights of access to children dressed up as superheroes and scaled various London landmarks. Their most subversive act of protest came in May 2004 when campaigners threw purple flour at Blair in the Commons chamber, raising fears of a poison attack.

- Council Tax protests—Pensioners got in on the protest act when hundreds marched on Downing Street in October 2004, angered by steep rises in Council Tax, a property-based levy set by local councils to help pay for services like policing and refuse collection.

These protests varied greatly in size and style. Some protesters were doubtless instrumental, seeking to achieve specific ends whatever their means. Other protestors did as they did for expressive reasons, marching or protesting simply in order to vent their feelings. Occasionally, politicians attempted to ally themselves with protestors. Liberal Democrat leader Charles Kennedy spoke at a big anti-war rally in February 2003, while Conservative leader Iain Duncan Smith backed the earlier "Countryside" march. However, their involvement was peripheral and added little to either event. In contrast, the media played a central role. Some of these protests, notably the "Fathers4Justice" stunt, were designed deliberately as media events. In some cases, the media also provided the venue for individual protests aimed directly at politicians. In February 2005, a woman called Maria Hutchings used a live television debate to reprimand Blair for the government's decision to phase out special-needs schools for children with learning difficulties.[64]

Protests were even evident during the 2005 election campaign. In the run up to voting, hauliers attempted to stage another fuel protest, while Greenpeace activists climbed on to the roof of Deputy Prime Minister John Prescott's home and installed solar panels to highlight the desirability of renewable energy. As has already been noted, many voters felt that insufficient attention was being paid to certain issues during the campaign. Some were willing to take direct action in an effort to raise the profile of the issues that concerned them.

Recent protests have thus been characterized by the participants' shared rejection of conventional means of obtaining the redress of grievances and influencing public policy. Together with the declines in turnout and party membership, such acts suggest that the political system is no longer as party-centric as it once was. For a growing proportion of the electorate, traditional politics, when defined as joining, supporting and voting for a political party, is something that other people do.

Restlessness at the Ballot Box:
Stirrings in the Party System

In many ways, the most significant manifestations of discontent were to be found at the ballot box. Voters' behaviour was increasingly characterized by anti-establishment and protest voting and pointed to a growing dissatisfaction with the traditional choices provided by the two major parties.

As has already been noted, British electoral politics has been a two-horse race for much of the postwar era (see Figure 3.1). At the 1951 and 1955 elections, Labour and the Conservatives between them secured over 96 per cent of the popular vote. From 1974, voters' willingness to vote for these two parties declined, although electoral competition was still framed as a dichotomous choice. Between 1945 and 1970, the two major parties secured, on average, 91.2 per cent of the vote. After 1970, their average combined share dropped by nearly 20 points to just 73.8 per cent. Then in 2005, the two parties polled their lowest combined share of the popular vote in postwar history: just 67.5 per cent. The previous low had come in 1983, when it reached

Figure 3.1 Major Parties' Combined Share of the Vote in General Elections, 1945–2005

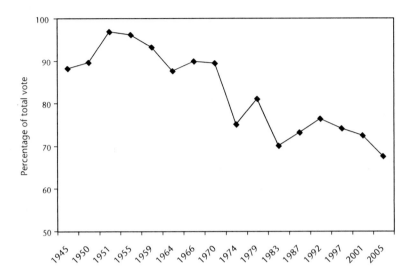

Sources: House of Commons Library, Research Papers, 04/61 and 05/33.

70.0 per cent, but this election occurred after a major split in the Labour ranks and the formation of a new party, the Social Democratic Party (SDP) in 1981. The emergence of Respect, the anti-war party led by George Galloway, a former Labour MP known for his pro-Iraq sympathies, as an alternative to New Labour after the 2001 election was simply not on the same scale as the SDP twenty years earlier. That makes the combined Labour and Conservative share of the vote in 2005 all the more remarkable.

The most obvious qualification to the "two-horse race" description of British politics has been the success of a third party in elections since 1970. After 1945, the Liberals, which had been the principal electoral rival to the Conservatives until the early 1920s, looked dead and buried. In 1974 there was a resurrection of sorts (see Table 3.5), and the party has been attracting on average 19.4 per cent of the vote ever since. In a FPTP system, these votes have effectively been wasted: third place in British elections is nowhere. Nevertheless, the Liberals, who later formed an alliance with the Social Democratic Party (SDP) before merging to create the Liberal Democrats in 1988, have functioned as the "plague on both your houses" party in British general elections. Indeed, its fortunes since 1970 suggest that large numbers of voters have been unhappy with the Conservative–Labour choice for the past three decades. The 1983 election saw the Liberal Party's best postwar result, although this had much to do with the split in the Labour Party. However, the Liberal Democrats' fortunes have been waxing again in recent elections, indicating, perhaps, voters' growing unhappiness with the two major parties.

More striking, however, is the fact that votes have lately been going to other parties. Minor parties have always existed in Britain. Fifty years ago, there was a Communist Party of Great Britain and British Empire Party, as well as the Scottish and Welsh nationalists (SNP and Plaid Cymru). But such parties were fringe parties. Then in the 1970s, things began to change. In Wales and Scotland, Plaid Cymru and the SNP picked up more votes (see Table 3.5) and other parties also began to attract support, although the increase in the reference books' "Other" column chiefly reflected the transformation of politics in Northern Ireland. For historical reasons, the Ulster Unionist party—which then represented the Protestant community in Ulster, and which had been allied with the Conservatives—split, while a new party, the Social Democratic and Labour Party, was formed at the same time to represent the nationalist community. Between them, these new parties accounted for the core of the "Other" vote in elections from 1970 onwards. However, the last three general elections have seen a marked increase in the votes won by minor parties that have nothing to do with Northern Ireland. This increase suggests that many voters are finding the two major parties—and indeed all three main parties—increasingly unattractive.

Voters' willingness to go elsewhere was demonstrated most clearly in the 2004 European Parliament elections, a nationwide poll in which Labour and the Conservatives failed to secure even half of the popular vote between them. When the Liberal Democrats' share of the vote was added to those of Labour and the Conservatives, just 64.2 per cent of voters opted for what might be termed the establishment parties.[65] The Conservatives were the "winners" of the election with 26.7 per cent of the vote. Labour secured just 22.6 per cent. Surprisingly, the third-placed party was the United Kingdom Independence Party (UKIP) with 16.2 per cent. UKIP's whole *raison-d'être* was to campaign against Britain's membership of the European Union. It was a party defined almost entirely by being against something. These elections also saw support for the Greens, who secured 6.2 per cent of the vote, and the far-right British National Party (BNP), which achieved 4.9

Table 3.5 The Liberal, Nationalist and Other Parties' Shares of the Vote in General Elections, 1945–2005

Election	Liberal	Nationalist	Others
1945	9.0	0.2	3.4
1950	9.1	0.1	1.4
1951	2.6	0.1	0.5
1955	2.7	0.2	1.1
1959	5.9	0.4	0.5
1964	11.2	0.5	0.9
1966	8.5	0.7	1.0
1970	7.5	1.7	1.4
1974 (Feb)	19.3	2.6	3.1
1974 (Oct)	18.3	3.4	3.3
1979	13.8	2.0	3.4
1983	25.4	1.5	3.1
1987	22.6	1.7	2.7
1992	17.8	2.3	3.6
1997	16.8	2.5	6.8
2001	18.3	2.5	6.8
2005	22.1	2.2	8.2

Sources: House of Commons Library, Research Papers, 04/61 and 05/33

Notes: The Liberal column refers to Liberal votes for 1945–1979, SDP–Liberal Alliance votes for 1983–1987 and Liberal Democrat votes for 1992–2005. The nationalist column refers to the combined support for the Scottish Nationalist Party (SNP) and Plaid Cyrmu per cent. The last time that any minor party did so well at a national election was 1989 when the Greens attracted 14.9 per cent of the vote in that year's European Parliament elections. Their support in 1989 appears to have been at the expense of the then newly formed Liberal Democrats.

No one knows whether the fringe parties' increased support reflected voters' true policy preferences or amounted to no more than "anti-them" protest voting. Some doubtless voted Green, UKIP or BNP because they genuinely supported significant aspects of their platforms. Others, however, were almost certainly voting for such parties to register discontent with the established choices. Although we cannot be sure, a spate of votes that were obviously protest votes cast in the last few years suggests that many voters have been using the ballot box to show how fed up they are. In the 2000 London mayoral elections, for example, voters rejected Labour, the Conservatives and the Liberal Democrats and voted for Ken Livingstone, a former Labour MP and gadfly to New Labour. Later elections for directly elected mayors witnessed even more anti-establishment voting. In May 2002, voters in Hartlepool elected Stuart Drummond, also known as H'Angus the Monkey, the mascot of the local football team, who campaigned on a platform of free bananas for school children.

Voters' willingness to vote for fringe parties has in turn generated a market for single-issue and protest organizations. The most high-profile party formed in the run up to the 2005 election was Veritas, established by Robert Kilroy Silk, a one-time Labour MP and former chat-show host, who portrayed himself and his party as a voice for the discontented. Other protest parties were also formed, often fighting on local issues but occasionally trying to broaden their support. The objective of the "Blair Must Go Party", for instance, was obvious. The Electoral Commission estimated that almost half of the new parties were simply special-interest groups or parties campaigning on a single issue.[66] Few sought to provide voters with a broad programme for national government.

The electorate's mood was clearly evident when Britain went to the polls in 2005. Nationally, as has already been noted, turnout was again low while the two major parties obtained their lowest combined share of the vote in postwar history (67.5 per cent). Just over two-thirds of British voters thus voted for one of the two main parties in a system based on only two political forces: government and opposition. Labour was returned to power with just 35.2 per cent of the popular vote, the lowest share of the vote obtained by a winning party since the Great Reform Act of 1832.[67] Support for Labour appeared to leak to a wide variety of parties rather than to the official opposition as would once have been expected. The Liberal Democrats picked up votes but many went to a range of other parties (including nationalists), whose combined share of the vote reached 10.3 per cent, the highest such figure of any postwar general election. UKIP (2.2 per cent), the Greens (1.0 per cent) and the BNP (0.7 per cent) achieved their best ever showing at any general election, although Veritas (0.1 per cent) fared badly.[68] Britain's party system after 2005 can no longer accurately be described simply as a two-party system. In only 335 out of 646 United Kingdom constituencies did Labour or the Conservatives finish in either of the top two places.

There were even clearer signs of disaffection at the local level. Three protest candidates won election to Westminster. Richard Taylor was re-elected in Wyre Forest, a seat he first took in 2001, campaigning on the issue of closure of parts of a local hospital. Peter Law, a former Labour member angered by an all-women shortlist adopted by the party, held Blaenau Gwent against the official Labour candidate. George Galloway, a former Labour MP, defied all expectations and won the seat of Bethnal Green and Bow for Respect after campaigning almost exclusively on the issue of Iraq. The results in Wyre Forest and Blaneau reflected local grudges. The result in Bethnal Green was slightly different because it reflected a more general concern about Iraq amongst Muslims: the constituency is home to a large number of British Muslims. Indeed, Respect did well in several other constituencies with large numbers of Muslim voters, coming second in three.[69] In areas with small Muslim communities, it fared abysmally. Elsewhere, an independent came third in Mansfield, which had previously elected an independent council, while the Greens came third in Brighton Pavilion.

An independent, Reg Keys, also did well in Tony Blair's constituency of Sedgefield, coming fourth with 10.3 per cent of the vote. His candidacy was itself an act of protest, prompted by the death of his son, killed on active service in Iraq. Disturbingly, the far-right BNP came third in Barking, and narrowly missed third spot in six other constituencies troubled by racial tensions.

In many ways, the unusual voting behaviour before and during the 2005 election suggested that the electorate had become more dissatisfied than ever with the established parties. However, it is also worth considering briefly the possibility that voters had simply acquired a habit for voting in new ways. In this respect, the PR systems that Labour introduced for elections to the European Parliament and the devolved bodies in Wales, Scotland and London, provide another possible source of restless voting. On the one hand, the electorate has had more opportunities to vote and register a protest. On the other hand, these more proportional systems allow voters to back their first preferences without their vote being wasted, as it may be under the system for Westminster elections. The electorate may thus have gained new voting habits in a relatively short time, perhaps unlocking discontent with the major parties that had been just beneath the surface for years. At any rate, the parties that did well in the 2005 election were certainly helped by successes in previous second-order elections.

Conclusion

To return to a question posed at the beginning of this chapter: has the electorate's mood affected the political parties' once central place in British political life?

Within the party system, support for the main parties has fragmented. Just 1,409 candidates contested 630 seats at the 1955 election. Over twice that number, 3,552 contested 646 seats in 2005.[70] Although British general elections really still offer voters a choice between Labour and Conservative governments, "two-party" is an unsatisfactory description for British electoral politics. British politics more generally appears to have become less party-centred. Fewer electors are party members or activists or are willing to vote, and more take part in extra-party protest activity. Changes in media coverage have added further to the sense that the historic domination of the two major parties is being eroded. It may be little more than cosmetic, of course, but current affairs programmes are more willing now to interview and invite on to panels non-politicians, whether experts or celebrities. Kevin Marsh, the editor of the influential early morning *Today* programme on BBC Radio 4, for example, claims that politics is now "multipolar" and that broadcasters should aim to "bring in voices beyond the mainstream".[71] Television and radio producers, at least, sense the decline of parties in the public imagination, and their reluctance any longer to focus exclusively on them may in turn have contributed further to the decline.

These stirrings have important consequences for the functions that parties are supposed to fulfil. Some were unaffected. Parties still frame the choice of government, while recruitment to governmental office is still defined more or less in party terms. Successful independent candidates are still rare and elections remain fundamentally party-centred, despite the best efforts of men in monkey costumes. However, parties were increasingly unsuccessful in communicating political messages and also in mobilizing and integrating voters into the political process. These functions appeared increasingly to be undertaken by the media and single-issue protest groups. Similarly, questions were asked as to whether parties themselves were setting the political agenda or slavishly following the media's lead. Some commentators claimed, for instance, that the parties were following the *Daily Mail*'s hard-line lead on immigration.[72] In years gone by, it was generally accepted that "the parties monopolise the national agenda".[73] Before the 2005 election, this no longer appeared to be the case.

There have also been consequences for other functions that parties have traditionally fulfilled. Parliamentary democracy and broad-based parties have traditionally provided an institutional structure for involving voters in the process of governing the country as a whole. As more and more voters eschew these structures, however, their views risk becoming ignored. Moreover, the rise in protest activity risks undermining democratic channels. Extreme groups can wield disproportionate influence and, like all single-issue interest groups, may work against the public good.

The ability of parties to fulfil what has been termed a "latent function"—conferring legitimacy on elected officials—is also at risk as a result of the stirrings in the system. With lower turnouts and more fragmented voting, MPs and governments are being elected with more tenuous mandates. In

2005, for example, just 213 MPs received 50 per cent or more of the vote, and not a single MP was elected by 50 per cent of the eligible electorate.[74] Indeed, four MPs were elected by less than 20 per cent of the eligible voters in their constituencies.[75] At a national level, Labour was re-elected in 2005 with the support of just 21.6 per cent of the registered electorate, the lowest proportion ever to return a single-party government with a large majority. Surprisingly, however, there appeared to be little discontent with the overall result of the election. It may simply be that a majority, however they cast their ballots, wanted Labour rather than the Conservatives to win.[76] At any rate, very few people, if any, took to the streets in protest at the outcome.

The observation that parties were struggling to fulfil certain functions in recent years is framed by the context of what has generally been considered the "normal" state of affairs in British politics: two parties—Labour and the Conservatives—competing for office and acting as the prime movers in politics. What has passed for normal, however, is in many ways a myth of the postwar settlement. Until the early 1920s, Britain had a two-party system centred on the Liberals and the Conservatives. Labour gradually supplanted the Liberals during the interwar period and emerged as the chief electoral rival to the Conservatives after 1945. But if we regard the two major parties' share of the vote as the key measure—though it is not ideal—Britain has had just twenty-five years of normal two-party politics (1945–70) and thirty-five years of abnormal two-and-a-half party politics (1970–2005). With hindsight, it therefore seems odd that the immediate post-1945 era should have been regarded as the norm for so long.

By this reckoning, it is probably time to reappraise what "normal" is. It might also be time to reconsider whether the electoral system needs reforming to recognize the new patterns of competition. Some voters may be voting for other parties because they are unhappy with the established choices; but these voters may in turn become more disaffected with politics if their votes are not reflected in parliament. The depth of this possible source of discontent is difficult to gauge, but it seems limited at present to the *Independent* newspaper and Liberal Democrat supporters who have long advocated electoral reform.[77] Perhaps the most important argument for a review, however, is the issue of legitimacy. Almost no one questioned Labour's right to govern in 2005. But if future elections result in governments being elected by equally small proportions of voters, there could be problems.

However, one final point is worth making. The recent discontent with politicians and politics may simply reflect a humdrum malaise of democracy. As the commentator Martin Kettle noted before the 2005 election, "We hate our politicians, but we've never had it so good".[78] For the last ten years, British voters have enjoyed relatively high levels of employment, economic stability and growing affluence. In the long term, they have benefited from a welfare state, a National Health Service, personal freedom and relative security. In all respects, political processes, based on politicians and political parties, have delivered the goods. Some of the electorate's discontent documented in this chapter may thus strike the reader as the equivalent of grumpy old men and women finding fault with everything rather than as constituting a growing yearning for change. Voters, unlike customers, can sometimes be wrong.

Notes

1. Lord Butler interview, "How not to run a country", *Spectator*, December 11, 2004.
2. Rod Liddle, "If only we could vote them all out", *Sunday Times*, April 17, 2005.
3. S.E. Finer, *The Changing British Party System, 1945–1979* (Washington, DC: American Enterprise Institute for Public Policy Research, 1980), p. 165.
4. For an early discussion of party functions, see Anthony King, "Political Parties in Western Democracies: Some Sceptical Reflections", *Polity*, 2 (1969), 111–41. See also Finer, *The Changing British Party System;* and Paul Webb, David M. Farrell and Ian Holliday, eds, *Political Parties in Advanced Industrial Democracies* (Oxford: Oxford University Press, 2002).
5. Paul Webb, "Political Parties in Britain: Secular Decline or Adaptive Resilience?" in Webb, Farrell and Holliday, *Political Parties in Advanced Industrial Democracies*.
6. David Easton, *A Systems Analysis of Political Life* (New York: John Wiley and Sons, 1965).
7. Anthony King, "In office, but out of touch and out of favour", *Daily Telegraph*, September 9, 2003.
8. Averages based on data from the MORI website, http://www.mori.com.
9. Figures from MORI, http://www.mori.com.
10. Martin Paldam, "The Distribution of Election Results and the Two Explanations of the Cost of Ruling", *European Journal of Political Economy*, 2 (1986), 5–24.
11. John Bartle, "Why Labour Won—Again", in Anthony King, ed., *Britain at the Polls: 2001* (New York: Chatham House, 2002), p.187.
12. See MORI's "Final Aggregate Analysis" of voting behaviour, http://www.mori.com.
13. George Jones, "Voters prepared to back Blair again despite doubts on war", *Daily Telegraph*, October 9, 2004.
14. "It's Tough Being a Tory", *The Economist*, September 30, 2004.
15. Anthony King, "Poll gap stays just as wide no matter who wins the arguments", *Daily Telegraph*, April 29, 2005.
16. Harold D. Clarke, David Sanders, Marianne C. Stewart and Paul Whiteley, *Political Choice in Britain* (Oxford: Oxford University Press, 2004), p. 289.
17. Catherine Bromley and John Curtice, "Where Have All the Voters Gone?" in Alison Park, John Curtice, Katarina Thomson, Lindsey Jarvis and Catherine Bromley, eds, *British Social Attitudes: 19th Report* (London: Sage, 2002), p. 146.
18. David Denver, *Elections and Voters in Britain* (Basingstoke, Hants.: Palgrave, 2003), pp. 61–5.
19. Clarke et al., *Political Choice in Britain*, pp. 182–5.
20. Andrew Marr, *Ruling Britannia: The Failure and Future of British Democracy* (London: Michael Joseph, 1995), p. 17.
21. Anthony King, "Public confidence in politicians falls as 'sleaze' factor returns to haunt Labour", *Daily Telegraph*, November 29, 2004.
22. *Daily Telegraph*, November 29, 2004.
23. Charles Pattie, Patrick Seyd and Paul Whiteley, *Citizenship in Britain* (Cambridge: Cambridge University Press), pp. 37–8.
24. "Members of Parliament are okay but . . . ", *New Society*, 23:7, March 1963.

25. John Curtice and Ben Seyd, "Is There a Crisis of Political Participation?" in Alison Park, John Curtice, Katarina Thomson, Lindsey Jarvis and Catherine Bromley, eds, *British Social Attitudes: 20th Report* (London: Sage, 2003), pp. 101–2.
26. These figures are a combination of those agreeing and strongly agreeing with the statement "People like me have no say in what the government does". Data from the BESIS website, http://www.besis.org.
27. Anthony King, "Shift in balance of power", *Daily Telegraph*, April 28, 2003.
28. Anthony King, "Don't know, don't care", *Daily Telegraph*, March 7, 2005.
29. Electoral Commission, *An Audit of Political Engagement 2* (London: Electoral Commission, 2005), p. 16.
30. Pattie, Seyd and Whiteley, *Citizenship in Britain*, p. 62.
31. Steven Barnett, "Will a Crisis in Journalism Provoke a Crisis in Democracy?" *Political Quarterly*, 73 (2002), 400–8.
32. See, for example, Nick Cohen, "What is a Briton?" *Observer*, September 7, 2003; and George Monbiot, "Extreme measures", *Guardian*, March 2, 2004.
33. David Wooding, "Trough at the top", *Sun*, October 22, 2004.
34. Alastair Campbell, "It's Time to Bury Spin", *British Journalism Review*, 13 (2002), 18.
35. Tim Dowling, "We only work for croissants", *Guardian*, April 14, 2005.
36. Peter Riddell, *Honest Opportunism: The Rise of the Career Politician* (London: Indigo, 1996).
37. Anthony King, "Swing to Tories will not be enough to topple Blair", *Daily Telegraph*, March 25, 2005.
38. Anthony King, "Economy fails to stretch Labour poll lead", *Daily Telegraph*, April 8, 2005.
39. Meg Russell, *Must Politics Disappoint?* (London: Fabian Society, 2005), pp. 22–3.
40. Jean Blondel, *Voters, Parties, and Leaders: The Social Fabric of British Politics* (London: Penguin Books, 1967).
41. Mary Ann Sieghart, "In a strictly electoral sense—I'm anybody's", *The Times*, April 28, 2000.
42. Martin Kettle, "Society is disintegrating, and single-issue politics is back", *Guardian*, April 19, 2005.
43. Robert Putnam, *Bowling Alone: The Collapse and Revival of American Community* (New York: Simon and Schuster, 2000).
44. Russell Dalton, *Citizen Politics* (Chatham, NJ: Chatham House, 2002).
45. Ronald Inglehart, *Culture Shift in Advanced Industrial Society* (Princeton, NJ: Princeton University Press, 1990).
46. Russell, *Must Politics Disappoint?*
47. Campbell, "It's Time to Bury Spin", p. 18.
48. Anthony Downs, *An Economic Theory of Democracy* (New York: Harper and Row, 1957).
49. Based on data contained in House of Commons Library, Research Papers, 04/61 and 05/34.
50. Peter Kellner, "Britain's Culture of Detachment", *Parliamentary Affairs*, 57 (2004), 830–43.
51. House of Commons Library, Research Paper, 04/50.
52. Constitutional Affairs and ODPM: Housing, Planning, Local Government and the Regions Committee, *First Joint Report, Electoral Registration*, HC 243-I 2005-04, para. 51.
53. Ibid., para. 52.
54. David Butler and Gareth Butler, *Twentieth Century British Political Facts 1900–2000* (Basingstoke, Hants.: Macmillan, 2000), p. 141.

55. See Paul Webb, *The Modern British Party System* (London: Sage, 2000), endnote 1, p. 248.
56. Patrick Seyd and Paul Whiteley, "British Party Members: An Overview", *Party Politics*, 10 (2004), 355–66, at p. 357.
57. Seyd and Whiteley, "British Party Members", p. 358.
58. Rosemary Bennett, Sam Lister and Angus Macleod, "Labour faces poll disaster in May", *The Times*, February 18, 2003.
59. Seyd and Whitelely, "British Party Members", p. 359.
60. "Empty Vessels?" *The Economist*, July 22, 1999.
61. Dalton, *Citizen Politics*, p. 65.
62. Curtice and Seyd, "Is There a Crisis?" pp. 101–2.
63. Clarke et al., *Political Choice in Britain*, p. 288.
64. Steve Bird, "Irate mother confronts Blair live on TV show", *The Times*, February 17, 2005.
65. House of Commons Library, Research Paper, 04/50.
66. Tania Branigan, "Poll line-up grows as single issue parties flourish", *Guardian*, April 1, 2005.
67. The figure of 35.3 per cent relates to the whole of the United Kingdom. Great Britain only figures are more useful comparators these days, because Northern Ireland had become entirely detached from the British party system. On this basis, Labour obtained 36.2 per cent of the popular vote.
68. House of Commons Library, Research Paper, 05/33.
69. The three seats were West Ham, East Ham, and Birmingham Sparkbrook and Small Heath.
70. House of Commons Library, Research Papers, 04/61 and 05/33.
71. Andrew Bounds, "Tough detachment", *Financial Times*, August 28, 2004.
72. Nick Cohen, "Howard's one-way street", *Observer*, April 24, 2005.
73. Finer, *The Changing British Party System*, p. 174.
74. Excluding Northern Irish MPs. These figures were calculated from the British Parliamentary Constituency Database, 1992–2005.
75. The four MPs were George Galloway, Respect, Bethnal Green and Bow; Roger Godsiff, Labour, Birmingham, Sparkbrook and Small Heath; Jim Fitzpatrick, Labour, Poplar and Canning Town; and Ann McKechin, Labour, Glasgow North.
76. Throughout the election campaign, YouGov asked a question obliging respondents to choose between a Labour and Conservative government. Labour won this "forced choice" contest hands down. See http://www.yougov.com.
77. After the 2005 election, the *Independent* began a spirited campaign for electoral reform. See "Campaign for democracy", *Independent*, May 10, 2005.
78. Martin Kettle, "We hate our politicians, but we've never had it so good", *Guardian*, February 8, 2005.

4

The Reluctant European: Europe as an Issue in British Politics

David McKay

"Europe" has figured prominently in British politics and British election campaigns at least since the early 1960s. In this period the issue has taken on many guises—membership of the Common Market (as it used to be called), membership of the Exchange Rate Mechanism (ERM) and more recently the single currency (the euro), negotiations over the British budget rebate, enlargement and the status of the European Union (EU) constitution. Until very recently, three constants have notably moulded the terms of the debate.

The absence of intra party unity: Initially the main schism afflicted the Labour Party with the battle lines drawn between the then "modernizers", such as Harold Wilson and Roy Jenkins, who saw Europe as a vehicle for making British industry more competitive, and the traditionalists of the left, such as Tony Benn and Michael Foot, who viewed Europe as a rich man's capitalist club. As will be developed later, although Labour remains divided on the issue, it does so along quite different and also much attenuated lines. Instead, it is the Conservative Party that is now deeply divided on Europe. Most Conservative MPs—and even more so Tory Party activists—oppose any further deepening of European integration and especially British membership of the euro. At the same time a smaller but high profile elite within the party including such figures as Kenneth Clarke, the former Chancellor of the Exchequer and Michael Heseltine, the former Deputy Prime Minister, continue to be strong supporters of further integration including membership of the single currency. Of the major parties only the Liberal Democrats have been consistent in their almost unqualified support of the further integration of Britain into Europe.

Low political salience among the electorate: While the political classes tend to have very strong feelings on Europe, most voters do not. From the very beginning the salience of the issue among the mass public has been low. Very generally, voters are Eurosceptic—that is, they distrust what they see as a Brussels elite intent on ever-greater integration. They have also been consistently opposed to British adoption of the euro and a proposed EU constitution. However, apart from a minority of (mainly Tory) voters most tend not to hold these views very strongly. In every general election since 1970 other issues, most notably the economy, the quality of the public services and law and order, have trumped Europe. As we will see, this dissonance between the intensity of political party feelings on Europe and the relative indifference of voters has had important political and electoral consequences.

Britain's unique position as a Eurosceptic nation: Britain is the only country in the EU where both the detail and even the status of membership have been contested over the whole period since 1970. Until very recently "Europe" had approached the status of a "valence" (or consensual) issue in almost all of the member states.[1] Major political parties were supportive of further integration and mass publics assumed that "ever closer union" was broadly in the public interest. And although recent events including the rejection of the EU Constitution by France and the Netherlands have dented this solidarity, Britain retains the status as the "spoiler of Europe". As a result British political leaders have rarely assumed the status of major players in the EU, and in particular as enthusiasts of further European integration. This applies even to Tony Blair, who, in spite of his self-image as a Europhile, had by 2005 taken on the "traditional" British role of reluctant European.[2]

To understand how these three factors have shaped political debate in the period since the 2001 general election it is necessary to highlight some of the more important developments involving Europe during the eighteen years of Conservative government from 1979 to 1997.

Preamble: Labour, the Conservatives and Europe, 1983–97

Nothing better illustrates the dramatic transformation of the Labour Party's position on Europe than the shifting content of party manifesto promises during the period.

In its 1979 manifesto Labour was hostile to what it saw as a capitalist and free-trade Europe: "We aim to develop a Europe which is democratic and socialist, and where the interests of the people are placed above the interests of national and multinational capitalist groups, but within which each country must be able to realize its own economic and social objectives, under the sovereignty of its own Parliament and people". By the time the 1983 manifesto was written, this hostility had grown into a pledge, under the new leader Michael Foot, to withdraw completely (and rapidly) from the European Economic Community (EEC), as "Europe" was then known: "On taking office we will open preliminary negotiations with the other EEC member states to establish a timetable for withdrawal; and we will publish the results of these negotiations in a White Paper". It is worth noting in passing that two young MPs, Tony Blair and Gordon Brown, were first elected on the 1983 manifesto that pledged British withdrawal. Under Neil Kinnock's leadership, however, the 1987 and 1992 manifestos were much more conciliatory. In 1987 the manifesto pledged, "Labour's aim is to work constructively with our EEC partners to promote economic expansion and combat unemployment". In 1992 the pro-EEC trend continued with a promise to use European integration to "promote Britain out of the European second division into which our country has been relegated by the Tories".[3]

By 1997 the transformation was complete. The "New Labour" manifesto of that year was highly positive on Europe, proposing that Britain should stay in the EU but also play a leading role. In addition, and in contrast to 1987 and 1992, the manifesto devoted much more space to the European issue (248 words compared with a mere sixty-two in 1987).[4] Finally, the 1997 manifesto offered the British people the opportunity to vote in a referendum on the single currency. While important, this policy U-turn was not as significant in electoral terms as the other policy changes undertaken by Labour during the later 1980s and the 1990s. Pledges not to reverse the trade union reforms and income tax reductions of the Thatcher governments, the re-writing of Clause 4 of the Labour Party constitution, and continued support for improved public services were all more salient to voters in 1997 than was the European issue.[5] In one respect, however, Labour's U-turn on Europe was to the party's electoral advantage: by 1997 Labour had replaced the Conservatives as the major party with the least negative stance towards EU membership. This had the effect of cutting across the traditional class divide of British politics. In other words, as an issue Europe became partly decoupled from the left/right policy cleavage that had divided the parties in the past. The Conservatives were now viewed as the more Eurosceptic and Labour as the more Europhile of the two major parties (for voter attitudes on Europe by party, see Figure 4.1).

Figure 4.1 EU Attitudes by Vote, 1964–1997

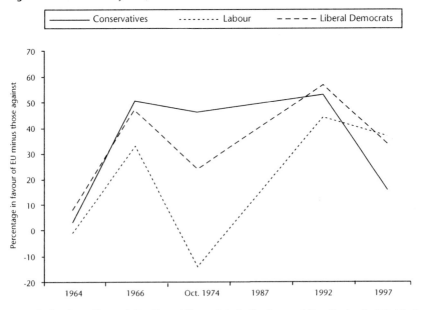

Source: Geoffrey Evans, "Europe: A New Electoral Cleavage", in Geoffrey Evans and Pippa Norris, eds, *Critical Elections: British Parties and Voters in Long-Term Perspective* (London: Sage, 1999) pp. 207–22, at p. 212, fig. 11.2. Reprinted by permission of Sage Publications Ltd. ©1999 Geoffrey Evans.

Another dimension to the European debate was what might be called the "technocratization" of the issue. By 1997 the Maastricht Treaty, which greatly extended the competence of the EU, had been ratified and those countries that had not opted out of the single currency (such as Denmark and the United Kingdom) were well on course to the adoption of the euro in 1999.[6] Even in opposition Labour's stance on the issue was ambivalent. As party leader Tony Blair was broadly supportive, while the shadow chancellor, Gordon Brown, had deep misgivings about the impact that the single currency would have on the British economy.[7] This divide persisted all the way through to the 2005 general election and, indeed, beyond.

By 1997, therefore, Labour was broadly supportive of the EU and the remaining divisions were centred on the largely technical question of membership of the single currency. These divisions were, moreover, concentrated in the party elite and in particular in the personages of Blair and Brown.

The Conservative Party had been the most pro-European of the two major parties and led Britain into the Common Market in 1973. As a new leader Margaret Thatcher campaigned for Britain to stay in Europe in a referendum held in 1975 and supported Europe again in the 1979 general election. In office she clashed with European leaders over Britain's contribution to the budget and won a rebate, which Britain retains to this day. Thereafter, she championed the creation of a single market, but steadily became more alarmed by the growing power of the EU and the emerging "social dimension", which was promoted by Germany in France. Her reluctance to accept further integration contributed to the resignation of her deputy prime minister, Sir Geoffrey Howe, provoked a leadership challenge by Michael Heseltine and her eventual defeat in November 1990.[8] Her successor, John Major, adopted a largely agnostic position on the single currency but was constantly challenged not only by pro-European cabinet members such as Kenneth Clarke and Michael Heseltine, but also by Eurosceptics such as Home Secretary Michael Howard or Defence Secretary Michael Portillo. In addition Major faced increasing criticism from a party membership whose opposition was increasingly directed not just at the euro but at the whole EU project and those in the parliamentary party who had brought about the downfall of their heroine.

Every time the European issue blew up it merely served to highlight Tory divisions and cost them support.[9] These factors help to explain the cautious 1997 manifesto position on Europe which was broadly similar to that of Labour: "If, during the course of the next parliament, a Conservative government were to conclude that it was in our national interest to join a single currency, we have given a guarantee that no such decision would be implemented unless the British people gave their express approval in a referendum".[10] Perhaps unsurprisingly, Europe was not an important issue in the ensuing election, which was dominated by concerns about the quality of public services (particularly health and education), law and order, unemployment and the economy.[11]

The Conservatives, New Labour and Europe, 1997–2001

The staggering extent of the defeat imposed by Labour on the Conservatives led to the resignation of John Major and his replacement by the Eurosceptic William Hague. Hague immediately set about the task of appointing a shadow cabinet that was almost entirely in agreement with his position on the euro and the EU. Several prominent Europhiles, such as Kenneth Clarke, declined to serve in the shadow cabinet. For the first time, therefore, the Conservative parliamentary leadership was united in its opposition both to the euro and to further European integration. At the same time Hague declared that joining the single currency was off the party agenda for the foreseeable future. To bolster his position he balloted party members who voted overwhelmingly (84.4 per cent) in support of his position.[12]

By 2001, this development was to assume some electoral significance because the Tories' new stance shifted the policy agenda on the issue in a significantly Eurosceptical direction. This development was to do the Tories considerable electoral damage because their resolutely hostile stance towards Europe was not reflected in public opinion. There are two parts to this claim. As can be seen from Figure 4.2, public support for European Monetary Union reached a low point around the end of 1996 but recovered significantly thereafter.

Admittedly, opinion remained firmly negative throughout, but slightly less negative when respondents were asked what they would do if the government took a strongly pro-EMU stance. More importantly, EMU and the Europe issue in general was never very salient among voters. Although the Tories wanted to fight the 2001 election on the twin issues of Europe and tax, a MORI *Sun* survey in May 2001 showed that only 10 per cent of the public

Figure 4.2 UK—Balance of Opinion over European Monetary Union, June 1991–June 2001

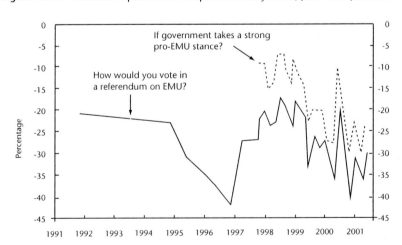

Source: MORI, June 22, 2001, http://www.mori.com/polls/2000/ssbsep00.shtml.

rated tax as an important issue and just 5 per cent rated Europe so.[13] When asked not to name the most important issue but to identify issues that would decide which party they would vote for, Europe was never identified by more than 29 per cent of a more general MORI sample during the whole of the January–June 2001 period (see Table 4.1). Even more revealing was the fact that more members of the public (45 per cent) thought that Labour more closely represented their views on the subject, than the Tories did (40 per cent).[14]

In other words, the decision by the Conservative leader William Hague to elevate the single currency issue to the top of the political agenda proved to be a major miscalculation.[15] Time and again in the subsequent election campaign Hague solemnly declared his intention to "save the pound". As the Tory manifesto declared, "*We will* keep the pound. Labour's plan for early entry into the euro is the single biggest threat to our economic stability. By keeping the pound we will keep control of our economic policy, including the ability to set interest rates to suit British economic conditions".[16]

Hague's position on the issue was, in a sense, a double miscalculation, for not only was the electorate largely unexcited on the question, but also the position of the Labour government was hardly diametrically opposed to that of the Conservatives. On the contrary, at least since the autumn of 1997 when Chancellor Gordon Brown elaborated his five economic tests for membership of the single currency system, Labour had been hedging its bets on membership, and this continued through the 2001 campaign. As Robert Shrimsley of the *Financial Times* noted during the election campaign, "Labour's manifesto offers no modifications to its cautious euro policy. It reiterates the 1997 statement by Gordon Brown, who said Labour favours euro membership in principle, but would not recommend participation in European monetary union unless five economic tests were met. The manifesto says an assessment of the tests would be made early in the next parliament. Tony Blair said in February that the assessment would be no later than two years after the election, but the manifesto does not repeat that timetable".[17]

In other words there was no clear indication that Labour intended to join the single currency system—something that the pro-Labour but anti-euro *Sun* tabloid newspaper noted in an editorial just a week before the election: "Tony Blair will have no mandate to take Britain into the single currency when he wins the election. The election of 2001 has not been fought on the Euro . . . when William Hague says there are only days to save the pound he is wrong. When Hague loses, the pound will not be dead".[18] The *Sun* was, of course absolutely right, for Brown's five economic tests were framed in such a way that they could always be interpreted to suit the government of the day. The five tests were (and indeed remain) as follows:

- whether the British economy has achieved sustainable convergence with the economies of the euro area;

- whether there would be sufficient flexibility to respond to shocks if Britain joined the euro area;

- the impact on investment in Britain;
- the impact on the British financial services industry; and
- the impact on employment.[19]

These tests were the product of Brown's Treasury and were, therefore, designed to give the chancellor the maximum room for manoeuvre over the issue. Indeed tests 1 and 2 were particularly hard to pass, if only because no time frame was applied to "sustainable convergence" and no definition of "flexibility" offered. They were, in other words, tailored to fit the chancellor's personal misgivings over membership of the single currency system. In contrast, Blair was an enthusiastic supporter of membership, which he saw primarily as a political project—although he was not averse to invoking economic arguments if it suited his purpose. Indeed, one of the more celebrated rows between Blair and Brown over Europe involved Blair's apparently harmless comment on the May 17, 2000: "The fact is that as long as we are outside the Euro, there is little that we can do to protect industry against destabilizing swings in the value of sterling".[20] Brown's reaction to this comment was, apparently, vociferous, and he insisted that all speeches on the subject had to be cleared with the chancellor before they were delivered.[21]

For the rest of the period until the general election an uneasy truce on the issue prevailed between the prime minister and the chancellor. The official line remained "prepare and see" or wait until that time when the economic (and by implication, the political) circumstances were right. And while Blair had a number of cabinet allies who supported his position—notably the secretary of state for trade and industry, Peter Mandelson, and the foreign secretary, Robin Cook—they were kept firmly in check by the Brown camp. Blair's position was weakened when both these supporters of the euro later resigned from the cabinet, though not over Europe.[22]

A further important dimension to the European debate during this period was the increasing tendency for Tony Blair to take on the role of a European rather than merely a British statesman. In a historic speech in Warsaw in October 2000, he called for Europe to become a "superpower, but not a superstate" and argued for his vision of Britain's role in this newly enlarged Europe:

> Britain will always be a staunch ally of all those European democracies applying to join the EU; a staunch ally wielding its influence at the centre of Europe.

> It was not always like that. British policy towards the rest of Europe over half a century has been marked by gross misjudgements, mistaking what we wanted to be the case with what was the case; hesitation, alienation, incomprehension, with the occasional burst of enlightened brilliance.

> I have said the political case for Britain being part of the single currency is strong. What does have to be overcome is the economic issue. Join-

ing prematurely simply on political grounds, without the economic conditions being right, would be a mistake. Hence our position: in principle in favour; in practice the economic tests must be met. We cannot and will not take risks with Britain's economic strength.[23]

It is worthy of note, however, that even when playing the European statesman, Blair felt obliged to repeat, yet again, the official "prepare and see" line on the single currency.

Parties, Voters and the European Issue, 2001–2005

In the four years before the 2005 general election, the political and electoral significance of the European issue was to be transformed out of all recognition. Many of the reasons for this relate to events outside the control of British political actors. Some, however, relate to specifically British events or to a combination of domestic events and developments throughout Europe. Let us look at each of these in turn.

The Conservatives

A second resounding defeat at the hands of the Labour Party led the Tories into further soul-searching and as in 1997 also to changes in the leadership selection process. William Hague almost immediately stood down as leader and on the final leadership ballot consisting of Tory Party members rather than MPs, deeply Eurosceptic candidate Iain Duncan Smith won 61 per cent of the vote as against Europhile Kenneth Clarke's 39 per cent. Duncan Smith had been a leader of the Euro-rebels who very nearly killed off John Major's attempts to win ratification of the Maastricht Treaty in the early 1990s.[24] Not surprisingly, therefore, his shadow cabinet reflected his anti-European views, with all the leading posts occupied by Eurosceptics. Under the leadership of Iain Duncan Smith the Conservatives' position on the single currency changed from "possibly sometime in the future, but not in the next five years", to "never". Much of the debate between the parties in the two years after the election was, therefore, over the government's proposed referendum on the subject.

However, events were to render this debate almost moot by 2003, for in that year the Parliamentary Conservative Party, following a period of what was widely regarded as inept leadership, removed Duncan Smith. He was replaced unopposed by the shadow chancellor, Michael Howard. While Howard was also a convinced Eurosceptic, he was aware that the Tories would not return to power at the next election by keeping the European issue at the top of the political agenda. From 2003 through to the election in 2005, Europe was, therefore, gradually de-emphasized in favour of those issues that more concentrated the minds of the voters, and notably the quality of the public services, law and order, and immigration and asylum. As can be seen from Table 4.1, as a voting cue, Europe declined in importance from 29 per cent in early 2001 to 19 per cent in April 2005. By this date, moreover, no less than eleven other issues trumped Europe as an issue that might determine how people vote.

The Labour Government

In the two years after the election, debate within the Labour party continued much as before. Gordon Brown wavered not one jot from his five economic tests criteria, while Tony Blair continued to hint that a referendum on the single currency could be held within the current parliament. Initially momentum seemed to be with the Blair camp. The Welsh Secretary and Leader of the House of Commons Peter Hain remarked almost casually in August 2001 that the decision could not be "put off for ever".[25] And in September a widely cited report *Winning the Euro Referendum: A Guide to Public Opinion and the Factors that Affect It* argued that because the issue was so vague in the minds of the voters, it was ripe for exploitation by a united government campaign in support of membership.[26]

Table 4.1 Importance of Key Issues to Voting, 1995–2005

Q. Looking ahead to the next general election, which, if any, of these issues do you think will be very important to you in helping you to decide which party to vote for?

	Jul 1995	Mar 1996	Jul 1996	Feb 1997	Apr 1997	May 1998	Jul 1999	Jan 2000	Jul 2000	Feb 2001	Sep 2003	Sep 2004	Feb 2005	Apr 2005
Asylum											39	37	36	37
Animal welfare	–	–	–	–	10	12	11	9	8	10	9	8	7	14
Constitution/ devolution	–	–	–	–	7	8	8	7	6	5	10	5	7	8
Defence	10	16	9	8	12	12	12	13	10	13	20	24	15	19
Education	52	66	51	56	61	62	52	55	52	52	53	47	46	61
Europe	17	24	19	26	22	26	30	24	26	29	22	21	19	19
Health care	61	68	60	63	68	66	61	71	67	65	62	54	57	67
Housing	24	30	17	19	22	23	21	18	15	16	20	19	20	27
Iraq														18
Law & order	43	52	45	45	51	45	43	49	54	47	49	45	45	56
Managing the economy	30	38	26	29	30	34	28	28	29	27	27	24	23	35
Pensions	25	34	29	28	39	36	32	31	35	28	42	40	39	49
Protecting the natural environment	21	31	20	22	20	22	22	21	19	18	19	18	20	28
Public transport	12	19	12	15	18	23	28	26	27	27	25	19	17	26
Taxation	30	30	26	28	33	32	32	30	36	31	32	33	28	42
Trade unions	4	9	5	5	9	5	4	4	3	3	7	3	3	
Unemployment	53	65	48	47	49	50	42	36	35	25	24	22	18	25
Other	2	1	2	1	2	1	3	1	3	3	2	3	2	2
Don't know	6	4	4	4	2	5	6	5	4	6	5	5	6	4

Source: MORI, http://www.mori.com.

Note: The table shows the percentage of respondents mentioning each issue.

As can be seen from Figure 4.3, however, the government had a long way to go. For even when respondents were asked how they would vote if the government "strongly urged" them to support membership the balance against joining remained firmly negative in 2001 and 2002. Note also, however that the total number of respondents answering positively or negatively rarely exceeds about 85 per cent of the total. Moreover, the "Don't knows" tended to increase in number when support for the Euro went up, suggesting that opinion on the issue was shallow and poorly developed. This is, of course, precisely what the authors of the *Winning the Euro Referendum Report* were arguing. All that was needed was for the government to educate and inform up to and during the referendum campaign, for public opinion to swing in favour of membership.[27] Part of this effort would be devoted to countering the views of the popular and tabloid press, almost all of which—with the notable exceptions of the *Guardian, Independent, Mirror* and *Financial Times*—were strongly opposed to British membership.[28]

By late 2004, however, the argument that the government could win a future referendum had almost passed from public discourse, and for three reasons. First, on June 9, 2003, Gordon Brown announced to the House of Commons that only one of the five economic tests had been met (the competitiveness of British financial services) and above all the British economy had not converged with that of the euro area. This effectively put paid to any thought of a referendum on the euro until after the next general election, by

Figure 4.3 UK Public Opinion in a Single Currency Referendum, 1997–2002

Q2. If the government were to strongly urge that Britain should be part of a single European currency, how would you vote?

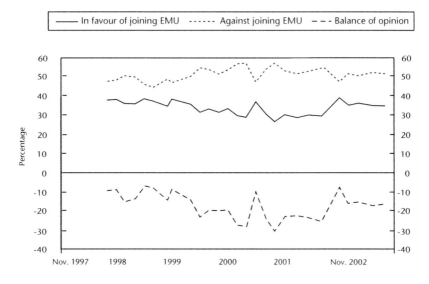

Source: MORI, http://www.mori.com/polls/2002/sssb-nov.shtml.

then widely expected to be held in the spring of 2005. Brown's position was bolstered by external events and in particular the relative position of the British economy in relation to the euro economies. As can be seen from Table 4.2 Britain outperformed the fifteen members of the EU in the 1990–2001 period and in particular the key euro area countries of France, Germany and Italy. This trend has continued since 2001 and most of the economic projections for the euro area are deeply pessimistic.[29] This is not to say that all the economic woes of the euro area are attributable to the euro. They are not. However, the mere fact that the euro area was doing badly while Britain was doing relatively well was enough for politicians and pundits to draw negative inferences about the effects of the euro.

These negative perceptions were compounded by the continuing problems associated with the Stability and Growth Pact, which was designed to police the borrowing requirements of the euro member states. By 2003 several countries including France, Germany and Portugal were in formal breach of the rules, and in particular the requirement that public borrowing should not exceed 3 per cent of gross domestic product (GDP). The outcome was a suspension of the Stability and Growth pact rules by the Council of Ministers who in effect overthrew the Commission's constitutional duty to enforce the rules. And although a subsequent European Court of Justice ruling favoured the Commission's position, by 2005 it was not clear what rules, if any, applied to the national accounts of the states using the euro.[30] These events undoubtedly strengthened further Gordon Brown's resolve not to join the euro.

Second, the pro-euro camp received a further blow to their cause when, in September 2003, the Swedes voted decisively by 56 to 42 per cent to reject the euro. The Swedish referendum result was particularly poignant because not only the incumbent government but also all the major political parties had campaigned vigorously for a "yes" vote. Moreover, this vote came in spite of the wave of public sympathy for the recently assassinated finance minister, Anna Lindh, who had been the government's main spokesperson on

Table 4.2 Output, Productivity and Employment in Selected Countries, 1990–2001

	USA	Can.	Aus.	Japan	Ger.*	Fr.	It.	UK	OECD†	EU-15‡
Average rate of growth of GDP	2.8	2.5	3.3	1.7	1.5	1.9	1.7	2.3	2.5	2.0
Of which:										
Labour productivity	1.6	1.3	1.9	1.3	1.7	1.1	1.6	1.8	1.6	1.5
Employment	1.2	1.2	1.4	0.4	-0.2	0.8	0.1	0.4	0.9	0.6

Source: Maria Maher and Michael Wise, "Product Market Competition and Economic Performances in the United Kingdom", Working Paper 433, OECD, Paris, 2005, Table 1.

Note: USA–United States; Can.–Canada; Aus.–Australia; Ger.–Germany; Fr.–France; It.–Italy; UK–United Kingdom.

*Average growth 1992–2001.
†OECD, except Austria, Luxembourg, Poland and Turkey.
‡EU, except Austria and Luxembourg.

the issue. What all this implied was that even if the Labour government were to run a highly effective campaign, there was still a serious prospect of defeat. In fact the Swedish case was doubly worrying, because public opposition to the euro had always been more muted than in Britain, as had opinion as expressed by the popular press.[31] Perhaps most tellingly, the Swedish anti-euro campaign had been built around the claim that Swedish employment and economic growth levels were superior to those in the euro area. This was, of course, precisely the same argument as was being invoked by the anti-euro forces in Britain and was regularly repeated in the Eurosceptic press.

Third, the political salience of the euro was for all intents and purposes displaced at the centre of debate on Europe by debate on the new EU Constitution. At the December 2000 meeting of the European Council in Nice, a declaration was adopted proposing a wide-ranging debate on the future of Europe followed by an Intergovernmental Conference to look at the ways in which the various treaties on European Union relate to one another. The major impetus to this initiative was the imminent enlargement of the EU from fifteen to twenty-five states, which would render the existing decision-making mechanisms cumbersome. Eventually, a Convention on the Future of Europe met between February 2002 and July 2003, when a draft treaty on a new constitution was published. After some amendments the heads of states and governments signed the treaty on October 29, 2004. There then followed a period of ratification, where the approval mechanisms were to be decided by the member states. In some, parliamentary approval was sufficient, in some judicial assent was necessary and in others the final ratification would be decided by national referendums.

Publication of the draft constitution immediately sparked off debate in Britain, with the forces aligned much along the same lines as in the euro debate. However, there were some subtle differences in comparison with the euro controversy. From the word go, the Conservatives opposed the constitution and the government and Liberal Democrats broadly supported it. However, the Conservatives were almost certainly on stronger electoral and political ground than they had been in their opposition to the euro. For one thing it was inordinately difficult to clarify exactly what the constitution was proposing. Most of the document was devoted to a codification of existing treaties, but important changes in the decision rules to be taken by the Council of Ministers and the European Parliament were proposed and a Charter of Fundamental Rights including trade-union rights was to be enshrined into EU law.[32] Given the length and technicality of the constitution it was relatively easy for the Conservatives to project it as the embodiment of a new European superstate intent on undermining British sovereignty. In a speech on June 1, 2004, Tory leader Michael Howard clarified his position which clearly exaggerated the centralizing elements in the constitution:

> [T]he EU will have a President and a Foreign Minister to set policy. The
> EU, instead of Britain, will have new powers to make treaties with

other countries. The European Court could have new powers to review the actions of the British army. So I am totally opposed to the European Constitution. Countries have constitutions and I do not want to be part of a country called Europe. Even more worryingly, we have learned in the last few days that plans are already being drawn up to take us beyond the European Constitution.

The Constitution is described as the start of a political Europe. The discussion document reveals proposals for a Europe-wide tax, a European minimum income, and giving the European Union "political territory". It is an explicit commitment to create a fully-fledged European state in the next twenty years.[33]

However, in contrast to earlier debates on the euro, the Conservatives framed their opposition in terms of a generally positive stance towards many other aspects of the EU including its recent enlargement to twenty-five members. So they went out of their way to stress that they wanted Britain to be at the centre of Europe, and in particular to open dialogue with the new member states, while remaining implacably opposed to joining the euro and to the constitution. They proposed holding a national referendum on the issue, which, given that the public were even more opposed to the constitution than they were to the euro, they were confident they would win (see Table 4.3).

Meanwhile events were also crowding in on the government. During the constitutional convention, the British delegation had argued for the retention of the national veto in a number of key areas and some assurance that the Charter of Fundamental Rights would not dilute British industrial relations law. At a 2004 press conference Blair outlined the British position:

[The constitution] gives a role to national parliaments of a greater degree than ever before, and it ensures that where in those areas we need in the interests of Britain as well as other states to have qualified majority voting, we have it, but in those areas where it is essential that we retain the ultimate power, we retain that power. And so for exam-

Table 4.3 Public Opinion on the EU Constitution, January 2005

Q. Should the United Kingdom approve the treaty establishing a constitution for the European Union? If the referendum were held tomorrow, would you vote Yes or No in response to that question or would you not bother to vote?

	Total (%)	Con (%)	Lab (%)	Lib Dem (%)
Vote Yes	24	7	40	40
Vote No	45	78	29	31
Would not vote	7	2	3	2
Don't know	25	12	29	27

Source: YouGov/Daily Telegraph survey at http://www.yougov.com/archives.

ple in relation to economic policy, that remains within the control of the nation state, the veto on tax is kept, so taxes cannot be harmonised, the veto on social security is kept, foreign policy and defence is still subject to unanimity. We retain of course full control of our armed forces, we retain our veto over our budget rebate and the negotiations about the future financing of the Union, and the Charter of Rights is expressed specifically in such a way that it means that the industrial relations law of our country cannot be altered by the European Court of Justice through the Charter of Fundamental Rights.[34]

Initially, the government was silent on whether the treaty would be subject to a national referendum, but in April 2004 Tony Blair announced to the House of Commons that a referendum would be held. This decision had all the hallmarks of political panic about it and may have been influenced by concerns about the response of the Eurosceptical press, particularly the *Sun*, which was owned by Rupert Murdoch.[35] Above all, the prime minister wanted to avoid the issue dominating the upcoming election campaign, and given the apparent strength of public opinion against the treaty, a referendum after the election would effectively defer debate until an electorally safe time. While this pleased the more sceptical of his cabinet colleagues including Foreign Secretary Jack Straw and Chancellor Gordon Brown, it enraged the constitutional enthusiasts such as the Education Secretary Charles Clarke and disappointed euro enthusiasts.[36] But these were minor political costs to pay. Instead of suffering a bruising campaign dominated by Europe, the government could go into the election secure in the knowledge that all three main political parties supported at least the idea of a referendum (the Liberal Democrats agreed the issue should be put to the vote and promised that they would campaign hard for a "Yes" vote).

Eurosceptic Parties

The referendum decision might also have served to weaken support for the United Kingdom Independence Party (UKIP), which advocated total withdrawal from the EU. In 1997 the Referendum Party, funded by the financier Sir James Goldsmith, had fought the election demanding a referendum on Britain's relationship with Europe. Despite lavish expenditure and fielding 547 candidates, the party won just 2.6 per cent of the vote. The Referendum Party was replaced by UKIP in 2001 and received further financial support from the Eurosceptic Yorkshire businessman, Paul Sykes. It fielded some 428 candidates and although it polled just 1.5 per cent of the vote and failed to win one seat, the party could represent a threat to all the main parties, at least at the margin, especially if the European issue had come to dominate the campaign.[37] Indeed in the 2004 elections for the European Parliament UKIP secured a staggering 16.1 per cent of the vote and won twelve seats, with the help of £1.4 million in funding from Sykes.[38] Labour, by contrast, polled just 22.6 per cent of the vote and won nineteen seats. This result was widely regarded as a disaster for Labour, especially as the decision to hold a referendum had not had the anticipated effect of bolstering the Labour vote.[39] Labour's only consolation was that the turnout at this election was a mere 38.2 per cent. Eurosceptics in the Conservative Party again used the result to suggest that UKIP represented a threat to the party especially in the south west of England and that it had to maintain its opposition to Europe.

The UKIP vote in the 2004 European elections proved, however, to be a mere blip on the electoral radar screen. UKIP itself underwent serious (some would say terminal) internal problems. One of their most prominent members and the newly elected member of the European Parliament (MEP) for the East Midlands, the former talk-show host Robert Kilroy-Silk, quickly fell out with the party. He alleged that the party's leader, Roger Knapman, had reneged on a deal to let him become party leader. Kilroy-Silk's call for UKIP to "kill" the Conservative Party finally led Paul Sykes to withdraw financial support.[40] He also fell out with his fellow UKIP MEPs in Strasbourg and resigned in January 2005 to form a competing party (Veritas). The new party was launched with much fanfare and promised to bring "honesty" to politics.

The divisions on the Eurosceptic wing of British politics did neither UKIP nor Veritas any favours and they gained unsympathetic coverage in the mainstream media. At the 2005 general election UKIP polled just 2.2 per cent of the vote in 2005, up just about a third from their 2001 result. Veritas did appallingly badly, attracting around 40,000 votes and with Kilroy-Silk just about managing to retain his deposit by polling 6 per cent of the vote in the Erewash constituency. After the election he was criticized for his leadership and he later announced that he would stand down as leader.[41]

Europe, the 2005 General Election and After: Blair Embattled and Blair Redux

No doubt the poor showing by Eurosceptic parties reflects the low electoral salience of the issue in 2005. All three major parties held a common position on the need for a referendum on the constitution. In April 2005 a survey of respondents ranked it equal twelfth among issues that might determine their vote (Table 4.1). Indeed, all three main parties gave it a low priority in their manifestos. In comparison with previous campaigns the Conservatives were almost conciliatory on the issue: "Conservatives support the cause of reform in Europe and we will co-operate with all those who wish to see the EU evolve in a more flexible, liberal and decentralised direction. We oppose the EU Constitution and would give the British people the chance to reject its provisions in a referendum within six months of the General Election. We also oppose giving up the valuable freedom which control of our own currency gives us. We will not join the Euro".[42]

And while Labour was committed to "campaign wholeheartedly for a 'Yes vote' in the referendum", they were also strong advocates of extending membership to Turkey, the Balkans and Eastern Europe.[43] Together with their "prepare and see" stance on the euro this was tantamount to supporting EU decentralization, for further enlargement would likely weaken rather than strengthen the powers of EU institutions in relation to those of the member states.[44]

Following Labour's third straight victory in 2005, the government was preparing itself for a struggle in the referendum campaign in 2006, when all the indications were that they would lose. The referendum issue might not only be damaging to the government in relation to the Tories, but also to relationships within the cabinet. Blair was much more enthusiastic about the constitution than was his chancellor, Gordon Brown, who was widely assumed to be his heir apparent. A referendum defeat might well have hastened his departure given that he was increasingly seen as an electoral liability to the party and had announced prior to the election that he would go sometime during the parliament elected in 2005. Events, however, were to evolve to the prime minister's advantage, so that just weeks after the election his position both on Europe and more generally were greatly strengthened.

On May 29, 2005, the French voted in a national referendum to reject the EU constitution by 55 to 45 per cent. A few days later on June 1, the Dutch rejected the constitution by an even greater margin of 62 to 38 per cent. If two of the six founding members of the original European Community rejected the new treaty, then it was effectively dead—something that Jack Straw was to acknowledge on June 6, when he announced that legislation to introduce the referendum bill would be postponed indefinitely.[45]

Later in the month Blair's position was boosted further when the issue of Britain's budget rebate, originally negotiated by Margaret Thatcher, surfaced as a major issue on the EU negotiating agenda. In effect, the French and the Germans were lobbying for the rebate to be rescinded. They argued that because Britain's relative economic position had improved considerably since the 1980s there was a case for a reworking of the algorithm used to determine the British contribution to the EU budget. In a rare display of unity both Blair and Brown grabbed at the chance to use this issue as an opportunity to open a "fundamental debate" on the whole system of EU finances, and in particular the funding of the Common Agricultural Policy (CAP). Everyone knew that the CAP system of agricultural subsidies rewarded the least efficient farmers, most of whom were concentrated in France and other Continental countries, but notably not in Britain.[46] Major reform of the system could only mean net benefits for Britain and net costs for a number of other states.

By mid 2005, therefore, the European issues that historically caused divisions both within and between the political parties seemed to have almost passed from the political agenda. Given all the problems afflicting the euro area, membership of the single currency was effectively ruled out for the foreseeable future. The European constitution was effectively dead and the one issue where Britain had been a consistent critic for over thirty years, the CAP, had returned to the centre of the political stage. Unlike the euro and the constitution, however, this was hardly a divisive question in terms of domestic politics. On the contrary, all the main parties and the press agreed with the government's call for root and branch reform.

Conclusion

Perhaps the most remarkable feature of the European issue in British electoral politics over the last several decades is how emotions on the subject have been periodically raised to high levels—at least among political elites—while objectively very little has actually changed in terms of the EU affecting the lives of ordinary voters. For while it is true that the EU regulatory regime has become more extensive and intrusive over the years, there is little evidence that this has been the source of political opposition to further European integration.

Instead, political leaders have become excited about what *might* happen should Britain adopt the euro or be bound by the EU constitution. The one major change in policy over the years that was reflected in political party differences was the reversal of John Major's opt-out of the Social Chapter negotiated as part of Britain's support for the Maastricht Treaty. When reversed by the Blair government in 1997, the issue passed from political discourse together with the Conservative's opposition to the Social Chapter's provisions which included improved working conditions for part-time and low-paid workers.[47]

This is not to say that the same would have happened with the more fundamental questions of the euro and the constitution, but it does illustrate the general point that discourse on the European issue has been largely confined to the rarefied world of elite and media speculation, rather than the real world of policy implementation in such areas as health, education, transport, the economy and, more recently, terrorism and the war in Iraq. No doubt this helps explain the relatively low electoral salience of the issue over the whole period.

It should also be noted that by 2005 the issue had come full circle with Britain playing its traditional role not so much as reluctant European, but more as spoiler in the Franco-German camp. Putting to one side the question of whether, in a much enlarged EU, this role will take on a new meaning, it does have significance in terms of British domestic politics. For with the euro and constitution issues now dormant, the Blair government found itself broadly in tune not only with public opinion on the budget rebate and reform of the CAP, but also with the views of the Conservatives and their allies in the popular press.

Notes

1. On the distinction between "valence" and "position" issues, see Donald Stokes, "Spatial Models of Party Competition", *American Political Science Review*, 57 (1963), 368–77.

2. For an account of Britain's troubled relationship with Europe through to the 1990s, see Hugo Young, *This Blessed Plot: Britain and Europe from Churchill to Blair* (London: Macmillan, 1999).

3. All manifesto quotes are from Political Science Resources, University of Keele, http://www.psr.keele.ac.uk/area/uk/man.htm.

4. Political Science Resources.

5. Anthony King, "Why Labour Won", in Anthony King, ed., *New Labour Triumphs: Britain at the Polls* (Chatham, NJ: Chatham House, 1998), pp. 177–208.

6. For an account of the Maastricht negotiations and their aftermath, see Kenneth Dyson and Kevin Featherstone, *The Road to Maastricht: Negotiating Economic and Monetary Union* (Oxford: Oxford University Press, 1999).

7. James Naughtie, *The Rivals: The Intimate Story of a Political Marriage* (London: Fourth Estate, 2001), pp. 130–4.

8. Alan Watkins, *A Conservative Coup: The Fall of Margaret Thatcher* (London: Duckworth, 1992).

9. Geoff Evans, "Euroscepticism and Conservative Electoral Support: How an Asset Became a Liability", *British Journal of Political Science*, 28 (1998), 573–90.

10. Political Science Resources.

11. Anthony King, "Why Labour Won".

12. Philip Norton, "The Conservative Party", in Anthony King, ed., *Britain at the Polls, 2001* (Chatham, NJ: Chatham House, 2002), pp. 75–112, at p. 82.

13. MORI, 2001 Election Commentary, May 10, 2001, http://www.mori.com/pubinfo/rmm/ec0510.shtml.

14. MORI, 2001 Election Commentary.

15. John Bartle, "Why Labour Won—Again", in King, *Britain at the Polls, 2001*, pp. 164–206.

16. Political Science Resources.

17. "Labour's manifesto at a glance", Ft.com, http://specials.ft.com/ukelection2001/FT3XJO5GTMC.html.

18. "The Sun, Blair and Euro", *Sun*, May 28, 2001.

19. Paul Temperton, *The UK and the Euro* (London: Wiley, 2001), p. 57.

20. Naughtie, *The Rivals*, p. 146.

21. Ibid.

22. Mandelson resigned over allegations that he had interfered with an application for a passport made by one of the Indujah brothers, who were sponsors of the Millennium Dome, one of his pet projects. He was later cleared of any wrongdoing. Cook resigned in March 2003 over the Iraq War.

23. "A superpower, but not a superstate", *Guardian*, October 7, 2000, http://www.guardian.co.uk/print/0,3858,4073335-105579,00.html.

24. For a vivid account of the internecine battles affecting the conservatives in the ten years down to 2001, see Simon Walters, *Tory Wars: Conservatives in Crisis* (London: Politico's, 2001).

25. "'Tough' Blair can win euro referendum, say backers", *Guardian Unlimited*, http://observer.guardian.co.uk/euro/story/0,10818,545723,00.html.

26. Mark Leonard and Tom Arbuthnott, eds, *Winning the Euro Referendum: A Guide to Public Opinion and the Issues That Affect It* (London: Foreign Policy Research Centre, 2001).

27. These events also produced a small flurry of pro-euro and anti-euro pamphlets and books, see, for example, John Redwood, *Just Say No: 100 Arguments against the Euro* (London: Politico's 2001); Anthony Brown, *Should Britain Join?* (London: Icon Books, 2001).

28. On this theme, see Rob Evans, "Science in the Democratic Process: The Euro in the UK General Election", Working Paper Series No 33, Centre for Study of Knowledge, Expertise and Science, Cardiff University, 2003.

29. Organisation for Co-operation and Development, Economic Survey of the Euro Area 2005: Executive Summary, http://www.oecd.org/document/27/0,2340,en_2649_201185_35103963_1_1_1_1,00.html.

30. See David McKay, "Economic Logic or Political Logic? Economic Theory, Federal Theory and EMU", *Journal of European Public Policy*, 12 (2005), 528–44.

31. "Results cheer British anti-euro campaigners", *The Times*, September 15, 2003.

32. EU Draft Constitution, http://europa.eu.int/constitution/futurum/constitution/index_en.htm.

33. Michael Howard's website, http://www.michaelhowardmp.com/sp010604.htm.

34. Downing Street press release, June 18, 2004, http://www.number-10.gov.uk/output/page5988.asp.

35. Martin Kettle, "Rupert Murdoch may be the man who saved Europe", *Guardian*, June 14, 2005.

36. Philip Stevens, *Tony Blair: The Price of Leadership* (London: Politico's, 2004), p. 377.

37. House of Commons Library, Research Paper, 01/54 (revised), http://www.parliament.uk/commons/lib/research/rp2001/rp01-054.pdf.

38. Sarah Hall, "How UKIP splashed out for the Euro poll", *Guardian*, December 23, 2004.

39. "In Depth: Vote 2004", http://news.bbc.co.uk/1/hi/in_depth/uk_politics/2004/vote_2004.

40. Helen Rumbelow, "Kilroy-Silk claims monopoly on the politics of truth", *The Times*, February 3, 2005.

41. "Kilroy quits as Veritas head", *Guardian*, July 30, 2005.

42. Political Science Resources.

43. Political Science Resources.

44. On this theme, see Mika Widgren, "Enlargements and the Principles of Designing EU Procedures", in Charles B. Blankart and Dennis C. Mueller, eds, *A Constitution for the European Union* (Cambridge, Mass., and London: MIT Press, 2004), pp. 85–108.

45. Downing Street press release, http://www.number-10.gov.uk/output/Page7585.asp.

46. "Blair and Brown turn up heat in rebate row with French", *The Times*, http://www.timesonline.co.uk/article/0,,13509-1649078,00.html.

47. The other important act regarding Europe in this period was the government's decision to incorporate the European Convention on Human Rights into British law. However, the convention is, strictly speaking, not a part of the EU institutional apparatus.

5

The Politics of Fractured Federalism

Iain McLean

The United Kingdom now has, in principle, elected subnational governments in four of its twelve standard regions: Scotland, Wales, Northern
Ireland and London.[1] A proposal for an elected assembly in a fifth, the North-
East of England, was heavily defeated in a referendum in November 2004.
And the Northern Ireland Assembly is currently suspended. Therefore we
may assume that for the lifetime of (at least) the 2005 parliament, either three
or four of the United Kingdom's standard regions will have an elected assembly of one sort or another; and either eight or nine will have none. This has
important implications for the development (or not) of federalism, and for the
continued unity of the United Kingdom.

The four sets of elections use, between them, three electoral systems.
Only Scotland and Wales use the same system. None of the systems is the
same as those used in elections to the House of Commons, to local authorities, or to the European Parliament. Thus, even before we consider the results
of these elections, it is clear that the United Kingdom has stumbled into a system of fractured federalism. As Karl Marx said wisely, "Men make their own
history, but they do not make it just as they please; they do not make it under
circumstances chosen by themselves, but under circumstances directly
encountered, given and transmitted from the past".[2] Or, to put the same point
in the less elegant language of modern social science, the development of relationships between national and subnational government is path-dependent;
and, furthermore, electoral systems and voting behaviour are deeply endogenous to (that is, both causes and effects of) one another. As is shown below,
electoral systems shape voting behaviour, and hence electoral outcomes. But
electoral outcomes, both past and anticipated, also shape electoral systems.

How We Got Here

The devolution settlement in both Scotland and Wales is driven by events
as long ago as 1967; that in Northern Ireland can probably be traced back to
Oliver Cromwell and William III, but brevity precludes discussion of them.
The demand for London-wide government also has an interesting history but
limitations of space preclude detailed discussion of that case.

Table 5.1. Attitudes towards Devolution, Regions of Great Britain, 1970

	England (%)	Wales (%)	Scotland (%)	North (%)	Yorkshire (%)	North-West (%)	West Midlands (%)	South-West (%)	East Midlands (%)	East Anglia (%)	South East (%)	Greater London (%)	South (%)	Total* (%)
Leave as they are	14.0	15.2	6.5	10.7	15.8	8.5	14.7	20.6	12.2	16.6	13.7	16.4	10.9	12.9
Keep things much the same but more govt understanding	24.1	27.1	20.2	26.4	23.3	19.2	23.0	28.2	22.6	24.3	28.6	24.4	23.1	23.8
Keep the present system but more regional decisions	24.0	21.1	26.1	25.8	23.5	30.0	26.1	19.6	26.2	17.2	20.6	23.6	19.9	23.9
Have a new system of governing the region	20.2	23.4	24.2	20.1	20.0	23.7	17.7	17.2	21.3	21.3	20.0	18.8	25.0	21.4
Let the region take over complete responsibility	16.1	12.9	22.1	15.7	16.0	15.4	17.1	12.4	17.7	20.1	15.8	14.3	20.5	16.7
Don't know	1.6	0.3	0.9	1.3	1.4	3.1	1.4	1.9		0.6	1.3	2.4	0.6	1.3
Total	100	100	100	100	100	100	100	100	100	100	100	100	100	100
n	3,058	697	815	154	478	409	459	196	150	158	436	460	144	4,569

Source: Social Community and Planning Research Data, June 1970 [computer file]. Colchester, Essex: UK Data Archive [distributor], 1977. SN: 173.
*Unweighted.

Scotland

Scottish devolution first leapt to prominence when the Scottish National Party (SNP) snatched what was then the safest Labour seat in Scotland in the Hamilton by-election of November 1967. It was part of then-Prime Minister Harold Wilson's statecraft to send difficult issues such as devolution and trade-union reform to a stately Royal Commission with a distant reporting date. His response to Hamilton was to appoint the Crowther (later Kilbrandon) Royal Commission on the Constitution, which was set up in 1969 and reported in 1973. This body commissioned research on attitudes to devolution, which remains the only survey of the whole of Great Britain whose samples were big enough in each region of England, as well as in Scotland and Wales, to compare attitudes to devolution across each of them. They turned out to be remarkably uniform (see Table 5.1).

Table 5.1 shows that Scotland was, as predicted, the region where the demand for self-determination was highest, but it was closely followed by East Anglia and the South of England. However, the East Anglia National Party and the Southern Separatist Party failed to materialize. Demand for self-determination was lowest in Wales and in South-West England; albeit within a narrow range.

Although there was no evidence that demand for devolution was higher in Scotland than elsewhere, and some evidence that it was weaker in Wales than elsewhere, the Royal Commission proposed a legislative assembly for Scotland when it reported in 1973. By this time, the SNP was rising fast again, because it had discovered its most effective campaign slogan ever: "It's Scotland's Oil . . . " The SNP won a by-election in a "safe Labour" seat of Govan in Glasgow within a week of Kilbrandon finally reporting.

In the February 1974 general election, the SNP won 22 per cent of the Scottish vote. The first-past-the-post (FPTP) or "plurality" electoral system protected Labour by giving the SNP only 10 per cent of the Scottish seats for this 22 per cent of the vote. It was soon realized, however, that if the SNP vote share were to rise to somewhere between 30 and 35 per cent, the system would have flipped from punishing the SNP to rewarding it. This is simply because the plurality electoral system treats parties differently according to whether their vote is geographically concentrated or dispersed. Small geographically concentrated parties—as the SNP was in 1970, and Welsh nationalists have always been—can achieve their population share of seats or more, because their votes are efficiently distributed to win seats in just the few places where they are strong. So the SNP won the Western Isles in 1970, and Plaid Cymru has held at least one of the half-dozen Welsh-speaking seats since 1966. Large concentrated parties, by contrast, are penalized when their vote slumps, as did the Tories in 1906 and 1997. They retain seats in their "heartlands" but lose seats elsewhere and end up with a smaller share of seats than votes.

Dispersed parties suffer or enjoy the opposite effects of FPTP. A small, dispersed party, such as the Green Party, will win no seats at all. When it was a small party within Scotland, neither did the SNP. But if support grew, dispersal would turn from a curse to a blessing. With an evenly distributed 35 per cent of the vote, it could win more than half of the seats in Scotland as Labour did in most elections. Were it to do so, moreover, it would start to negotiate for Scottish independence. Throughout 1974, Labour's national elite focused on retaining the party's capacity to govern the United Kingdom. This entailed shifting the basis of its appeal in Scotland from the welfare-state unionism that it had espoused for forty years to a policy of moderate devolution. There was the embarrassment in June 1974 when the Labour Party's Scottish executive resolved that devolution was "irrelevant to the needs of the Scottish people". In the notorious "Dalintober Street coup", the national Labour Party mobilized the big trade unions that were affiliated to the party, to impose on the Scottish Labour executive the view that they loved devolution after all.[3] Richard Rose has stated that the Labour devolution pledge was a panicky response to the threat to Labour posed by the SNP, sparked by an unpublished MORI poll which was interpreted (possibly mistakenly) as showing strong support for a devolution pledge. By revisiting this MORI poll (courtesy of MORI and the UK Data-Archive) we can test Rose's claim.[4]

Amongst MORI's respondents who expressed a vote preference, 41.4 per cent said they would vote Labour, compared to 25.2 per cent SNP, 26.1 per cent Conservative and 6.9 per cent Liberal. This suggested a swing since February 1974 away from the Conservatives and towards Labour and the SNP. However, rumours at the time suggested that poll evidence showed the Labour Party under threat. Bob (now Sir Bob) Worcester, the long-serving chairman of MORI, was reported as claiming that, if the Labour Party did not change its policy on devolution, the party would lose up to thirteen seats.[5]

In retrospect, the evidence in the MORI survey for strong support for devolution seems sparse. Without prompting, only 6.9 per cent of respondents mentioned the creation of a Scottish parliament/assembly as the most important issue, behind inflation (33.1 per cent), unemployment (17.3 per cent) and North Sea Oil (6.9 per cent), and just ahead of strikes (6.6 per cent), balance of payments (5.9 per cent) and housing (5.0 per cent). Of those who mentioned a Scottish parliament/assembly as the most important issue, 60 per cent were SNP supporters, the remainder split between Conservative and Labour.

Labour concern was sparked by a question presenting three options for Scottish constitutional reform:

Would you personally like to see . . . ?

- A completely independent Scottish parliament separate from England (20.8 per cent)

- A Scottish assembly part of Britain but with substantial powers (56.1 per cent)

- No change from the present system (17.2 per cent)

- Don't know (3.7 per cent)

The question, however, was asked as a follow up to one presenting more detailed options:

> For running Scotland as a whole which of these alternatives would you prefer, overall?

- Leave things as they are at present (10.3 per cent)

- Keep things much the same as they are now but make sure the needs of Scotland are better understood by the Government (17.2 per cent)

- Keep the present system but allow more decisions to be made in Scotland (26.6 per cent)

- Have a new system of governing Scotland so that as many decisions as possible are made in the area (21.7 per cent)

- Let Scotland take over complete responsibility for running things in Scotland (21.1 per cent)

- Don't know (2.7 per cent)

Asking the question in this way indicates support for the status quo plus tinkering (the first three options) at 54.1 per cent. Support for a devolved assembly came from only 21.7 per cent of the respondents. It is possible to analyse the data in multiple ways, all of which, it can be argued, show that the settled wish of the Scottish people was not for devolution, but for a bigger slice of the cake—especially the oil-cake (see Table 5.2).[6]

Table 5.2 Attitudes towards North Sea Oil by Party Preference, Scotland, 1974

	Con	Lab	Lib Dem	SNP	All
Profits from North Sea oil should be kept for the benefit of the Scottish people					
Disagree	42.7	19.8	32.1	12.1	24.7
Agree	45.5	71.9	51.8	83.5	66.5
Other/n.a.	11.7	8.3	16.1	4.4	8.7
Profits from North Sea oil should be used to help the less prosperous regions in the United Kingdom					
Disagree	27.7	35.8	26.8	44.7	35.3
Agree	54.5	45.9	62.5	43.2	48.6
Other/n.aa	17.8	18.3	10.7	12.1	16.1
Scotland gets less than its fair share of economic help from the British government					
Disagree	17.4	12.1	14.3	6.3	12.2
Agree	68.5	75.4	69.6	87.4	76.3
Other/n.a.	14.1	12.4	16.1	6.3	11.6

Source: Robert M. Worcester and Brian Gosschalk, MORI Labour Party Research Data, August 1974 [computer file]. Colchester, Essex: UK Data Archive [distributor], 1977. SN: 926.

Note: n=813. Lib Dem refers to the former Liberal Party.

Table 5.2 shows that Labour and SNP voters formed one cluster and Conservative and Liberal voters another. The first cluster believed strongly that "profits from North Sea Oil should be kept for the benefit of the Scottish people" and that "Scotland gets less than its fair share of economic help from the British government". This confirms how dangerous the SNP oil campaign was to Labour. Labour promoted its policy to take a majority public stake in North Sea oil with the magnificently ambiguous slogan "Make Sure It's Your Oil, Vote Labour", which was used only in Scotland.[7] The almost complete segregation of the Scottish media from those serving the rest of the United Kingdom helped Labour pull this strategy off. Very few Scottish readers saw papers originating in England—the English broadsheets had trivial circulations in Scotland, and the mass-market papers all had Scottish editions. Because the Borders are thinly populated, almost nobody in Scotland picked up English news broadcasts.

The Conservatives were, therefore, on safe electoral ground when they abandoned their support for Scottish devolution in 1975. They had been the first of the major parties to swing towards devolution, with their "Declaration of Perth" in 1966. However, the accession of Margaret Thatcher to the leadership in 1975 swung them back. Abandoning the declaration, as Thatcher did in 1975, fitted her own constitutional instincts. The Conservatives' private pollster, ORC, provided her with evidence that it did not put their vote at risk. In the referendum held in early 1979 the Scots voted narrowly in favour of devolution, but the proposal fell when it failed to receive the support of 40 per cent of the eligible electorate. The general election of 1979 was forced when the incumbent Labour government lost a motion of no confidence in its devolution policy by one vote. Thatcher came to power, and immediately ditched all plans for devolution to Scotland or Wales.

Wales

It has ever been the fate of Wales to be tacked on to other people's devolution plans, usually with the condescending phrase "and to a lesser extent Wales". The majority report of the Kilbrandon Commission proposed an elected assembly for Wales: "some members would give it legislative functions and others deliberative and advisory functions". The minority report by Lord Crowther-Hunt and Alan Peacock proposed seven "Assemblies and Governments" of equal standing, one each for Scotland, Wales and five regions of England.[8]

As already noted, Wales began the 1970s with one of the lowest levels of support for devolution of any region in Great Britain. By February 1974 devolution was more popular, although the level of support for the proposition that "Wales should completely run its own affairs" was less than half that for Scotland, and support for the status quo was double the Scottish level. The 1979 British Election Study survey was undertaken after the devolution scheme in the Wales Act 1978 had been rejected by a four-to-one margin in the referendum of March 1979. This referendum result was the most comprehensive defeat of any devolution proposal up to that date.[9]

Wales was divided politically and socially between the rural, chapel-going, Welsh-speaking north and west and the rest of Wales. The Plaid Cymru vote was concentrated heavily in the former, which accounts for only about 20 per cent of the population of Wales. It has always been more a cultural nationalist party, and less a party of economic grievance, than the SNP.[10] Accordingly, the very features of Welsh devolution that appealed most to its Welsh-speaking supporters appealed least to its non-Welsh-speaking opponents. Both saw it as an institution that would preserve (privilege) the language and culture of north Wales. In 1979, the Welsh-language publicity produced by those advocating devolution stated that a "Yes" vote would protect the special status of the language. Its English-language publicity denied that it would give Welsh-speakers any special status. Unfortunately for the "Yes" campaign, the former perception leaked into Anglophone Wales. Accordingly, proposals for Welsh devolution were overwhelmingly rejected.

The Rebirth of Devolution

The Conservatives won their third general election in a row in 1987. But their support in Scotland, where they had piloted the Poll Tax, a uniform charge to fund local government that was not based on the ability to pay, was slipping. Indeed, all the Scottish ministers involved with introducing the Poll Tax lost their seats in 1987. This obviously sharpened old questions about the legitimacy of Westminster governments of one complexion imposing their will on outlying parts of the United Kingdom of another complexion—the issue that had caused the "Irish Question" to fester from 1886 to 1921. Therefore leading Labour and Liberal Democrat politicians in Scotland, with support from such bodies as churches and trades unions, created a Constitutional Convention which reported in 1995, outlining a scheme of devolution which was substantially that established in 1999.

In 1994 John Smith, the then Labour leader, sonorously proclaimed devolution to be "the settled will of the Scottish people". The Scottish referendum of 1997 validated the constitutional settlement proposed by the convention. In a dual vote with a 60 per cent turnout, 74.3 per cent of those who voted approved the Scottish Parliament, and 63.5 per cent of those who voted agreed that it would have a power to tax, although to date it has not used that power, nor does it look likely to in the near future. The Welsh referendum was held a week after the Scottish one in the hope of generating a bandwagon. The result could not have been closer. The National Assembly of Wales, which in theory is responsible for the whole range of domestic public services—especially health, education and personal social services—in Wales, was approved by just over 50 per cent of those who voted in the referendum, on a 50 per cent turnout. But devolution is path-dependent. The Scottish Parliament with its massive popular endorsement, and the National Assembly for Wales with its feeble popular endorsement, are equally part of the constitutional landscape. The institutions of politics and civil society adapted to their existence and now have a stake in their continuation. Above all, the Conservative Party has abandoned its historic role as last-ditch defender of the Union in favour of accepting the Scottish and Welsh assemblies and governments. Their systems of proportional representation gave the Conservatives a foothold that they would not have had under FPTP system that they continue (almost inexplicably) to favour.

Despite John Smith's certainty, we cannot say whether a popular groundswell for devolution pre-dated the creation of the Convention. There was a groundswell of grumpiness, as people in Scotland and Wales became aware that a government which they had not voted for introduced the highly unpopular Poll Tax. But, if public opinion in 1989 resembled that in the 1970s, it is unlikely that there was a strong demand for Scottish autonomy. However, by the time of the 1997 referendum campaign, a peak of 37 per cent of Scottish respondents wished to see Scotland independent of the United Kingdom. Most of those, however, voted for, not against, the offer of a devolved parliament. By the time of the first Scottish Parliament election in 1999, the Scots were more satisfied with what they had. Support for independence had dropped to 26 per cent, and over half (51 per cent) of respondents most preferred what they had got, namely a Scottish Parliament with tax-varying powers.[11]

This is not to deny that there was a big shift in Scottish opinion between the 1979 referendum and those of 1997, when both the parliament and its tax-raising powers were approved by comfortable majorities. But it is wrong to read that shift as reflecting something fundamental about Scottish culture or attitudes.

Wales

The place where opinion changed most between 1979 and 1999 was Wales. Whereas in 1979 support for a Welsh Assembly was highly localized to Welsh speakers and Plaid Cymru supporters, by 1997 it had spread to supporters of all parties except the Conservatives. The biggest movement was among those who generally thought of themselves as Labour. In 1979, Labour was perceived as divided (because it was). In 1997, although there were still Labour opponents of devolution, almost everybody in Wales perceived Labour, as well as Plaid Cymru, as favouring a "Yes"; the Conservatives, again correctly, as favouring a "No"; and they tended not to know where the Liberal Democrats stood. This sufficed to bring the majority of those who voted and thought of themselves as Labour into the "Yes" camp, and hence to the knife-edge "Yes" victory by less than 7,000 votes. Although fluent Welsh speakers were still the core of the "Yes" vote, the "Yes" camp, unlike in 1979, made significant inroads into the rest of the Welsh electorate.

However, only the higher turnout of Welsh-speakers delivered a "Yes" on the night.[12]

The second step-change was probably concentrated in the immediate run-up to the first National Assembly election in 1999. Labour leader Ron Davies's unacknowledged statecraft was to avoid creating a National Assembly with an overwhelming Labour majority in terms of seats, which might in itself have reduced the legitimacy of the National Assembly. However, Labour was so hegemonic in Wales that everybody expected it to control the National Assembly comfortably even with proportional representation (PR). In the event, Labour failed to get an overall majority of seats. Plaid Cymru benefited from differential turnout (like the "Yes" side in the 1997 referendum).

The logistic regression model shown in simplified form in Table 5.3 reveals the social bases of Welsh politics. Fortunately, it is not necessary to fully understand the qualities of this statistical model in order to appreciate its significance. Put quite simply, Table 5.3 shows that attitudes to constitutional futures and national identity were the best predictors of a vote for Plaid Cymru. Welsh speakers were less inclined to vote for any of the other parties than were non-Welsh speakers. Otherwise, the strongest predictors of vote for or against the two big parties in the United Kingdom were factors that were generally significant across the whole of British orientations, such as social class (significant only for Conservative voting) and attitudes to issues that affected the whole United Kingdom. As is so often the case, Liberal Democrat voters were harder to characterize.

In both Scotland and Wales, the second devolved assembly elections, in 2003, had a feel of a return to normal politics. In Scotland, support for independence had dwindled from its peak of 37 per cent at the time of the referendum to 26 per cent, while support for the new status quo of a Scottish Par-

Table 5.3 Significant Predictors of Welsh National Assembly Vote by Party, 1999

	Lab	Con	Plaid Cymru	Lib Dem
Class		+++		
Born in Wales	+			--
Constitutional preference		---	+++	--
Welsh speaker	---	---	+++	-
National identity scale			++	
Against UK government	---	+++	++	
Welsh issues			+++	
UK considerations	+++	++	-	

Source: D. Trystan, R. Scully and R. Wyn Jones, "Explaining the 'Quiet Earthquake': Voting Behaviour in the First Election to the National Assembly for Wales", Electoral Studies, 22 (2003), 635–50, Table 4.

Key: +++, ---   p<0.01
      ++, --   p<0.05
      +, -   p<0.1

Blank cell: Variable is not a significant predictor of voting for or against the party.

For descriptions of variables (where not obvious) and direction of coding, see source.

liament with taxing powers was the modal preference, at 48 per cent. In Wales, too, the status quo was the modal preference—41 per cent opting for an assembly without taxation or law-making powers. It was, however, rather grumpy support. The blissful dawn of both assemblies had turned into grumbling; and most people by 2003 believed (once again) that the Westminster government had more influence than the devolved assembly on how their country was governed. Most Scots and Welsh respondents thought that their assembly had made no difference to the quality of their government, although those who thought it had got better outnumbered those who thought it had got worse by about 20 points.[13] In both countries, the nationalist parties fell back sharply in the 2003 elections (see Table 5.4).

Northern Ireland

The territory with the strongest popular endorsement for constitutional change is, ironically, the one where constitutional change has hit a brick wall. Without going back to Cromwell, as threatened above, we can identify the Northern Ireland constitutional problem as the remaining unfinished business of the Irish Question. In the most brilliant stroke of his Welsh wizardry, Prime Minister David Lloyd George achieved an Irish settlement in 1921 that reconciled the irreconcilable for fifty years.[14] But it left the insoluble problem of Northern Ireland behind. In Northern Ireland, the Protestant majority was grimly determined to hold on to power; the excluded Catholic minority faced unappetizing choices of participation (as a permanent minority) in the Northern Ireland parliament at Stormont outside Belfast; abstention; and violence. A renewal of paramilitary violence (at first on the Protestant side, soon matched on the Catholic side) in 1969 led directly to the abolition of the parliament and government of Northern Ireland in 1972. British ministers then imposed direct rule, and spent most of the time up to 1998 vainly trying to restore devolved government. The final push was begun by the outgoing Conservative Prime Minister John Major, and concluded by his successor Tony Blair. The Belfast ("Good Friday") Agreement of 1998 won 71 per cent support; and in the parallel referendum in the Irish Republic, the proposal to abandon the Republic's irredentist claims over Northern Ireland won 95 per cent.[15] Support for constitutional change in Ireland was therefore stronger than in Scotland, and much stronger than in Wales. However, the Northern Ireland Assembly, unlike those in Scotland and Wales, has failed. It has been suspended twice over the failure of the paramilitaries there to disarm. Although a second election to the suspended Assembly was held in 2003, the deadlock has continued, and the new Assembly has never met. The general election in the United Kingdom of 2005 has strengthened the extremes at the expense of the middle. Westminster elections in Northern Ireland always do—partly because of the electoral system. But opinion in both the nationalist and unionist communities has undoubtedly moved in favour of the hard-liners.

Devolved Election Results since 1998

Table 5.4 shows how the parties have fared in the Westminster and devolved elections since 1998. Elections to the House of Commons are held under the single-member, FPTP electoral system. Elections to the legislatures of all the devolved administrations (DAs) are by versions of proportional representation. Scotland and Wales use the Additional Member system (AMS); Northern Ireland uses the Single Transferable Vote (STV) system. The three electoral systems in use in the elections covered by Table 5.4 therefore produce very different votes-to-seats mappings. As electors in the DAs have become familiar with the variety of electoral systems in use there, the system also affects the willingness of people to vote for parties of different sorts in different context. It is therefore necessary to interpret the figures in Table 5.4 one territory at a time and one electoral system at a time. Vote shares and seat shares each tell an important story, but they are different stories.

Scotland

In Scotland, Labour has retained its hegemonic position in all four elections since 1999. However, its hegemony in votes is less secure than its hegemony in seats. In the second Scottish Parliament election in 2003, its share of the vote dropped to 32 per cent. It was vulnerable to the left (the Scottish Socialist Party and the Green Party) as well as to the Scottish National Party (SNP). Table 5.4 shows that Conservative performance in Scotland has been flat. Their improvement from the nadir of the 1997 general election, when they won not a single seat in Scotland, has been entirely due to the way that the new system translates votes into seats, not to an improvement in their share of the vote. The Liberal Democrats were similarly flatlining until the 2005 general election, which took their vote share from either third or fourth place in the preceding elections to second place, forcing the SNP into third place in Scotland for the first time since 1992. Labour performed better, and the SNP worse, in elections to the House of Commons than in elections to the Scottish Parliament. Table 5.4 shows that in the general election of 2005, the Conservatives came fourth in Scotland.

Wales

In Wales, Labour was also hegemonic, but never to the extent of winning more than half of the popular vote. Unlike in Scotland, the Conservatives made a real recovery between 1999 and 2001, and have retained their slightly higher share of the vote since then. The Liberal Democrats have a similar profile in Wales to Scotland, but their gain in 2005 was less dramatic. Plaid Cymru has done distinctly badly, dropping from nearly 30 per cent of the Welsh vote in the first National Assembly to only 12.6 per cent in the 2005 general election. But as in Scotland, voting behaviour seems to differ in

Table 5.4 Votes and Seats in Scotland, Wales and Northern Ireland, 1998–2005

Scotland

	Scottish Parliament 1999				House of Commons 2001				Scottish Parliament 2003				House of Commons 2005			
	Vote Share	Seats	Seat Share	Seat/Vote	Vote Share	Seats	Seat Share	Seat/Vote	Vote Share	Seats	Seat Share	Seat/Vote	Vote Share	Seats	Seat Share	Seat/Vote
Labour	36.2	56	43.4	1.20	43.9	56	77.8	1.77	32.0	50	38.8	1.21	39.5	41	69.5	1.76
Lib Dem	13.3	17	13.2	0.99	16.4	10	13.9	0.85	13.6	17	13.2	0.97	22.6	11	18.6	0.82
SNP	28.0	35	27.1	0.97	20.1	5	6.9	0.35	22.4	27	20.9	0.94	17.7	6	10.2	0.57
Conservative	15.5	18	14.0	0.90	15.6	1	1.4	0.09	16.1	18	14.0	0.87	15.8	1	1.7	0.11
Other	7.0	3	2.3	0.33	4.0	0	0	0	16.1	17	13.2	0.82	4.4	0	0	0
	100.0	129	100.0		100.0	72	100.0		100.0	129	100.0		100.0	59	100.0	

Wales

	National Assembly 1999				House of Commons 2001				National Assembly 2003				House of Commons 2005			
	Vote Share	Seats	Seat Share	Seat/Vote	Vote Share	Seats	Seat Share	Seat/Vote	Vote Share	Seats	Seat Share	Seat/Vote	Vote Share	Seats	Seat Share	Seat/Vote
Labour	36.6	28	46.7	1.28	48.6	34	85	1.75	38.3	30	50.0	1.31	42.7	29	72.5	1.70
Lib Dem	13.0	6	10.0	0.77	13.8	2	5	0.36	13.4	6	10.0	0.75	18.4	4	10.0	0.54
Plaid Cymru	29.5	17	28.3	0.96	14.3	4	10	0.70	20.5	12	20.0	0.98	12.6	3	7.5	0.60
Conservative	16.2	9	15.0	0.93	21.0	0	0	0	19.6	11	18.3	0.94	21.4	3	7.5	0.35
Other	4.8	0	0	0	2.3	0	0	0	8.3	1	1.7	0.20	4.9	1	2.5	0.51
	100.0	60	100.0		100.0	40	100		100.0	60	100.0		100.0	40	100.0	

Northern Ireland

	NI Legislative Assembly 1998				House of Commons 2001				NI Legislative Assembly 2003				House of Commons 2005			
	Vote Share	Seats	Seat Share	Seat/Vote	Vote Share	Seats	Seat Share	Seat/Vote	Vote Share	Seats	Seat Share	Seat/Vote	Vote Share	Seats	Seat Share	Seat/Vote
DUP	18.1	10	9.3	0.51	22.5	5	27.8	1.23	25.7	30	27.8	1.08	33.7	9	50.0	1.48
UUP	21.3	28	25.9	1.22	26.8	6	33.3	1.24	22.7	27	25.0	1.10	17.7	1	5.6	0.31
SDLP	22.0	24	22.2	1.01	21.0	3	16.7	0.79	17.0	18	16.7	0.98	17.5	3	16.7	0.95
Sinn Fein	17.7	18	16.7	0.94	21.7	4	22.2	1.02	23.5	24	22.2	0.95	24.3	5	27.8	1.14
Other	20.9	28	25.9	1.24	8.0	0	0	0	11.1	9	8.3	0.75	6.8	0	0	0
	100.0	108	100.0		100.0	18	100.0		100.0	108	100.0		100.0	18	100.0	

Sources: BBC election websites 2001, 2005; Electoral Commission; Constitution Unit; A. Trench, ed., *Has Devolution Made a Difference?* (Exeter: Imprint Academic, 2004), Figure 4.7.
Notes: Vote share in Scottish and Welsh assemblies: unweighted average of constituency vote and list vote for each party.
Vote share in Northern Ireland assembly: share of first preference vote for each party.

Westminster and Welsh elections. Labour performed better, and Plaid Cymru worse, in elections to the House of Commons than in elections to the National Assembly for Wales.

Northern Ireland

In Northern Ireland, each main community contains a relatively moderate and at least one relatively extreme party. With few exceptions, Protestants vote for unionist parties and Catholics vote for nationalist parties. In the unionist community, the relatively moderate party is the Ulster Unionist Party—UUP in Table 5.4; the main relatively extreme party is the Democratic Unionist Party of the Reverend Ian Paisley—DUP in Table 5.4. Other unionist parties with links to Protestant paramilitaries won seats in the Legislative Assembly elections, but not in general elections. In the nationalist community, the relatively moderate party is the Social Democratic & Labour Party—SDLP in Table 5.4. The relatively extreme party is Sinn Fein, which is widely believed to be intimately connected with the main republican paramilitary organization, the Irish Republican Army (IRA). Sinn Fein's parliamentary leaders, Gerry Adams and Martin McGuinness, have always denied that they serve on the IRA's governing councils, although Unionists believe that McGuinness is a member of the IRA's Army Council.[16] There is relatively little cross-community voting. The non-sectarian Alliance Party has never won seats at Westminster, although it did win some at Stormont in 1998 and 2003, as did the Northern Ireland Women's Coalition in 1998. The SDLP's gain of Belfast South in the 2005 general election may indicate the first cross-community voting by Protestants on any scale since the foundation of Northern Ireland.

Since 1998, the extremes have been gaining ground at the expense of the centre. The DUP has risen from an 18 per cent share of the vote in 1998 to 33.7 per cent in 2005. Sinn Fein has risen from 6.7 to 24.3 per cent over the same period. The UUP and SDLP have lost votes and seats. The UUP was reduced to one Westminster seat in May 2005, and David Trimble, its leader and Nobel Peace Prize winner, lost his seat in Upper Bann to the DUP. There has been a long-run tendency for the extremes in Northern Ireland to do better in first-past-the-post Westminster elections than in PR local elections. This tendency can neither be confirmed nor contradicted for the period since 1998. True, the centre parties were annihilated in the 2005 Westminster election, as has happened in Ireland in some past general elections, especially 1885, 1918 and both February and October 1974. For instance, in 1918 Sinn Fein, then a party determined to achieve independence for Ireland by violence if need be, wiped out the non-violent Irish Party in the House of Commons—but its popular vote was only double that for the Irish Party. However, Table 5.4 shows that the upward gradient for the extreme parties has been continuous since the Good Friday Agreement, so their triumph in 2005 cannot be wholly ascribed to electoral system effects.

The Endogeneity of Votes and Electoral Systems

Despite these observations, Table 5.4 does shows that electoral systems matter profoundly for the future of devolution within Britain. The electoral systems did not change during the second Blair term, but systems introduced at the start continued to work their effects in subtle ways through the politics of representation and finance, which are examined in subsequent sections of this chapter. Past British governments introduced proportional representation in (Northern) Ireland and Scotland for quite deliberate reasons, which overrode the winners' natural reluctance to disturb the first-past-the-post system that gave them their victories in elections to Westminster. The STV system was introduced in both parts of Ireland as long ago as 1918, in order to protect local minorities—that is, Protestants in southern Ireland and Catholics in Northern Ireland. In both parts of Ireland, incumbent governments have tried to abolish it in order to bring back the winner's bonus associated with first-past-the-post. In both parts they failed in the long term, although in Northern Ireland the incumbent Unionists temporarily got rid of it between 1929 and 1973. In Scotland, the architect of devolution, Donald Dewar, the former Secretary of State for Scotland, was quite explicit. He forced PR through against the will of many of his Labour Party colleagues, who knew that they stood to lose seats. As Labour would probably have easily won an outright majority of its seats on a minority vote had the FPTP Westminster system applied in Scotland, Dewar called this "the best example of charitable giving this century in politics".[17] However, it guaranteed the legitimacy of the Scottish Parliament and made it harder for the SNP to gain a majority in it. In October 1974, the SNP had come perilously close to winning a majority of Scottish seats on a minority of the vote.[18] AMS in the Scottish Parliament makes that unlikely.

Wales, as usual, was an afterthought. There was no comparable reason of Unionist statecraft for imposing PR on the National Assembly, but consistency with Scotland, and perhaps some desire to break up the single-party (Labour) fortresses of the South Wales Valleys, led Labour to introduce the AMS system there too. This decision accidentally saved Labour from significant losses in the elections held in 1999, but in general it has constrained Labour more than it has liberated it in Wales.[19]

Votes, seats and electoral systems are endogenous to one another. This makes separating out the unique effects of each on either of the others very difficult. That the SNP and Plaid Cymru do better in devolved than in Westminster elections almost certainly reflects two things: that there are people who sincerely support them in the first but not in the second; and that there is more tactical point in voting for them under PR than under first-past-the-post. For both of these reasons (which cannot be easily disentangled), they are entrenched in their respective assemblies despite their weakening performance during the second Blair term. The tendency for the centre in Northern Ireland to do better under STV than under FPTP cannot be confirmed for sure during this period. Diminishing policy appeals almost certainly underlie the weakening of the centre in 2003 and its collapse in 2005; namely, the failure of republican paramilitaries to disarm and the knock-on disillusionment of unionists with the UUP politicians who had trusted the republicans' good faith.

The simplest summary measures of the electoral system effects on devolution are seat/vote ratios. These are shown in Table 5.4 as the fourth column of figures for each parliament. The seat/vote ratio for a party is simply its share of seats expressed as a proportion of its share of votes: that is, the third column in each block of Table 5.4 divided by the first. In a pure PR system, the seat/vote ratio would always be 1.00. Under FPTP the ratio for the leading party will almost always exceed 1.00, the ratio for the second party is sometimes above and sometimes below 1.00, and the ratio for third and lower parties is almost always below 1.00. The ratio for any party which fails to gain a seat is, of course, zero.

In all three territories, the locally dominant party has a ratio greater than 1 at Westminster elections. For Scotland and Wales, this is always Labour; in Northern Ireland, it was the UUP until 2001, and is now the DUP. Opposition parties whose vote is spatially distributed in a way that is efficient under FPTP may have seat/vote ratios of close to 1 and so they may, by sheer good luck, be proportionally represented. Examples are the Liberal Democrats in Scotland (though not in Wales), the SDLP and Sinn Fein. The see-saw movements in Table 5.4 arise from the switching fortunes of other parties, which are penalized under FPTP but do well under PR. This especially describes the Conservatives in Scotland and Wales, and the "Others" (which include the smaller unionist and cross-community parties) in Northern Ireland.

But Table 5.4 shows that no DA's electoral system is truly proportional. If they were, the ratio for all parties would converge towards 1 at both the 1998/9 and the 2003 time points. The DUP had a ratio of only 0.51 in 1998. This is probably an intended effect of STV, which is designed to favour centrists over extremists. If centrists exchanged second preferences for one another's parties, their seat share would be boosted, and that for extreme parties correspondingly depressed. The DUP was a victim of this in 1998, but has not been since then. The Northern Ireland electoral system failed to restrain the more extreme parties in 2003. Disillusionment with the Good Friday Agreement had gone too far by then.

In both Scotland and Wales, the incompletely proportional AMS system retained some of the seat advantage that Labour would have had under FPTP. The Labour politicians who wrote the Scotland and Wales Acts 1998 intended this, and they have not yet been disappointed. But the seat advantage was too small to deliver Labour majority administrations. There has been a Labour–Liberal Democrat governing coalition for the whole lifetime of the Scottish Parliament so far. However, Table 5.4 shows that all parties including "Others" got a seat/vote ratio close to 1 in the 2003 Scottish Parliament. Two left-wing parties—the Greens and the Scottish Socialists—did well in the regional list vote, and some single-issue candidates did well in the constituency vote. The presence of seven Greens and six Scottish Socialists in particular shapes the policy choices of the governing coalition. In Wales, Labour has governed at times alone as a minority administration, and for a spell in coalition with the Liberal Democrats. In the second National Assembly, since 2003, it has reverted to single-party minority government. Its minority status means that it, too, has to care more about opposition party interests than does its counterpart at Westminster.

Policy Divergence since Devolution

Scottish politics from 1997 to 2003 seemed to be about just one thing, namely the cost of the Scottish Parliament building in Edinburgh. From initial estimates of below £40 million, the cost progressed inexorably to a final bill in excess of £430 million.[20] This threatened the reputations especially of two eminent deceased people—Donald Dewar, architect of devolution and first First Minister of Scotland, and Enric Miralles, the Catalan architect of the building. The Fraser Report exonerated Dewar (but not Miralles). It spread its blame both before and after the date when the parliament took responsibility for its own affairs in 1999. Two months later, the permanent secretary to the Scottish Executive announced that no civil servants were to be disciplined for their role in the parliament building fiasco.[21] The building is rather grand and carries uplifting quotations from Robert Burns on the wall facing the Canongate.

Holyrood certainly damaged the reputation of the parliament and government of Scotland. But the damage came early. There is no time-series question specifically on the performance of parliament or government, nor on the parliament building. But data from the Scottish Political Attitudes time-series show that the slump in the proportion of Scots saying that the devolved institutions have given "ordinary people a say in how Scotland is governed" has slumped from 64 to 44 per cent between the 1999 and 2000 surveys, and has since dropped to 39 per cent. However, a similar twenty-point drop occurred in Wales between the 1999 and 2001 surveys.[22] In Wales, there were some issues with the assembly building, but they were much smaller than in Scotland. The slump in public confidence probably owes more to an onset of realistic expectations about what the parliament can achieve than to Holyrood.

Below the surface, devolution was bedding in. The Scottish Parliament spends money that other people raise. The SNP flirted briefly with the idea of using the parliament's tax-raising power but was bitterly attacked by all the other parties, and it backed down. This has forced serious discussion of redistribution and public finance to the margins. Distributive politics marked the beginning of differences with the British government—more by not doing things that the Blair New Labour administration was doing in England than by doing things that it was not. On student fees; reform of the NHS; and use of the Private Finance Initiative to fund public infrastructure, Scotland and Wales refused to act when Westminster (or Whitehall) acted. In December

2002, First Minister Rhodri Morgan announced that he would put "clear red water" between Welsh Labour and the Labour government in London. As in Scotland, this would take the form of not doing things that the British government was doing. Morgan singled out proposals to create "foundation hospitals" for attack.[23] The Welsh government has also refused to introduce comprehensive performance assessment for local authorities and league tables of school performance.

This divergence flows from Celtic resentment at being used as an experiment for unpopular policies of a Conservative government, under Margaret Thatcher, that held very few seats in Scotland or Wales. The Labour government in Westminster (as opposed to the Labour Party of Wales) holds no seats there. In Scotland, the Labour–Liberal Democrat governing coalition had to look over its shoulder at the Greens and the Scottish Socialists; in Wales, the minority Labour administration was vulnerable to opportunistic attacks, for instance on student fees. The divergence opens up a policy gap among the four nations and makes it possible to compare the effect of public policy in different parts of the United Kingdom. On education, the comparison mostly shows confusion; on health, it shows interesting contrasts.

The Land Reform (Scotland) Act 2003 abolishes feudalism in Scotland.[24] At Westminster, Scottish land reform might have been blocked in the House of Lords; even had it found legislative time. As it involves reforming Scots law, it is right that Scots law should now come under the Scottish Parliament, restoring a link that was broken in 1707 (when the Act of Union was passed). Less brave was the parliament's 2003 ducking of a Green MSP's civil partnerships bill, which would have extended some of the rights of married people to same-sex couples. This was a matter within the devolved powers of the parliament to determine. But in 2000 the parliament had been savagely attacked by a cardinal and a busman over its (ultimately successful) repeal of the misnamed "Section 28" clause banning the public endorsement of homosexual lifestyles.[25] This time round, the parliament avoided a fight by passing a so-called "Sewel motion". Sewel motions remit a devolved matter back to Westminster for legislation. They are a voluntary surrender of devolution. They have been used much more than commentators anticipated in 1999. Sometimes there are good technical reasons why it suits both sides to let Westminster legislate on a devolved matter. But over civil partnerships, it was sheer cowardice.

As to Wales, the National Assembly's finest moment came in February 2000. Its vote of no confidence in Alun Michael, Blair's nominee as first minister, forced him out in favour of Rhodri Morgan, whom Blair had been trying to block since devolution in Wales began.[26] The focus of controversy had been additional Whitehall funding for "West Wales and the Valleys", an artificial confection that had been granted "Objective One" status by the European Union. This confection gained extra European funding, which the National Assembly asked Whitehall to match. Whitehall refused, and Michael was blamed. Objective One areas are the poorest areas in the Union, with less than 75 per cent of average European Union gross domestic product (GDP) per head. The actual politics of Objective One are less noble than the principled defenestration of Alun Michael would suggest. It amounts to a distinctly "Old Labour" policy of rewarding an area for its poverty and throwing museums and steam railways at it to get it out of poverty. It may well have distracted the Labour administration in the National Assembly from growth-promoting economic policy.

Much of the energy of the National Assembly was directed inwards. The Government of Wales Act 1998 gave it the powers and structure of a local authority, and therefore no separate legal recognition of the assembly government as an entity distinct from the National Assembly. Also, the National Assembly has no primary legislative powers. It has the power to enact secondary legislation (statutory instruments), but these powers are ill-matched to the policy areas that are devolved to it. The constitutional framework therefore rapidly proved unworkable. The assembly appointed a commission under the Labour politician Lord Richard to review the case for giving the assembly primary legislative powers. The commission reported in March 2004. With one dissenting member, it called for the National Assembly to be given primary legislative powers on the same lines as Scotland. A tax-varying power, as in Scotland, would be "desirable but not essential". The assembly should be replaced by a legally distinct parliament and executive, as in Scotland. The sixty-member assembly elected by AMS should be replaced by an eighty-member assembly elected by STV.[27]

In response, Secretary of State for Wales Peter Hain said that the criterion of constitutional change should be whether it made the lives of people in Wales better, dropping heavy hints that in his view the Richard proposals would not do so. The Commission's proposal for a National Assembly elected by STV angered those whose seats it imperilled; its recommendation of greater powers for the assembly (and hence fewer powers for MPs for Wales) angered forty MPs, most of them from Labour. Nevertheless, the May 2005 Queen's Speech announced a Government of Wales Bill, which might (or might not) contain primary legislative powers. A White Paper and possibly a further referendum on primary powers are promised.

The Northern Ireland Assembly was suspended in October 2002. The 2003 election was delayed in the hope that the parties could agree on conditions for the lifting of the suspension. No conditions were agreed; the assembly remained suspended; a delayed election (whose results have already been analysed) was held in November 2003 to an assembly that has never met and on current conditions is never likely to. The root cause of break-down has been the failure of the IRA to prove that it has decommissioned its weapons. This has led Protestant and Unionist voters to lose faith in the Good Friday Agreement. A deal on decommissioning seemed tantalizingly close in December 2004, when DUP leader Ian Paisley and Sinn Fein leader Gerry Adams seemed, however improbably, poised to agree terms for resumption of the assembly. However, the talks failed over whether the IRA would be forced to produce photographs of the process of destroying its weapons. Soon afterwards, agreement disappeared over the horizon as IRA members were implicated in rapid succession in a huge bank robbery in Belfast; a money-laundering operation in the Irish Republic; and in the cover-up after a Catholic, Robert McCartney, was murdered outside his local bar in a republican area of Belfast.

Northern Ireland is therefore governed by direct rule ministers and the Northern Ireland Civil Service. The most encouraging fact is that life goes on: the incidence of sectarian murders and violence has sharply declined; there have been no terrorist bombs or attacks since the appalling Omagh bomb of 1998, which killed twenty-nine people. Direct rule ministers could do things that elected ministers would find difficult, such as close down public services in areas of declining population or widen the tax base. Northern Ireland escaped the Poll Tax and still levies domestic rates. The Treasury thinks that Northern Irish householders pay too little towards the cost of local services. Otherwise, the politics of devolution in Northern Ireland is largely the politics of not changing things that have been changing in England, leading to a natural experiment where education and health have started to diverge. In July 2005 the leaders of Sinn Fein and the IRA announced that the latter had ended its military campaign; in September they announced that they had put all their arms beyond use. The decommissioning was observed by a Catholic and a Protestant clergyman, and approved by the Canadian head of the body set up to supervise disarmament. However, the IRA did not allow any photographs to be taken. As this book goes to press, it is too early to say whether any of this will lead to the reactivation of the assembly.

Since 1918, there have been five distinct school systems in the United Kingdom. They did not map exactly on to the four territories. One covered England and Wales. Scotland and Northern Ireland each had two systems. One was non-denominational (which meant "Protestant"); the other Roman Catholic. The cause of integrated schooling is raised from time to time in Northern Ireland (and, less often, in Scotland). But the firm opposition of the Roman Catholic hierarchy means that integration is not practical politics. The new responsibility of the National Assembly for school education in Wales has not led to any radical change in the second Blair term. In due course it may become possible to compare the United Kingdom's four, or six, school systems using international comparisons of achievement, or on cost per pupil. But the most relevant international comparison has missing data— embarrassingly, too few schools in England supplied data for the latest OECD international comparison of school standards for valid inferences to be made. So the fact that considerably more is spent per pupil in the devolved administrations—especially in Scotland and Northern Ireland—than in England has consequences which are not adequately measured.

It is in higher education that policy has diverged the most. Higher education is a devolved function, but scientific research is a "reserved" function for the parliament at Westminster. This fact cuts across the way that universities are funded. So does the fact that a student whose domicile is in any part of the United Kingdom may go to university in any other part of the United Kingdom. As indeed may a student from anywhere in the European Union (where by EU rules they must pay the same fees as British students attending the same university). In 2003–2004 the British government decided to enact a Higher Education Bill that made profound changes to university funding in England. The bill was controversial among Labour MPs. Both main opposition parties saw a handy bandwagon and jumped on to it, opposing the bill's provision for graduates to be liable for a fee of up to £3,000 per annum, reclaimable through their income tax after graduation and only once their income had crossed a certain threshold. The bill finally scraped through the Commons with a majority of five on second reading. If English MPs alone had voted on it (and MPs from the other three territories had refrained from voting), it would have been defeated by six votes.[28]

Ministers and their advisers in the British government did not stop to consider the knock-on consequences of their bill for Scotland, Wales and Northern Ireland. Some of these were obvious. There would be a predictable surge of English students to Celtic universities as they sought to avoid the new fees. But the burden of funding these students would mostly fall on the devolved administrations' budgets. More subtly, the act and associated spending reviews sharply increase the universities' budget for research. Some of this flows, in England, through the Department for Education and Skills. This money carries something that experts lovingly refer to as a "Barnett consequential" for the three devolved administrations, so that they get their population share of this flow. But the rest flows through the Department of Trade and Industry, which is the sponsoring ministry for scientific research. The DTI is a ministry which covers the whole of the United Kingdom; therefore its own allocation mechanisms (delegated to the research councils) also cover the whole United Kingdom. The devolved administrations would get their population share of this flow only if their university scientists had exactly the same rate per head of successful grants from the research councils as those in England. They do not.

On health policy, the political scientist Scott Greer has tracked the divergence among the four territories of the United Kingdom.[29] He characterizes the medico-politics as *professionalism* in Scotland; *markets* in England; *localism* in Wales, and *permissive managerialism* in Northern Ireland:

> The Scottish health policy landscape is ... densely populated with groups based on very high-status, important medical institutions who are willing and able to participate in policy. . . . Welsh health policy's guiding themes—new public health, localism, and trust in the public service—stem from a policy community dominated by believers in, and workers in, local public services. . . . [B]eing an insider with advice and acquiescence still matters in Northern Ireland, while the outlines of policy changes still travel from Britain to Belfast via the civil service.[30]

The most important contrast that separates all three of the DAs from England is that all three have reverted to a style of NHS politics that pre-ante-dates the partial marketisation introduced by the Thatcher administration in the late 1980s. England, by contrast, has pressed on. After pulling back in the first years of New Labour, the Blair administration has now taken the market approach further.

The performance of the National Health Service (NHS) has visibly improved in England according to tangible measures; whereas in all three other territories it has stagnated or got worse. The latest available news from the Constitution Unit's quarterly "Monitoring Reports" include the following tit-bits of information:

- Northern Ireland: "an outpatient queue lengthening by more than 17,000 over the calendar year" (April 2005 report, p. 47).

- Wales: Assembly Minister for Health removed in January 2005 after criticism of poor NHS performance; highly critical audit report on NHS waiting times in Wales; Secretary of State for Wales Peter Hain interferes in a devolved matter by urging the assembly government to adopt English methods of cutting waiting times (April 2005 report, pp. 6, 23–4).

- Scotland: "Health policy is clearly the area where the Executive is having the greatest difficulty in 'delivering'". Whichever targets Ministers choose, they not only seem to be missed, but things appear to be getting worse rather than better" (April 2005 report, p. 42).[31]

Tony Blair and his advisers may be permitting themselves a sly smile or three. It seems their market-based approach is outperforming the "Old Labour" solutions so loved elsewhere.

The Barnett Formula Limps On

The block grant that finances devolved services in the three DAs is based on something called the "Barnett Formula". This means that changes in the block grant from HM Treasury to the DAs reflect their shares of the British population. The formula is unsustainable in the long run for a variety of reasons. The issues are rather technical.[32] Briefly:

- *The Barnett Formula is not efficient* . . . because it gives no incentives to the DAs to seek economic (or, more narrowly, tax) efficiency. All three DAs manage public expenditure. None of them manages public revenue except relating to local government finance (Council Tax; business rates; domestic rates in Northern Ireland). So in none of the DAs do the decision makers face a budget constraint. A rational politician would rather spend more than less (because a marginal pound of public spending, financed out of non-local taxation, should always improve their chances of re-election) up to the point where Barnett sets a hard constraint or where the marginal effect of extra taxation in that territory outweighs the marginal benefit from the spending. The largest DA (Scotland) contains less than 10 per cent of the population of the United Kingdom. Therefore, extra public expenditure in Scotland would have to cost around ten times the benefit it brings before the Scottish people would rationally rebel against it.

- ... *nor equitable.* Public spending per head, across the twelve standard regions of the United Kingdom, ought to be inversely related to GDP per head (that is, highest in poor areas and lowest in rich areas). At the moment, there is no statistical relationship at all between the two. There are, moreover, three regions that seem to receive significantly more spending than they should. They are Scotland, Northern Ireland and London. It has been argued that their higher relative expenditure per head derives not from greater need but from the more credible threat to the Union of the United Kingdom that they pose, compared to the other nine standard regions.[33]

- *It gives perverse incentives to the DAs.* The incentive to spend what Australians call a "ten-cent dollar" (five-cent dollars in Wales; three-cent dollars in Northern Ireland) has already been mentioned. The DAs have no incentive to broaden their tax bases because they do not see the proceeds; and they have an incentive to switch their block grants from capital spending (which brings benefits after the next election) to current spending (which brings benefits before the next election).

- *DAs cannot control their block grant* because it depends on spending in England on each devolved service. Spending in England is tightly controlled by the Treasury's biennial spending reviews, to which the DAs have no input.

- *But their decisions have consequences for macroeconomic management in the United Kingdom,* notably because of the temptation just mentioned for the DAs to switch money from capital programmes to current spending. This could interfere with the British government's fiscal rules (currently called the "Golden Rule" and the "Sustainable Investment Rule", which are likely to be followed by British governments of all complexions).

On the surface, there has been little movement over the Barnett Formula, and the one movement that occurred tended to preserve it, as explained below. But the academic consensus that it was unsustainable was shared, publicly or privately, by civil servants in all three DAs and at the centre. The first green shoots of post-Barnett thought started to appear. The Fraser of Allander Institute commissioned a paper on fiscal federalism which turned that from a fine phrase into a careful proposal for the first time. Others have proposed that the Barnett mechanism should be scrapped and replaced by a non-partisan grants commission modelled on an Australian example, which would allocate block grant either to the four nations of the United Kingdom or to its twelve standard regions.[34]

The English Question According to Prescott and Brown

In the parliament of 2001–2005, Deputy Prime Minister John Prescott (representing Hull) and Chancellor Gordon Brown (representing Fife) took a close interest in the so-called "English Question". Their agendas overlapped but were not identical. In the 2001 election campaign, Prescott threatened that there would be "blood on the carpet" over the apparently unfair distribution of public expenditure around the United Kingdom, with the northern English regions getting suspiciously little. He was immediately slapped down by the prime minister's press secretary, Alastair Campbell, who denied that Prescott had said the words captured on the journalist's tape-recorder. Nevertheless, Prescott returned to the fray, his then deputy Nick Raynsford telling the *Newcastle Journal* in 2004 that the time had come to review the Barnett formula.[35] On something so sensitive, Raynsford must have been speaking with Prescott's authority.

The Prescott agenda was zero-sum. Scotland was getting too much; northern England was getting too little. The solution might be elected assemblies in each English region, or at least the northern ones. A plan was developed for assemblies with quite limited powers, in those regions that wanted them. If they voted for an elected assembly, the people of any region must simultaneously agree that local authorities in the region would all become single-tier. This provision was said to have been inserted by Tony Blair, anxious that the scheme would not be condemned as "too many politicians". But that is exactly what happened in the only region that finally went to a referendum. This was the North-East, thought to be the standard-bearer for regionalism, because complaints against Barnett are loudest there. However, the "No" campaign fought feistily. Its mascot was an inflatable white elephant. The result, on November 4, 2004, crushed the Prescott agenda. In an all-postal ballot with a turnout of 47.7 per cent, the vote against an elected regional assembly was 696,519 (77.9 per cent); the vote in favour was 197,310 (22.1 per cent).[36]

This left only the Brown, non-zero-sum, agenda in play. It owed a lot to Brown's long-standing adviser Ed Balls, Chief Economic Adviser to the Treasury from 1997 to 2004. Multiple Treasury documents since 2000—Budget books, Pre-Budget Reports, and Spending Reviews—have drawn attention to unequal economic growth in the regions of England, with London and the South-East leading and the rest lagging. The latest spending review commits the Treasury and Prescott's department, the Office of the Deputy Prime Minister (ODPM), to "make sustainable improvements in the economic performance of all English regions by 2008, and over the long term reduce the persistent gap in growth rates between the regions, demonstrating progress by

2006". That is a large and tough agenda. To measure improvements in the economic performance of the English regions, governments first need to know what it is. Two reports during the 2001–2005 parliament (the Allsopp and McLean reports) led to improvements in regional statistics being introduced or promised.[37]

Conclusion

The United Kingdom is indeed in a state of fractured federalism. Finance is unstable because the Barnett Formula is unsustainable. Serious thought as to what might replace it is just beginning. The answer may well not come in the parliament that will presumably run between 2005 and 2009–2010, but it will have to come soon. In representation, the ancient "West Lothian Question" again reared its head because both university student fees and foundation hospitals were enacted in England only through the votes of MPs from the other territories, where these polices were not to apply. With the reduced Labour majority in the 2005 parliament, this is likely to recur. The West Lothian Question asks why MPs have different powers over policy in different parts of the United Kingdom: for instance, why can MPs from Scotland vote to decide education policy in England, whereas no MPs can vote to decide education policy in Scotland, which is solely the responsibility of the Scottish Parliament? The stable solutions are either a more symmetrical federalism, with assemblies for England or the regions of England (unlikely in the near future after the North-East referendum), or further reduction in Scottish and Welsh seats in the House of Commons. Scotland is represented in proportion to population; Wales is overrepresented. Perhaps the least unfair solution to the West Lothian Question is to reduce their representation to about two-thirds of their population share, in line with the arrangements for Northern Ireland when domestic politics was securely devolved, between 1920 and 1972.

Policy divergence is just beginning: partly (as in higher education) it reveals only confusion all round, while partly (as in health) real consequences from real decisions are beginning to emerge. A more mature system requires that those who spend are also those who tax, at least at the margin. Then (but probably only then) it will be possible to see whether the coalitional governments likely to be thrown up by PR in Scotland and Wales (and Northern Ireland if and when it returns) truly involve a different style to the majoritarian government of the United Kingdom. Britain is sleepwalking towards federalism.

Notes

1. Earlier versions of some of this material have been previously published in Anthony Seldon and Dennis Kavanagh, eds, *The Blair Effect* (Cambridge: Cambridge University Press, 2005), and Iain McLean and Alistair McMillan, *State of the Union* (Oxford: Oxford University Press, 2005). I express my thanks to Alis-

tair McMillan for permission to adapt some of this chapter from our earlier joint work.

2. Karl Marx, *The Eighteenth Brumaire of Louis Bonaparte*, in K. Marx and F. Engels, *Selected Works* (1852; repr. London: Lawrence and Wishart, 1968), p. 96.

3. McLean and McMillan, *State of the Union*, chapters 7 and 8 passim.

4. Richard Rose, *Understanding the United Kingdom: The Territorial Dimension in Government* (London: Longman, 1982), pp. 189–90; Robert M. Worcester and Brian Gosschalk, MORI Labour Party Research Data, August 1974 (computer file), Colchester, Essex, UK Data Archive (distributor), 1977, SN: 926.

5. Michael Keating and David Bleiman, *Labour and Scottish Nationalism* (Basingstoke: Macmillan, 1979), p. 168. Worcester made "a clandestine trip to Glasgow in the summer, posing as a visiting American sociologist", in order to gauge feeling within the Scottish Labour Party. "Unfortunately . . . the sample consisted of those who were on the telephone, lacked prior engagements and were interested in talking to American sociologists, and was dominated by academics with English accents". See p. 208, n. 28.

6. Which we do in McLean and McMillan, *State of the Union*, Tables 8.3 to 8.12.

7. David Butler and Dennis Kavanagh, *The British General Election of October 1974* (Basingstoke: Macmillan, 1975), p. 131.

8. Lord Kilbrandon (chairman), *Report of the Royal Commission on the Constitution*, Cmnd 5460 (London, HMSO, 1973), para. 1217; *Minority Report*, Cmnd 5460-I, para. 16.

9. Full citations to the relevant surveys are in McLean and McMillan, *State of the Union*, chapters 7 and 8.

10. According to the Kilbrandon Survey in Wales, there was some association between attitudes towards constitutional change and those respondents who spoke Welsh, especially those who spoke it fluently. Fluent Welsh speakers were more likely to favour a new system of regional government or the option of letting government take over complete responsibility.

11. Lindsay Paterson, *New Scotland, New Politics?* (Edinburgh: Polygon, 2001), Table 6.1.

12. Richard Wyn Jones and Dafydd Trystan, "The 1997 Welsh Referendum Vote", in Bridget Taylor and Katarina Thomas, eds, *Scotland and Wales: Nations Again?* (Cardiff: University of Wales Press, 1999), pp. 65–93, data from Tables 4.1 and 4.3.

13. John Curtice, "Restoring Confidence and Legitimacy? Devolution and Public Opinion", in Alan Trench, ed., *Has Devolution Made a Difference: the State of the Nations, 2004* (Exeter: Imprint Academic, 2004), pp. 217–36; data from Figures 9.6 to 9.8.

14. Iain McLean, *Rational Choice and British Politics: An Analysis of Rhetoric and Manipulation from Peel to Blair* (Oxford: Oxford University Press, 2001), pp. 169–203.

15. Brendan O'Leary, "The Belfast Agreement and the Labour Government", in Seldon and Kavanagh, *Blair Effect*, pp. 449–87.

16. In July 2005 they seemed close to admitting their membership for the first time, in stories saying that they had resigned. See, for example, "Adams 'resigns from army council'", *Belfast Telegraph*, July 23, 2005.

17. *Parliamentary Debates*, Commons, vol. 312, May 6, 1998, col. 803.

18. Iain McLean, *The Fiscal Crisis of the United Kingdom* (Basingstoke: Palgrave, 2005), p. 67.

19. Iain McLean, "The National Question", in Seldon and Kavanaugh, *The Blair Effect*, pp. 429–47, esp. 440–3.

20. Lord Fraser of Carmyllie QC, *Holyrood Inquiry: Final Report* (Edinburgh, HMSO, 2004), para. 16.5, from the web version at http://www.holyroodinquiry. org.
21. Scottish Executive News Release, "No disciplinary action after Holyrood Inquiry", November 25, 2004, http://www.scotland.gov.uk/News/Releases.
22. John Curtice, "Restoring Confidence and Legitimacy? Devolution and Public Opinion", in Alan Trench, ed., *Has Devolution Made a Difference? The State of the Nations 2004* (Exeter: Imprint Academic, 2004), pp. 217–36, Figure 9.3.
23. Rhodri Morgan, "Clear Red Water", speech at University of Wales, Swansea, December 11, 2002, quoted by John Osmond, "Nation Building and the Assembly: The Emergence of a Welsh Civil Consciousness", in Trench, *Has Devolution Made a Difference?* pp. 43–77, at p. 52.
24. Yes, really. See http://www.semplefraser.co.uk, under "Latest Industry Briefings".
25. Cardinal Thomas Winning, then head of the Roman Catholic Church in Scotland, and Brian Souter, founder of Stagecoach plc (McLean, "National Question", p. 430). The campaign was misnamed because it was Section 2A, not 28, of the relevant Scottish Act.
26. McLean, "National Question", pp. 442–3.
27. Lord Richard (chairman), *Report of the Richard Commission: Commission on the Powers and Electoral Arrangements of the National Assembly for Wales* (Cardiff: National Assembly, 2004), chapter 14, "Desirable, but not essential", at 14.35, from the web version at http://www.richardcommission.gov.uk/content/ finalreport/report-e.pdf.
28. Guy Lodge, "Devolution and the Centre: Quarterly Report" (London: Constitution Unit, 2004), Figure 5, from the web version at http://www.ucl.ac.uk/ constitution-unit/index.php.
29. Scott L. Greer, *Territorial Politics and Health Policy: UK Health Policy in Comparative Perspective* (Manchester: Manchester University Press, 2004).
30. Greer, *Territorial Politics*, pp. 78 (Scotland); 156 (Wales); 193 (NI).
31. All of these quotations and précis are from the Quarterly Monitoring Reports from the Nations and Regions Programme, Constitution Unit, University College, London. Cited from web versions available from the index page at http://www.ucl.ac.uk/constitution-unit/index.php.
32. See especially McLean, *Fiscal Crisis*; Iain McLean and Alistair McMillan, "The Distribution of Public Expenditure across the UK Regions", *Fiscal Studies*, 24 (2003), 45–71; David Bell and Alex Christie, "Finance—The Barnett Formula: Nobody's Child?" in Alan Trench, ed., *The State of the Nations, 2001: The Second Year of Devolution in the United Kingdom* (Thorverton: Imprint Academic, 2001), pp. 135–51.
33. McLean, *Fiscal Crisis*; McLean and McMillan, *State of the Union*.
34. Ronald MacDonald and Paul Hallwood, "The Economic Case for Fiscal Federalism in Scotland" (Glasgow: Fraser of Allander Institute, 2004); McLean, *Fiscal Crisis*, chapters 8, 9, 11.
35. Peter Hetherington, "Scots and Welsh face subsidy axe", *Guardian*, April 24, 2001, p. 1; James Mitchell and Fraser Nelson, "The Barnett Formula and the 2001 General Election", *British Elections and Parties Review 12* (London: Frank Cass, 2002), 171–89; Nick Raynsford, interview in *Journal*, Newcastle upon Tyne, March 3, 2004, p. 3; Iain McLean, "Scotland after Barnett", in Gerry Hassan, Eddie Gibb and Lydia Howland, eds, *Scotland 2020: Hopeful Stories for a Northern Nation* (London: Demos, 2005), pp. 134–48.
36. Data from Electoral Commission, http://www.electoralcommission.org.uk/ election-data.

37. HM Treasury, *2004 Spending Review: Public Service Agreements, 2005–2008 Cm 6238* (London: HM Treasury 2004), p. 17; Iain McLean et al., *Identifying the Flow of Domestic and European Expenditure into the English Regions* (Oxford: Nuffield College, and London: ODPM, 2003), accessible at http://www.local.odpm.gov.uk; C. Allsopp, *Review of Statistics for Economic Policymaking: Final Report* (London: HM Treasury, 2004), accessible at http://www.hm-treasury.gov.uk/Independent_Reviews/independent_reviews_index.cfm.

6

The Labour Government and the Media

John Bartle

The relationship between the Labour government and the media has simultaneously been more continuous, more intense and more fraught than any other in British history. Indeed, for some critics, an obsessive concern with presentation, spin and controlling its press is the defining characteristic of New Labour. Sir Bernard Ingham, Margaret Thatcher's former press secretary, for example, declared: "It is a presentational government. It's not a policy government. It is not a conviction government because they don't believe in anything other than office. Everything is dedicated to remaining in office. They thought presentation was the way to do it: media, media, media. And they've just blown it".[1]

While it is hardly surprising that Tony Blair's political opponents should seek to downplay his substantial political achievements in creating a modern social democratic party, such assessments do appear to have an element of truth. In June 2000 the prime minister himself conceded, "I think we in government—and that means me—have to trust the people more. We don't have to fight over every headline". In May 2002, Peter Mandelson, Blair's closest confidant, cautioned, "Policy should no longer be presented as if it is being driven by tomorrow's headlines".[2] Shortly after her resignation as secretary of state for international development in May 2003, Clare Short argued, "We have a prime minister so focused on presentation that there is inadequate consideration of the merits of policy".[3]

The purpose of this chapter is to examine why Tony Blair and New Labour acquired such a reputation for being obsessed with presentation, the media and spin. It will then examine various pressure points, to provide specific illustrations of these developments. It will finally speculate about the effect of these developments on government policies and the election.

Government and Media Relations

Any explanation of why relations between the government and media have become so strained must focus on the prime minister, Labour strategists and their spin doctors. The government, after all, sets the tone of debate, has enormous resources at its disposal and great authority. Primary responsibility for any deterioration in the relationship must inevitably fall on it. In order to produce a rounded account, however, it is first necessary to examine why the government felt compelled to expend so much time, energy and resources on ensuring that it got a good press.

Government versus Media

Conflict is hard-wired into the relationship between governments and the media in any properly functioning democracy. Ministers, civil servants and their advisers have all kinds of reasons for wanting to present themselves and their actions in the most favourable possible light, not least in order to win re-election. The media, by contrast, have reasons for presenting the government in different lights. Some newspapers exist simply to promote the political goals of their proprietors, goals which may conflict with those of the government of the day. Most have commercial motives to sell papers by producing news and entertainment and pursue these objectives whether or not it suits the government. Some, though by no means all, journalists also think of themselves as professionals with a duty to inform, whether or not it helps government. This motive is particularly important to public service broadcasters, such as the BBC, who are also required to "educate and inform" the public. Yet, whatever the precise nature of the media's interests, the struggle between government and media is as old as the hills (or at least as old as the invention of the printing press).

In Britain the relationship between the government and the media is complicated by the way that successive governments have preferred to conceal the processes by which they make decisions. Collective responsibility requires ministers not to reveal internal government debates. Yet journalists crave inside information in order to understand the reasons for policy and the processes by which governments have reached decisions. Many have developed very close links with government. Ministers, advisers and officials selectively leak information to strengthen their positions or communicate their disagreements. These relationships can be mutually advantageous, providing a way of communicating private views and producing good copy. It can also lead to mutual resentment when one side feels that it is being manipulated by the other.

The relationship is further complicated by the fact that the government has a responsibility for the regulation of the media. To be sure, the British newspaper industry is one of the most lightly regulated in the world. It is merely required to "take care not to publish inaccurate, misleading or distorted information" and is subject to self-regulation by a toothless Press Complaints Commission.[4] Newspapers remain free to be as biased, partisan and plain nasty as they like. Governments have, therefore, largely tried to persuade rather than bludgeon the press. The broadcast media, however, are subject to extensive regulation. The BBC, ITV and Sky were all established under statute and are either regulated by the Board of Governors (in the case of the BBC) or the Office for Communications (in the case of ITV and Sky), both appointed by the government. This provides the government with indirect influence over broadcasters. The way in which the BBC is funded, by a licence fee set by the government, adds to the special pressure on the Corporation. Although it has fought long to establish its independence, there has always been a danger that it might shy away from criticizing governments for fear of the consequences.

Recent Developments

Conflict between the government and media is, to repeat, hard-wired into both institutions. Recent developments and circumstances, which coincided with the rise of New Labour, have, however, increased the probability of conflict and made any conflict more bruising. One factor promoting conflict is simply the ease and speed of modern communications. In the past a letter of protest could be written by a party official one day, read by an editor or producer the next and acted on some time later. In the era of the email, mobile phone and pager, a whole series of exchanges can take place in the course of a single morning. Both sides may simply have little time to reflect or cool down. Conflict may also have been increased by the way in which both sides have greatly increased the number of people employed to manage relations with the other. Political parties have invested in rebuttal units and broadcasters in complaints departments. Those employed to manage relations, however, may seek to justify themselves by hyperactivity. Indeed, if the minions on either side are not properly supervised, minor disputes can quickly become major controversies.

Governments and parties have other reasons for being more sensitive about their press than in the past. The creation of New Labour resulted in ideological convergence, reduced the importance of "position" issues based on controversies and increased the importance of "valence" issues based on evaluations of competence (see Anthony King in Chapter 7). While positions are based on values, evaluations are based on facts. Values promote certainty and conviction, but what constitutes a fact is almost always uncertain. Have hospitals *really* got cleaner? Is Britain *really* safer from terrorism? All politics is a matter of interpretation (or spin), but valence politics particularly so. Political debates now turn on technical definitions, measurement and trust. The transition from position to valence politics has, accordingly, been accompanied by an increase in contestation.

As ideological differences have narrowed, membership of parties has also declined (see Nick Allen in Chapter 3). Parties can no longer rely on unpaid volunteers to display posters, knock on doors or argue the party's case. In order to compensate for this decline, parties have recruited professionals to ensure that their messages are conveyed via the media. Weaker party loyalties, moreover, have made voters more sensitive to the sorts of messages that they receive. These developments have further increased sensitivities: words are simply assumed to have a far greater *potential* impact.

The specific political circumstances of the eight years prior to 2005 also contributed to strained relations. New Labour's triumph in 1997 was widely welcomed after eighteen years of Conservative government. In the government's first few years ministers enjoyed a honeymoon with the media, which—reflecting the mood in the country—often accepted that responsibility for bad things lay with Labour's predecessors. Many conceded that the government needed time to put things right and Labour got used to having an easy ride. In time, however, the excuses ran out and the media—like voters—began to demand to know whether Labour had delivered. Increased scrutiny inevitably increased conflict. Relations with the BBC soured towards the end of the first term, especially after a BBC *Panorama* programme had questioned Labour's record on the National Health Service. In June 2001, one senior BBC Executive declared, "I can't remember a more fragile state of affairs between the BBC and the Labour Party".[5] Many journalists slowly came to think of Labour as "the new establishment": immovable, arrogant and likely to bend the rules. Paradoxically, the weakness of the Conservative opposition may have increased tensions. Alastair Campbell, Tony Blair's combative director of communications and strategy, complained that, "There was a growing sense that it was [the media's] job actually to stand up and try to do the job the Opposition was failing to do".[6]

Other factors promoting the conflict between government and the media relate to broader political developments. One reason is that both politicians and the media have sensed a growing disconnection between politics and the mass public; most starkly illustrated by the downward step-shift in turnout that occurred in 2001 (see Table 3.3). Journalists blamed politicians for promoting a culture of spin, while politicians, for their part, accused the media of fostering cynicism and focusing on process and personalities rather than substance.[7] Voter disengagement in its own way, therefore, became a further source of tension between government and media.

These developments were enough to make conflict more likely than ever. The Iraq War, however, made it almost inevitable. It aroused intense feelings on all sides. The media, like the country, were deeply divided on the merits of the conflict. Some supported the government; others vigorously opposed it. The BBC sought to remain neutral but was accused of bias. Some critics called it the "Baghdad Broadcasting Corporation" and accused it of overstating internal Iraqi opposition to the war. One radio report from Baghdad, by Andrew Gilligan, the *Today* programme's defence correspondent, particularly enraged Alastair Campbell, the prime minister's director of communications.[8] The planning for the conflict, moreover, vastly increased the pressures on the prime minister and his advisers. The pressure intensified as they prepared a series of dossiers cataloguing the threat posed by Iraq in order to persuade parliament and the public of their case. Two in particular caused controversy. The first became known, even in government circles, as the "dodgy dossier", because it was based on a doctoral thesis downloaded from the internet. The second, the so-called "September dossier", was based on intelligence sources about Iraq's programmes of weapons of mass destruction (WMD). It became the focus of controversy after the war when no WMD was found. For some critics the government's frantic attempts to justify the war constituted the apotheoses of spin. A small, but vocal, minority concluded that Blair had lied about the war. Many others believed that, at the very least, he had exaggerated the threat that had been posed by Iraq. Trust inevitably, therefore, became one of the most discussed issues in the 2005 election.

The Changing Media

The late 1980s and early 1990s witnessed changes in the media that also increased tensions. These changes would have sharpened the conflict between the media and any government in any event. They would also have prompted any government to increase its efforts to control the media, in turn, provoking the media to try to break free of any additional constraints.

Fragmentation and pluralism. As recently as 1987, there were just four national television channels, a dozen or so national newspapers and just a handful of national radio stations (four of which were controlled by the BBC). There was also a scattering of local radio stations (again, dominated by the BBC). A government that had good relations with the press and television could expect to receive at least some favourable coverage. This did not mean that it always received such coverage, but it did at least have a chance of ensuring that large parts of the media stayed on message. In recent years, however, governments have had to cope with a more fragmented and pluralistic media that defies all attempts at control.

In broadcasting, the scale and pace of change has been breathtaking. By 2005, those viewers with satellite or digital television could choose from hundreds of channels. Expanded choice reduced the audiences for the terrestrial channels, in particular their news programmes. In 1992 the combined audience for the main BBC news bulletins was 14.6 million. By 2005 that figure had fallen to 9.6 million, a fall of 34 per cent in just thirteen years. In 1992 the audience for the ITV news bulletins totalled 12.3 million. By 2005 it totalled only 7.1 million, a fall of 42 per cent.[9] There have also been major changes in the newspaper industry. In 1992, the major national newspapers sold a total of 13.5 million copies a day. By 2005 this had fallen to 12.3 million. The growing competitiveness of the industry has made it virtually impossible for anybody to ensure control of it. The Labour government was, from the outset, therefore, trying to control the uncontrollable.

The decline of the partisan press. Newspapers, unlike broadcasters, are free to editorialize on behalf of favoured parties, personalities and causes. Throughout most of the twentieth century, the vast majority of newspapers, like most voters, have aligned themselves with one or other of the major parties according to the interests of their proprietors. Since most were rich men, they invariably inclined to the Conservative Party and "Old Labour" got very used to the idea of having to suffer a "Tory press". The intensity of partisanship, however, varied. Hostility to Labour decreased in the 1950s during the period of the post-war consensus. It then increased in the 1970s and 1980s as Labour moved sharply to the left.

Just as events promoted the growth of a Tory press, so they led to its decline. The initial cause was Margaret Thatcher's brutal eviction from office in November 1990, which left many proprietors, editors and journalists disillusioned with the Conservative Party. Although most newspapers offered John Major strong support in 1992, many soon felt let down. When Britain was forced out of the European Exchange Rate Mechanism in September 1992, the *Sun* declared, "Now we've all been screwed by the cabinet!" (a headline that cunningly combined this most disastrous of policy failures with allegations of sexual impropriety). Disillusionment with the Conservatives, however, did not cause papers to flock to Labour, which—under John Smith's leadership—was still too like its old Labour self. It was only after Tony Blair became leader that papers considered switching sides.

Even when the switch came, the Tory press was not replaced by an equally enthusiastic Labour press or even a "Tony press".[10] The values and beliefs of the major papers remained unchanged. Some sought to reflect the spirit of discontent which they detected in the electorate by affecting a detached scepticism. Others became genuinely sceptical. Disillusionment with the Conservative Party thus provided Blair with an opportunity to attract parts of the press, but that support—like that of voters—might prove short lived. The very newness of the Blair–press relationship, moreover, meant that it required a great deal of nurturing and the expenditure of time, energy and resources. Unsurprisingly, many in the party were anxious not to get on the wrong side of the press if they could possibly avoid it.

Twenty-four-hour news. The changing character of the new media presented other challenges. Satellite and cable television promoted the rise of dedicated news channels such as BBC News 24 and Sky News, producing twenty-four-hour coverage. The terrestrial channels have also introduced regular short bulletins throughout the day, providing viewers with snippets of information. Ministers could be interviewed many times on the same subject on the same day. The risk that they would make a mistake or contradict themselves increased and, in the era of valence politics, such gaffes assumed greater importance. Other changes added to the pressures. Alastair Campbell claimed that the government felt that it had to produce more stories "because stories that are deemed to be new at eight o'clock in the morning are considered old by the time the newspaper journalists are writing".[11] Government has pumped out more press releases, more briefings and policy announcements simply to satisfy the demand for news. Intense competition between the media, however, made it impossible to control the message. Every media outlet looked for new angles. Campbell, again, claimed to detect a shift to a rumour-driven form of journalism because, "what may happen in the future is often deemed to be more important and more interesting than what is actually happening now".[12] He and his minions viewed it as their job to fight over headlines and to either jump on or inspire rumours to Labour's benefit.

Style of political coverage. The growing professionalism of the parties in turn prompted responses by the media. Many newspapers came to believe that they could not compete with television in the provision of news and so increased the amount of comment and opinion they published. Over time, the traditional distinction between the quality newspapers, which separated fact and comment, and tabloids, which freely mingled both, became blurred. Newspapers became driven by the need to obtain scoops to boost sales. Westminster, Whitehall and Fleet Street (as it was still known) increasingly resembled enormous, fast-turning rumour mills.

Structural change has also been accompanied by behavioural change. The shift towards valence politics, coupled with the growing professionalism of government communications, has made it necessary for journalists to try to get at the "reality" beneath the headlines. Few facts are taken at face value. Assertions are tested and official statistics questioned. Yet some politicians have become so adept at evading questions that journalists have had to adopt a more tenacious approach when interviewing them. A new breed of journalist, such as Jeremy Paxman of BBC2's *Newsnight* and John Humphrys of Radio 4's *Today* programme, are willing to tell interviewees that they have not answered questions, to contest claims and to interrupt. Politicians are, therefore, no longer able simply to deliver their sound bites and leave the studio. Those who were trained in the new methods in the 1990s now find that they need to think on their feet and maintain their composure. The frequently disputatious nature of interviews added to tensions and increased the tendency of the government to try to manage presentation. A few ministers, such as Jack Straw and John Reid, were considered safe hands and were offered for interviews on a range of subjects. The producers of the *Today* programme sometimes declined to interview these same people time and again. Understandably, some journalists felt that other ministers were escaping proper scrutiny.

The growing importance of valence politics has had other consequences. Governments are increasingly judged according to the results they produce rather than according to their ideology or rhetoric, but the data used to judge whether targets have been achieved or things have got better or worse are produced by the government itself. Not surprisingly, therefore, there has been a growth in investigative journalism. This is much more inquiring, disputatious and challenging of authority. In its extreme form, however, it can amount to "laser journalism", which "operates on the unstated belief that . . . mendacity is the rule, not the exception, and thus all that is needed is aggressive, directed investigation. In the diabolic account of our state, such figures as Alastair Campbell [Blair's press secretary] . . . naturally become vastly important. They are the liars-in-chief, the gatekeepers of vaults of dirty big secrets that wait for the deployment of journalistic diligence and courage to be discovered".[13]

This style of reporting arguably amounts to a modern response to the belief that "power tends to corrupt and absolute power corrupts absolutely".[14] It is particularly evident during a time of war, when the state is at its most powerful. For some critics, laser journalism lacks a sense of proportion and plays on the audience's ignorance of the policy context. This style of reporting was, however, itself a response to New Labour's approach to the media. Some on the left saw it as inherently right wing, because it cast doubt on the ability of politics to change things. It is unlikely, however, they would have felt quite the same if the Conservative Party was in power and subject to the same intense scrutiny.[15]

Blair, Campbell and the Media

Changes in the media have increased the chances of conflict occurring with the government of the day. It is probable that *any* government would have had a more fraught relationship with the media from the 1990s onwards. Characteristics unique to the Blair government, however, made conflict virtually inevitable and served to ensure that, when it did occur, that it would be more destructive than it would otherwise have been.

Preoccupation with the Media

Tony Blair entered office in 1997 as the most media-minded prime minister in history. All his experiences up that point suggested that the media were fundamental to political success. He was among the first generation to have learned his profession entirely during the media age and so took its importance for granted. As a young MP he was sensitive to the media and his advancement owed much to his telegenic qualities.[16] Like many others, he was convinced that the press onslaught on Neil Kinnock's character and Labour's tax policies in the 1992 election had cost Labour dear. Before his leadership campaign in 1994, he told supporters, "You have got to understand that the only thing that matters in this campaign is the media. The media, the media and the media".[17] He later came to believe that hostile coverage had helped to destroy the Major government. Moreover, when asked to explain Labour's (imminent) victory in the 1997 election, Blair told one journalist, "Nobody ... should underestimate the matchless importance to his victory of the endorsement [Labour] received on the first day of the campaign from the *Sun* newspaper".[18]

Most of Blair's closest advisers were noted far more for their media experience than for their policy expertise. Alastair Campbell, his press secretary, was a former tabloid journalist. Peter Mandelson, his closest confidant, was a former television producer. Philip Gould, Blair's pollster, warned Blair that, "Unless you handle the media well, you cannot govern competently".[19] Previous premiers had found the business of government so absorbing that they had quickly lost interest in matters of presentation. Blair, however, never did.

Campbell became the first press secretary to regularly attend cabinet and there were regular discussions about presentation in cabinet. Ministers' anxiety about their press turned on the belief, expressed by Tessa Jowell, the culture and media secretary, that, "With so many ways to get information—not just through tv and radio but also internet and mobile phone—it becomes increasingly hard to know where what we see or hear is coming from, who has made it and why".[20] In short, New Labour believed that voters could not be trusted to cut through the mediation and to focus on the bottom lines of prosperity, security or the quality of the public services. Ministers believed that, even if things had got better, they would get little credit from the electorate unless they got their message across. They needed to enlist the support of the media to extol the government's virtues.

Proprietors and Editors

As soon as Blair became Labour leader, he took steps to neutralize the impact of the press. He told Piers Morgan, then editor of the *News of the World,* "I want a good relationship with you. . . . I don't want to be chewed up and spat out like Neil Kinnock was by the *Sun.*"[21] He therefore pursued a twin strategy to win support. First, he sought to widen Labour's appeal by re-writing Clause 4 of Labour's constitution, removing commitments to public ownership, reducing spending commitments, pledging not to raise income tax and making it clear that the trade unions could have "fairness not favours". This last move was particularly important since most papers had had bitter experiences of union militancy. Secondly, he pursued "a deliberate and cynical course of seducing the leading figures of the Tory press".[22] He persuaded Lord Rothermere, owner of Associated Newspapers, the *Daily Mail* and London's *Evening Standard,* that his views on Europe, trade unions and families were sound. The Tory Lord enthused, "Tony Blair is a very capable, very charming, very astute man, full of enthusiasm and drive. He unquestionably comes from the British middle classes, as does his wife".[23]

However, Blair's most assiduous efforts to woo the press were focused on Rupert Murdoch, the owner of News Corp, the *Sun,* the Sunday paper the *News of the World, The Times,* the *Sunday Times* and Sky television (which, among other things, owned the rights to televise Premier League soccer). On July 17, 1995, Blair made a twenty-two-hour journey to Australia to deliver a speech to a News Corp "Leadership Conference".[24] He pleased the press baron at once by declaring that media policy should "create as much choice and diversity as possible" and, furthermore, that "the best way of achieving it is by an open and competitive environment".[25] The rest of his speech addressed the need to reconcile change, economic reform and social stability. Murdoch's personal fears about European integration were deflected by Blair declaring that "the Americans have made it clear they want a special relationship with Europe, not with Britain alone".[26] The owner of News Corp was impressed by the young leader and thought him a winner. However, his papers did not immediately endorse Labour. Relations with the *Sun* became warmer, but the party was kept on tenterhooks until the first week of the 1997 campaign when it was finally announced that, "THE SUN BACKS BLAIR".

Blair's readiness to consort with Murdoch carried risks. The Australian-born American's media empire, his defeat of the print unions in the mid-1980s and his support for Thatcher in the 1980s, meant that he was *the* hate figure on much of the left. The Labour leader's willingness to associate with him underlined the importance that he attached to the media. Blair's concern with the media, moreover, did not subside when he was prime minister. When Richard Desmond, a man who had made his fortune selling pornography, emerged as a possible buyer of the *Daily Express* and *Daily Star*, Blair invited him and his wife to tea at Downing Street.[27] As soon as the sale was sanctioned, Desmond donated £100,000 to Labour.[28] Lists of the guests invited to Chequers, the prime minister's country retreat, contained a large number of editors, commentators and journalists.[29] Piers Morgan, the former editor of the *Mirror*, records that he met Blair at "twenty-two lunches, six dinners, six interviews, twenty-four further one-to-one chats over tea and biscuits" and that there were "numerous phone calls".[30] Under Blair, therefore, the media "were not separate limbs or membranes in the anatomy so much as part of the lifeblood or nervous system".[31]

Alastair Campbell: His Role and Personality

Blair was anxious to ensure a good press. The man charged with responsibility for ensuring that he got one in both opposition and government was Alastair Campbell, a former *Mirror* journalist. He served as Blair's press secretary in opposition (1994–97), as the prime minister's press secretary (1997–2001) and then as the director of communications and strategy at Number 10 (2001–2003). None of these titles, however, provides any indication of Campbell's real influence. One well-placed source suggested that "To compare his influence to that of a mere Cabinet minister is to insult him".[32]

Campbell performed a number of roles for Blair. He was, first and foremost, one of the architects of the New Labour project and heavily involved in strategy. He was primarily responsible for managing Labour's relations with the media and acted as a go-between for Blair in his dealings with proprietors, editors and columnists, especially the tabloid press. It was also said that he was responsible for preparing the new leader for the inevitable attacks that would be directed at him and making him recognize people's darker motives.[33] In the years to come, however, this wariness verged on paranoia.

In opposition, Campbell had presided over the creation of the most professional political communications set-up in British history.[34] Labour spokespersons had received training in how to deal with the media and were equipped with pagers to provide them with the message for the day or suggested soundbites. Campbell had insisted that the party's communications were subservient to the office of the leader. This decision elicited accusations of control freakery and centralization but it did help the party stay "on message".[35] In time, Labour had acquired a reputation for having a disciplined communications strategy that was synchronized to the rhythm of the modern news room. The media marvelled at Labour's media machine and were flattered by the attention it lavished on them.[36]

In government, Campbell was given responsibility for media relations at Number 10 and Number 10, in turn, became central to the presentation of policy across the whole of government.[37] The newcomers quickly concluded, however, that government communications were inadequate. Many civil service information officers were replaced with special advisers (otherwise known as spin doctors) who better understood the requirements of the new media. A Strategic Communications Unit was brought in under Campbell's direction in Number 10 to co-ordinate the release of information. It established a "grid" containing details of political and non-political events in order to time and co-ordinate announcements. Campbell told one meeting of information officers that, "he wanted them to be able to predict what would be on the front page of the *Sun* the next day and help to write it".[38] The ministerial code was also revised to require all speeches, press releases and initiatives to be cleared by the Number 10 private office beforehand.[39] One well-respected commentator called the new code "the biggest centralisation of power seen in Whitehall in peacetime".[40]

Labour had come to power pledged to produce economic security and improvements in public services. Gordon Brown's decision to stick to Conservative spending plans for the first three years, however, meant that there was little extra spending on the public services during the first term. Many ministers and spin doctors, therefore, took to announcing the same expenditure, initiative or proposal time and time again, partly in order to ensure that the media and voters got the message but also to create the impression of greater delivery than had actually been achieved. In time, however, both the media and the public inevitably became suspicious of any government announcement. The impression that the government was obsessed with presentation increased further when it transpired that there had been a 163 per cent increase in government advertising between 1997 and 2001.[41]

In government Labour's spin doctors continued to try to exert the same pressure on the media that they had done in opposition. The producers of the highly influential *Today* programme on Radio 4 became inured to persistent allegations of bias and inaccuracies from government. Labour's spin doctors bad-mouthed journalists, cast doubt on their abilities and otherwise did them down. In one letter Campbell wrote to a political editor, "I know that questions of journalistic ethics do not keep you awake at night. . . . The fact that you would regard 'unprincipled and duplicitous' as a badge of honour for your brand of journalism only increases my utter contempt for you".[42] Others followed Campbell's lead. Even Peter Mandelson was forced to concede that Labour's media skills had been "allowed to fall into disrepute through overuse, and misuse when in inexperienced and overzealous hands".[43] Those at the centre of New Labour realized that their reputation for spinning was becoming a problem. They found it hard, however, to give up old habits, or to persuade their countless minions to do so.

Alastair Campbell himself gave a press briefing twice a day in which he would provide journalists with background information and insights into Blair's thinking. In contrast with previous convention, these were "on the record" and were reported as statements of the prime minister's official spokesman, rather than, as before, "sources close to the prime minister". This change ended some of the mystique surrounding government, but did not remove Campbell from controversy. On some occasions he inadvertently misled the press. He denied allegations, for example, that Blair had made an inquiry on Rupert Murdoch's behalf about the possible purchase of an Italian company with the Italian prime minister, saying, "That's crap, spelled C-R-A-P".[44] It was later revealed that Blair had indeed made the inquiry and Number 10 was forced to issue a series of embarrassing retractions, which made Number 10 look shifty. Campbell had apparently not known about the call and had instinctively denied the allegation. He also made an incorrect statement about Cherie Blair's purchase of a flat in Bristol, again simply because Cherie had been less than open with him.[45] Such misunderstandings were almost inevitable given the media's continuous demands for information, but some journalists came to believe the prime minister's press secretary was frequently less than honest.[46]

Campbell's personality contributed to tensions. He was highly partisan and suspicious of those who professed independence, notably the BBC. In a revealing comment, he once said, "I have much more time for frankly biased journalism than for people who just pretend they are reporting objectively".[47] It was as if he felt that every BBC journalist was a tabloid propagandist in disguise. Campbell was also an emotional man, prone to losing his temper and, according to some, to utter profanities. "Why should I waste my effing time talking to a load of wankers like you, when you won't print a word I say?" he once asked journalists.[48] Some in the lobby liked him all the better for his directness: others did not.

By the end of the first term Campbell had become the story himself. He compounded this problem in 2000 by co-operating in a documentary about his work. He told the documentary maker, "what I want to get across is that we fulfil a basic, necessary and legitimate function. We are not the horrible, Machiavellian people as portrayed".[49] In the event, however, it merely increased Campbell's reputation as "the king of spin". He regularly condemned the media for being "more interested in process than they are in policy and outcomes".[50] Such allegations had more than a little truth in them. The documentary maker reported that seventy journalists turned up to view the advance screenings and the programme received massive publicity.

Campbell made it clear that he wished to leave Number 10 after the 2001 election, but Blair was apparently so dependent on his advice that he persuaded him to stay. After the election he gave Campbell a new title and told him to adopt a more strategic role, but he was inevitably sucked back into day-to-day media management, especially in the run up to the Iraq War. Ironically, many of those who disliked him were most adamant in demanding his return. They preferred to speak to Campbell than the career officials who replaced him because only he could provide them with an insight into Blair's thinking. Neither his political master, nor his critics in the media, could do without Alastair Campbell.[51]

Pressure Points

Old Labour had an unenviable reputation for ineptitude in its relations with the media and many opponents in the press. In contrast, New Labour was regarded as thoroughly professional and had received the overwhelming—if not altogether enthusiastic—endorsement of the press in both 1997 and 2001. By the time of the 2005 general election, however, its reputation for professionalism had become damaging and its support in the press had weakened.

Daily Mail

The *Daily Mail* is one of the biggest successes in the British press industry. It combines a lively mixture of lifestyle, gardening, entertainment and "dream house" competitions with right-wing populism. It is thought to be the newspaper of choice of the aspirant middle classes, just the sort of swing voter targeted by Labour since 1994. *Mail* headlines were monitored carefully by the broadcasters and parties, simply because it was widely viewed as having its finger on the pulse of "Middle England". The *Media Guardian* declared, "Love it or loathe it, if you don't read the *Daily Mail* first thing in the morning, then you're playing catch-up for the rest of the day".[52]

The *Daily Mail* was initially intrigued by Blair. In 1993 Simon Heffer, a Thatcherite journalist, extolled him as a "devoted and active father . . . committed to family values".[53] Paul Dacre, the *Mail*'s editor, declared himself "enthralled by this man [Blair] who told [him] he was going to devote his government to restoring the family".[54] Lord Rothermere was so impressed he crossed the floor in the House of Lords to join Labour shortly before his death. In 1997 the paper was, accordingly, less hostile to Labour than in the past; though it did dutifully endorse the Tories. But this honeymoon did not last long and the *Mail* quickly found much wrong with Labour.

The growing rift has been attributed to a series of events such as the Ecclestone affair in late 1997, which made Labour appear just as sleazy as the Tories, and Blair's "forces of conservatism" speech in 1999, which was widely interpreted as an attack on all conservatives.[55] Dacre himself advanced another reason: "Blair's acceptance of money from Richard Desmond [owner of the *Express*] marked a new low in public life in this country".[56] While these events undoubtedly contributed to the rift with Labour, they concealed the importance of fundamental disagreements. Dacre himself admitted as much: "I very much regret that much of what . . . [Thatcher] did is slowly being unwound".[57] The *Mail* criticized Labour for imposing red tape on business and increasing taxes on the middle classes. It reserved special condemnation for "anti-family" policies, such as the decision to equalize the age of consent for gay sex and the repeal of a law that prohibited local authorities from promoting homosexuality. Labour was attacked for its failure to reform welfare, its commitment to Europe and its immigration policies. In 2001 the parlous state of William Hague's Conservative Party led the *Mail* to decline to endorse it, but its contempt for Labour was evident. By 2001 it had reverted to being Labour's implacable enemy, though some ministers still tried to placate it.

The *Mail's* early enthusiasm for Blair, his wife and his family was quickly transformed into intense personal dislike. Dacre declared Blair to be "a chameleon who believes what he said to the last person he talked to".[58] The *Mail on Sunday* relentlessly pursued Cherie Blair over allegations relating to the purchase of a flat in Bristol and the Blairs began to feel hunted. Alastair Campbell told a House of Commons Committee frankly that, "The *Daily Mail* loathes the prime minister, loathes me, loathes the government".[59] In the 2005 election the *Mail* focused on Blair's character and issues such as crime, immigration and asylum. Its Sunday edition ran a scare story that Labour would impose capital gains tax on house sales ("LABOUR 40% TAX ON HOUSE PROFITS"), a policy that would have constituted political suicide if it were true.[60] In the election itself the *Mail* evinced little enthusiasm for the Conservatives. It endorsed them but recommended "HOWEVER YOU VOTE, GIVE *BLAIR* A BLOODY NOSE".

The *Sun*

Rupert Murdoch ensured that the *Sun* endorsed Labour at the 1997 and 2001 general elections. The *Sun's* endorsement did not, however, amount to a wholesale endorsement of all that Labour stood for. In 1997 it made clear that it liked the leader ("THE SUN BACKS BLAIR") rather than the party, about which it harboured doubts. Like the *Mail*, its values and beliefs did not change and it never became part of the Labour movement in the way that the *Mirror* was. It remained a fun-driven, celebrity-packed, populist newspaper, fiercely patriotic, strong on law and order, critical of political correctness and sceptical about European integration. Although it offered Blair strong support over Iraq, it continued to run anti-Labour stories. In the first two terms it hammered the government over Europe, immigration and crime. It also continually warned the government not to introduce a right to privacy that would protect celebrities from tabloid intrusion.[61]

Despite its endorsement of Labour the *Sun* allowed one of its columnists, Richard Littlejohn, to continually pour scorn on Blair and his family. Littlejohn was the closest that Britain has ever had to a US-style "shock jock". His favoured approach was to report some act of political correctness and then exclaim "You couldn't make it up!" He accused Cherie Blair of personally benefiting as a lawyer from the introduction of the Human Rights Act, labelling her, among other things, "the wicked witch". Yet, under both David Yelland's and Rebekah Wade's editorships, the *Sun* continued to have close links with Labour. It was even alleged that it gave the government notice if it was going to publish something critical and a chance to reply and reassure readers.[62] The paper's influential political editor, Trevor Kavanagh, retained close links with Number 10. Like the paper itself, however, he became disillusioned. In April 2005 he wearily wrote, "Blair promises a brand new tomorrow, after eight years of yesterdays".[63]

In 1997 and 2001 the *Sun* had made clear its preference for a Labour victory at the start of the campaign. In 2005 it ostentatiously withheld its support, only finally declaring for Labour in the middle of the campaign. In imitation of the papal conclave, which had just met to elect the new pope, a puff of red smoke emerged from the *Sun*'s chimney to symbolize that it had backed Labour. A photograph of this momentous event was put on the front page. Ominously, however, the accompanying headline said "Give them one last chance".[64] The *Sun*'s support was hedged with qualifications. Grudging praise for Labour's management of the economy and improvements in the National Health Service (NHS) were mingled with strong criticism on immigration, crime and taxes. It endorsed Labour for two reasons: "Standing firm on Iraq and the lack of a real alternative", and it hinted that it might defect to the Conservatives in future. Littlejohn, however, was unconvinced. "I'd rather eat my own toenail clippings than vote for Labour", he declared.[65]

Murdoch seems to have backed Labour simply because most *Sun* readers had decided to do so and Labour was likely to win. His decision maintained the appearance that he had helped Labour win, but his evident preparedness to contemplate a switch will continue to provide him with leverage in his dealings with the government.

The *Mirror*

The *Mirror* had been for generations Labour's most loyal press supporter. It was the home of Andy Capp, the archetypal working-class cartoon character: the flat-capped, beer-drinking, wife-fearing (and, presumably, Labour-voting) British male of legend. The paper had supported Labour even in the dark days of the early 1980s. The *Mirror* was, therefore, Labour through and through, part of the Labour movement. In 1994 it had welcomed Blair's election as leader and in 1997 celebrated Labour's victory. Paul Routledge, the *Mirror*'s political editor, however, was an ardent supporter of Gordon Brown and regularly attacked Blair, Campbell and Mandelson (and, indeed, all that was "New" in Labour) in his columns.

The *Mirror*'s support was increasingly tempered by resentment of Labour's relationship with the *Sun*. A particular source of grievance was the way in which Campbell and Blair gave the *Sun* scoops, such as getting Bill Clinton to write for it.[66] This resentment was increased by the steep decline in the *Mirror*'s sales, which made it vital to recruit younger readers and gain advertising revenue. Given the cynicism of the young, it made little sense to support the government. In 2000 Piers Morgan, the editor, fired a warning shot by doing the unthinkable and endorsing the Tory candidate for London Mayor.[67] From 2001 onwards the *Mirror* was critical of proposals for foundation hospitals, increased student fees and the failure to adopt the euro (all of which were, of course, policies supported by the *Sun*). In marked contrast to that paper, moreover, the *Mirror* strongly opposed the Iraq War. On March 14, 2003, it published a front page headline, "Prime Monster?" which warned "Drag us into this war without the U.N. Tony and that's how history will judge you. For God's sake man, DON'T DO IT".[68] Relations between the paper and the party really improved only when Morgan resigned following publication of photographs of British soldiers attacking Iraqi prisoners that were subsequently revealed as fakes.

The *Mirror* behaved more traditionally following Morgan's resignation. The day after the 2005 election was announced, it published a handwritten note from Blair admitting to disagreements but urging readers to support Labour. In the campaign the paper gave Labour politicians space in which to state their case and defended Labour's achievements on the NHS, education and help for poor pensioners. When it came to its formal endorsement, however, it realized that it would be vain "to argue that this government has been perfect" and recognized that it had differences with Blair over the "illegal" Iraq war.[69] Its clinching argument was, therefore, negative. The "simple truth is that in most seats a vote that is not for Labour is a vote for Michael Howard's Tories and all that would mean for Britain".

The *Daily Express* and *Daily Star*

The *Daily Express* and *Daily Star* were bought by Richard Desmond shortly before the 2001 election. The *Express* had been the most loyal of all Tory papers. Indeed, it was the only paper to support John Major when he was challenged for the Tory leadership in 1995. The downmarket *Star* was similar to the *Sun* but had been relatively apolitical; it had not endorsed any party in 1992, but backed Labour in 1997. In 2001 both endorsed Labour. One journalist recalled that Alastair Campbell "treated us as if we were part of the Labour campaign team, not a newspaper".[70] As late as 2003, the *Express* declared, "There is not a glimmer of hope that this newspaper could support the Tories".[71] In April 2004, however, it changed its mind, "Mr Blair's cynical U-turn on the European constitution, offering a referendum AFTER the next General Election, a referendum that will probably never happen, is the final act of betrayal". It proclaimed, "YOU CAN'T TRUST A WORD BLAIR SAYS ANYMORE".

The *Daily Express* portrayed its defection as the result of Labour's "spin and deception". Political differences, however, played a part: "SO OFTEN rhetoric and reality have been poles apart in Blair's Britain. The rhetoric said tough on crime, the reality was a new early release scheme. The rhetoric was firm immigration controls, the reality was chaos and a trebling of immigration".[72] Commercial considerations were also a factor in the defection. Having secured government consent for his purchase of the paper, Desmond withdrew support after a discreet interval. Most *Express* readers voted Conservative anyway, so the defection was in many ways a return home. The *Star*, which had a high proportion of Labour voters, declined to endorse any party: "We're not going to tell you how to vote on May 5. It's not really our business—we're a newspaper, not the Vatican".[73]

Other Newspapers

New Labour's attempts to woo the *Mail*, *Sun* and *Express* often managed to alienate the *Guardian* and the *Independent*, two newspapers on the centre left. While both broadly approved of the government's domestic programme, they were alarmed by its authoritarianism, its tendency to ride roughshod over the parliamentary party and its keenness to criticize opponents. They expressed reservations about the anti-terror legislation that emerged after "9/11" and even greater reservations about the Iraq War. The *Guardian's* journalists and readers were just as divided as Labour itself over the war. The *Independent*, however, had transformed itself into a campaigning paper and was unequivocal in opposing British involvement. Many in government regarded both papers as irritants but had to keep an eye on them because so many Labour Party members read them.

In the election itself, both papers faced a dilemma about which party to endorse. The *Guardian* moaned, "It is an imperfect choice conducted under [an] imperfect electoral system" but then advised that "Only in a tiny handful of seats . . . is it safe for Labour voters to switch to the Liberal Democrats".[74] The *Independent* declared itself to be "tormented" by its choice.[75] Having opposed the war, however, it declared that Blair must be held accountable for the "most disastrous foreign policy decision since Suez". It noted, "It would be perverse if an anti-war protest vote inadvertently helped the Conservatives" and concluded "we seek an outcome in which there is a significantly larger force of Liberal Democrat MPs. And we hope that Mr Brown replaces Mr Blair as prime minister sooner rather than later". Its sister paper the *Independent on Sunday* backed the Liberal Democrats.

Of the remaining newspapers only the *Daily Telegraph* was straightforwardly partisan. It supported the Conservatives. It had been purchased by the Barclay brothers from Conrad Black's Hollinger Group in 2004, following a financial scandal involving Black. The *Telegraph* summarized its recommendation in the form of an equation "Small government + freedom + low tax = vote Tory".[76] *The Times* remained catholic in its political tastes. In 1997 it had recommended a vote for "Eurosceptics" in any party, in 2001 it endorsed Labour, in 2004 it recommended a vote for the Tories in the European elections and a vote for Simon Hughes, the Liberal Democrat candidate for London Mayor. Like the *Sun*, it supported the invasion of Iraq and university top-up fees. It declared that another Labour landslide "would leave a distorted picture of public sentiment and stoke the arrogance of power".[77] It regretted the anti-American sentiment expressed by some Tories in the wake of the Iraq War and advocated tactical voting to remove Old Labour MPs. It concluded, however, that: "The best result for Britain would be a smaller but viable Labour majority and a larger and renewed Tory opposition". The *Financial Times* endorsed Labour but without much enthusiasm.

Burying Bad News

On September 11, 2001, but before the full extent of the catastrophes in New York and Washington had become known, Jo Moore, Stephen Byers's Special Adviser at the Department of Trade and Industry (DTI) sent an email to a colleague, in which she suggested that it was a "good day to bury bad news".[78] When the email was leaked a few weeks later, Moore offered what was widely interpreted as an insincere apology and stayed in post. Not surprisingly, she continued to attract media attention. In early 2002, another email from Martin Sixsmith, Moore's colleague at the DTI, was leaked to the press. In it, Sixsmith had warned Byers against acting on Moore's alleged new suggestion that bad news should be published on the day scheduled for the funeral of Princess Margaret (the sister of Her Majesty the Queen).

In February 2002 Moore resigned and Sixsmith also departed.[79] Yet even these apparent acts of self-cleansing were bungled. It later emerged that Byers had announced the Sixsmith departure before the terms of his resignation had been agreed. The resulting furore culminated in Byers's own resignation in May. Remarkably for a government that had gained a reputation for its sophisticated handling of the media, it extracted no benefit at all from Byers' apparently honourable resignation. Indeed, the small window opened on the world of New Labour's spin doctors confirmed that they were obsessed with presentation, manipulative, cynical and heartless. Not surprisingly, the media and public alike became increasingly disillusioned with the government. Spin became for Labour what sleaze had been for the Conservatives between 1992 and 1997.

The Gilligan Affair and Hutton

On May 29, 2003, at 6.07 in the morning, John Humphrys interviewed Andrew Gilligan, the *Today* programme's defence correspondent, on BBC Radio 4. The topic was the government's case for war against Iraq, as set out in the so-called September dossier. Gilligan reported that "what we've been told by one of the senior officials in charge of drawing up that dossier was that, actually the government probably erm, knew that that forty-five minute figure was wrong, even before it decided to put it in".[80] Gilligan also reported that his source had claimed that intelligence sources were unhappy with the forty-five minute claim because it was based on an uncorroborated source. Later, in a *Mail on Sunday* article, he stated that his source had claimed that Alastair Campbell was responsible for the forty-five claim.[81]

Number 10 vigorously denied these allegations, insisting that nothing had been included in the dossier without the support of the Joint Intelligence Committee (JIC), comprised of senior intelligence advisers. Despite government complaints, however, the BBC declined to back down, protesting that Gilligan had *not* alleged that the government had lied; he had merely repeated an allegation made by someone who was well placed to know the truth. In subsequent days, Greg Dyke, the BBC's director general, and Gavyn Davies, its chairman, agreed that the BBC had to stand up to the government, not least because both men had been accused of being political appointees and likely to bend under pressure.

Campbell privately railed against the BBC to Blair and others in government. He then made his concerns public when he appeared before the House of Commons Select Committee on foreign affairs. He later accused the Corporation on *Channel 4 News* of a "fundamental attack on the integrity of the government".[82] Privately many at the BBC viewed Campbell as intent on vengeance for what he regarded as the BBC's anti-American, anti-government and anti-war agenda.[83] They treated him accordingly and hoped the issue would simply go away.

The story was further complicated when, in the following weeks, Dr David Kelly, a civil servant in the department of defence and former weapons inspector in Iraq, volunteered that he had met Gilligan, but denied that he was the source of Gilligan's allegations. The government made it known that an unnamed individual had admitted meeting Gilligan, but had denied being the source for his allegations. The press proceeded to find out who the individual was. Kelly's name was eventually made public. On July 17, 2003, he went missing and his body was found in the countryside close to his home. He was found to have committed suicide by slashing his wrists.

The tragedy of Dr Kelly's death dominated the news bulletins and front pages for months afterwards. It inspired lurid accusations about conspiracies and cover-ups, which were repeated by some of the government's opponents on both the left (who had opposed the war) and the right (most of whom had backed the war but hated Blair). One journalist directly asked Tony Blair, then in Japan, if he had "blood on his hands". The prime minister found himself under intense personal pressure and asked Lord Hutton, a Law Lord, to conduct an inquiry into Kelly's death. The hearings for the inquiry took place in the late summer and early autumn of 2003 at the Royal Courts of Justice in London. Although television cameras were excluded from the hearings, the media were provided with a continuous series of powerful images as key witnesses, including Campbell, Gilligan, Dyke, Davies, John Scarlett, the chair of JIC, and the prime minister himself, were filmed and photographed running the gauntlet of anti-war protestors gathered outside the court. It looked for all the world as if the government was on trial.

Between the close of evidence-taking and the publication of the report, there was endless speculation in the media about Hutton's conclusions. It was widely assumed that the report might result in the resignation of Geoff Hoon, the secretary of state for defence, and even Blair himself. In the event, however, Lord Hutton exonerated the government. He concluded that the forty-five minute claim was inserted by the JIC and that parts of Gilligan's report were, therefore, "unfounded".[84] He also found that Kelly had in all probability not told Gilligan that the government knew that the forty-five minute claim was wrong; that the government should have been given notice of the allegations and that the BBC's governors were culpable for not taking the government's complaints seriously.

The report was devastating for the BBC. Alastair Campbell immediately demanded the resignations of Dyke and Davies. Both left the Corporation the very same day. Some journalists protested that Gilligan had been "mostly right" and urged the BBC to stand its corner. However, Mark Byford, the acting director general of the BBC declared: "Mostly right isn't good enough for the BBC".[85] A subsequent internal report recommended that journalists should take more careful notes, try to avoid making grave allegations in live interviews and be aware that allegations made by third parties may be interpreted as being made by the BBC.[86] BBC journalists were also prohibited from writing for newspapers on contentious matters. Thus, the Corporation's new management sought to improve relations with the government while studiously maintaining its independence. Its coverage of the 2005 election was typically extensive, fair and balanced.[87] Jeremy Paxman in particular gave all three main party leaders a grilling in his televised interviews.

The Hutton inquiry—or at least the events that surrounded it—was, ironically, more devastating for the government than the BBC. While the final report exonerated Campbell, Blair and Hoon, the one-sided view taken by the judge fed the belief that report constituted a "whitewash". The inquiry had exposed New Labour's obsession with presentation and reliance on spin. Extracts from Campbell's diary showed that the government was desperate to gain "a win not a messy draw". He was widely thought to have pursued a vendetta and Blair was viewed as having failed to control him. The eventual failure to find WMD in Iraq, moreover, added to the feeling that the government had indeed exaggerated the threat; though whether this amounted to a "lie" was, of course, a more complex issue.

The public reacted in a measured way to the report. They criticized both the BBC and government for their dealings with Dr Kelly. An ICM poll found that only 23 per cent thought that the BBC had treated Kelly fairly, while 49 per cent did not (a net score of -26). The figures for the government were 19 per cent and 60 per cent (-41).[88] Yet, when asked who they trusted to tell the truth, 31 per cent chose the BBC and just 10 per cent the government. The Gilligan affair, like the Moore and Sixsmith affairs before it, helped to seal New Labour's reputation for exaggeration, dishonesty and spin.

Consequences

Old Labour was widely thought to have been a public relations disaster. New Labour, by contrast, was seen as a ruthless media machine. It wooed press barons, editors and columnists and exerted pressure on the media in order to get its message across. For a time it was astonishingly successful. By the time of the 2005 election, however, its hegemony was in doubt and its reputation for bullying and deceit had become a burden.

Relations with the Media

In 1997 fully 63 per cent of all readers took a paper that endorsed Labour. In 2001 this proportion rose to 67 per cent. But in 2005, with the *Express*'s defection, it fell to 58 per cent (see Table 6.1). These headline figures, of course, conceal a great deal. Newspapers such as the *Sun, The Times* and the *Independent* provided equivocal support for Labour, while the *Daily Mail* and *Daily Express* published excoriating attacks. Labour's efforts to simultaneously appeal to all these newspapers had failed: it had not appeased the right-wing press and had seriously disappointed its allies.

The government faced critics to both left and right, but had few friends. The consequent all-round lack of enthusiasm for Labour must surely have had some effect on the outcome of the election, though it is not possible to put a precise figure on the effect. If the Conservative Party succeeds in modernizing itself, moreover, both of Murdoch's papers could easily defect and that would be enough to tip the partisan balance in the Tories' favour. The *Mirror* and *Guardian* appear to be safe for Labour for the time being, but their support will be tested by government policies, especially in relation to the reform of the public services. The *Independent*'s new campaigning style makes it unlikely that it will ally itself with any government.

By the end of its second term, New Labour had acquired an unenviable reputation for spin. Every government announcement or statement was viewed with intense suspicion. The cumulative impact of this development was far from trivial. For example, on February, 25, 2005, a journalist asked Blair, "You talked this week, prime minister, about thousands of people still being at risk from a potential terrorist attack. Do you not think in the light of the absence of WMD in Iraq there is a danger that the general public will feel that you might be crying wolf again"?[89] Read after the events of July 2005, when bombs killed more than fifty people in London, the journalist's question seems ironic; but that it could be asked at all is a measure of the depths to which New Labour's reputation for veracity had sunk.

Table 6.1 Newspaper Circulation and Party Preference, 2005

Daily papers	Owner	Circulation (000)	Preferred winner
Daily Express	Desmond	926	Conservative
Daily Mail	Associated	2,380	Conservative
Daily Star	Desmond	851	None
Daily Telegraph	Barclay Brothers	912	Conservative
Financial Times	Pearson	427	Labour
Guardian	Scott Trust	367	Labour
Independent	Independent/O'Reilly	262	Labour/Lib Dem
Mirror	Trinity Mirror	2,185	Labour
Sun	News International/Murdoch	3,258	Labour
The Times	News International/Murdoch	685	Labour
Pro-Conservative circulation		4,218	34.4 % of total
Pro-Labour circulation		7,184	58.6 % of total
Total circulation		12,253	

Source: Circulation figures from ABC.

Labour found that trust, once forfeited, was difficult to re-establish, though they tried. In the wake of the Moore and Sixsmith affairs, Blair began holding press conferences broadcast live on television. To increase his visibility in parliament, he appeared regularly before a liaison committee composed of the chairmen of select committees in the Commons. The subsequent Gilligan affair and the Hutton inquiry represented major set-backs for his relations with the media, but the government continued to try to repair its fences. In 2004, a committee recommended that a new post of permanent secretary for government communications should be established and that all special advisers should be given training to uphold traditional standards of public service.[90] One well-respected commentator, sympathetic to the government, reckoned the government's immediate acceptance of these proposals constituted a "unilateral act of disarmament".[91] Others were, predictably, somewhat more cynical. The *Independent* observed: "The end of spin has been pre-announced, announced and re-announced many times".[92]

Tensions were relaxed somewhat when it was finally announced that Campbell would step down. His replacement, David Hill, attracted far less coverage. To no one's surprise, however, Campbell was soon back in Number 10 helping on Labour's 2005 campaign. He was immediately accused of leading a "dirty tricks" campaign by securing the release of certain documents, under the new Freedom of Information Act, that were damaging to the Conservatives.[93] Many documents relating to the 1992 Exchange Rate Mechanism disaster, which had done so much to damage the Conservatives, were released shortly before the 2005 election: just in time to remind voters why they could not trust the Conservatives on the economy. Despite Gilligan and Hutton, Labour continued to play hard ball with both their opponents and the media.

Policy

Blair once told Andrew Neil, the journalist, "How we treat Rupert Murdoch's media interests when in power will depend on how his newspapers treat the Labour Party in the run-up to the election and after we are in government".[94] It has often been suggested that Labour granted favours in return for favourable coverage. The clearest examples appear to relate to the commercial interests of the proprietors. Before ever getting into government, Labour abandoned plans to limit non-British ownership of the media. In government it declined to introduce a privacy law protecting people from media intrusion and has vetoed attempts to outlaw predatory pricing in the newspaper industry, enabling people like Murdoch to eradicate competitors.[95] Blair also approached Romano Prodi on Murdoch's behalf to see whether the Italian government would oppose the purchase of Berlusconi's Mediaset.[96]

Others maintain, however, that the media's influence goes far beyond commercial interests. Enthusiasts for European integration were quick to see Murdoch's influence behind the government's failure to adopt the European single currency during its first term. They saw the same malign influence behind the decision to hold a referendum on the proposed constitution in the second term (see David McKay in Chapter 4).[97] It was also alleged that Blair adopted "tough" decisions on welfare payments for lone parents in order to appeal to the *Daily Mail*.[98] Some felt that the large number of government initiatives on crime and frequent attacks on judges may have owed something to David Blunkett's eagerness to receive favourable coverage from that same source (see Tom Quinn in Chapter 1).

It is not possible to assess the impact of media considerations on Labour's policies accurately. There may be a tendency to overstate the influence of the right-wing press. In every case considered above, it can be argued that the policy pursued was in the interest of the minister, the government or the country. Blair may have promised a referendum on the European constitution, simply to deny the Conservative Party an easy line of attack in the 2005 election. Similarly, it is possible that Blunkett chose insensitive language in his dealings with judges because that is what his constituents in Sheffield expected.

While the motivations behind these policies must remain uncertain, it is quite certain that Labour's emphasis on presentation often made it more likely to adopt policies in order to attract headlines. Blair himself was as guilty as any of his ministers. In 2000 he announced that trouble-makers could be marched to cash machines in order to pay on-the-spot fines: just the sort of thought that would appeal to tabloid editors and headline writers. "The collection of cash is not a practical idea", reposted Sir John Evans, the sober chair of the Association of Chief Police Officers.[99] The policy might well have appealed to whoever was on the prime minister's sofa, but it was simply not practicable. There were numerous other examples of government ministers thinking aloud and having to issue retractions later. To that extent, the government deserved its reputation for government by headline and gimmick.

The Electorate

New Labour schmoozed with the press and spun largely in order to influence voters. Even critics such as Clare Short conceded that it had some effect and that "Blair and Campbell's ruthless focus on presentation increased [Labour's] majority" in 1997 and 2001.[100] In time, however, this reputation for spinning eroded trust in the government and threatened to undermine Labour's re-election prospects. By the end of the second term, 63 per cent of those polled thought Labour was not "honest and trustworthy".[101] Such evaluations damaged Labour both directly and indirectly. Honest governments are more appealing, other things being equal, than those that are not. Honest governments are also more likely to be believed when they claim that waiting lists have got shorter or the quality of education in schools has got better. Yet, at the end of the Labour's second term, ministers were frustrated by poll findings showing that, although many voters felt that their local hospitals and schools had improved, far fewer were prepared to give the government any credit. The same ministers were similarly alarmed by the way in which the decline in asylum applications failed to be translated into public confidence in the government's asylum policies. They thought that they had done rather well and inevitably blamed the Tory press or cynical media for the disparity. Labour's hyper-activity in the field of presentation and media management, however, reinforced the impression that it was simply not worthy of trust. By the time of the 2005 general election, spin had come to undermine Labour's achievements.

Notes

1. Andrew Billen, "I could be brutal but I had no power", *The Times*, September 9, 2003.
2. Peter Mandelson, "How spin turned on us", *Guardian*, May 17, 2002.
3. Clare Short, "The corrosion of integrity at Labour's heart", *Guardian*, September 7, 2003.
4. See the Press Complaints Commission code of practice at http://www.pcc.org.uk/cop/cop.asp.
5. Jason Deans, "BBC and ITV 'more biased than Sky'", *Guardian*, June 19, 2001.
6. Alastair Campbell, "It's Time to Bury Spin", *British Journalism Review*, 13 (2004): 15–23, http://www.bjr.org.uk/data/2002/no4_campbell.htm.
7. Campbell, "It's Time to Bury Spin".
8. Greg Dyke, *Inside Story* (London: Harper Perennial, 2005), pp. 257–8.
9. Data from Entertainment News, http://uk.tv.yahoo.com/050427/344/fhfqk.html.
10. David Deacon and Dominic Wring, "Partisan Dealignment and the British Press", in John Bartle, Simon Atkinson and Roger Mortimore, eds, *Political Communications: The General Election Campaign of 2001* (London: Frank Cass, 2002), pp. 197–214.
11. Campbell, "It's Time to Bury Spin".
12. Campbell, "It's Time to Bury Spin".
13. John Lloyd, "Media power", http://www.eurozine.com/pdf/2003-10-16-lloyd-en.pdf.

14. Anthony Jay, ed., *Political Quotations* (Oxford: Oxford University Press, 2001), p. 1.
15. Polly Toynbee, "Breaking news", *Guardian*, September 5, 2003.
16. John Rentoul, *Tony Blair: Prime Minister* (London: Little Brown and Co, 2001), chapter 7.
17. Rentoul, *Tony Blair*, p. 230
18. Hugo Young, "It's the Sun wot really runs the country", *Guardian*, October 30, 1997.
19. Patrick Wintour, "The Blair leak", *Guardian*, July 18, 2000.
20. "Tessa Jowell's Speech to the Oxford Media Convention", January 13, 2004. See http://www.culture.gov.uk/global/press_notices/archive_2004/dcms+speech_13_january_2004.htm?month=January&properties=archive%5F2004%2C%2Fglobal%2Fpress%5Fnotices%2Farchives%5F2004%2F%2C.
21. Piers Morgan, "Stop the f***ing lies", *Daily Mail*, February 28, 2005.
22. Rentoul, *Tony Blair*, p. 230.
23. Rentoul, *Tony Blair*, p. 334.
24. Rentoul, *Tony Blair*, pp. 279–80.
25. Tony Blair, *New Britain: My Vision of a Young Country* (London: Fourth Estate, 1996), p. 204.
26. Blair, *New Britain*, p. 210.
27. Kim Fletcher, "Gone to press: Why Desmond is dragging us down", *Daily Telegraph*, July 19, 2002.
28. Tom Leonard and Matt Born, "Labour, the porn king and 100,000 big ones", *Daily Telegraph*, May 17, 2002.
29. Colin Byrne, "Open House", *Independent*, June 20, 2005.
30. Piers Morgan, "Stop the f***ing lies".
31. Anthony Sampson, *Who Runs This Place? An Anatomy of Britain in the 21st Century* (London: John Murray, 2004), p. 207.
32. Robert Harris, "Machiavelli would have applauded Campbell", *Daily Telegraph*, November 13, 2001.
33. Anthony Seldon, *Blair* (London: Free Press, 2005), p. 299.
34. Seldon, *Blair*, p. 299.
35. Seldon, *Blair*, p. 299.
36. Nicholas Jones, *The Sultans of Spin: The Media and the New Labour Government* (London: Orion, 1999).
37. Peter Hennessy, *The Prime Minister: The Office and Its Holders since 1945* (London: Allen Lane, 2000), p. 485.
38. Seldon, *Blair*, p. 301
39. Hennessy, *The Prime Minister*, p. 484.
40. Hennessy, *The Prime Minister*, p. 476.
41. Andrew Grice, "Call for inquiring into Labour's £192m advertising splurge", *Independent*, July 26, 2001.
42. Michael Cockerell, "Lifting the Lid Off Spin", *British Journalism Review*, 11 (2000): 6–15, http://www.bjr.org.uk/data/2000/no3_cockerell.htm.
43. Mandelson, "How spin turned on us".
44. Cockerell, "Lifting the Lid Off Spin"; and Fran Abrams, "No. 10 denies Blair lobbied for Murdoch", *Guardian*, March 24, 1998.
45. Seldon, *Blair*, p. 546.
46. Peter Oborne, *The Rise of Political Lying* (London: Free Press, 2005).
47. Seldon, *Blair*, p. 296
48. Cockerell, "Lifting the Lid Off Spin".
49. Cockerell, "Lifting the Lid Off Spin".
50. Campbell, "It's Time to Bury Spin".
51. Cockerell, "Lifting the Lid Off Spin".

52. John Plunkett, "The Media 100", *Guardian*, July 18, 2005.
53. Rentoul, *Blair*, p. 230.
54. Bill Hagerty, "Paul Dacre: The Zeal Thing", *British Journalism Review*, 13 (2002): 11–22, http://www.bjr.org.uk/data/2002/no3_hagerty2.htm.
55. On the "Ecclestone affair", see Anthony King, "Tony Blair's First Term", in Anthony King, ed., *Britain at the Polls, 2001* (New York: Chatham House, 2002), pp. 1–44, p. 27.
56. Hagerty, "Paul Dacre".
57. Hagerty, "Paul Dacre".
58. Hagerty, "Paul Dacre".
59. See Campbell's evidence before the House of Commons Select Committee on Foreign Affairs, http://www.publications.parliament.uk/pa/cm200203/cmselect/cmfaff/813/3062514.htm.
60. Simon Walters, "Labour's 40% tax on house profits", *Mail on Sunday*, March 13, 2005.
61. "You hypocrite", *Sun*, May 26, 2001.
62. Jonathan Oliver, "Pop stars, football and The Sun's Asylum Week", *Mail on Sunday*, May 23, 2004.
63. Trevor Kavanagh, "Much to admire, but it has taken too long", *Sun*, April 14, 2005.
64. *Sun*, "Give them one last chance: Vote Blair & Brown", April 21, 2005.
65. Richard Littlejohn, "I'd rather eat my own toenail clippings than vote for Labour", *Sun*, May 5, 2005.
66. Morgan, "Stop the f***ing lies".
67. *Mirror*, "Sadly, Steve is best bet for London", May 3, 2000.
68. *Mirror*, "Prime Monster?" March 14, 2003.
69. *Mirror*, "Labour: The only choice", April 6, 2005.
70. Leonard and Born, "Labour, the porn king and 100,000 big ones".
71. *Daily Express*, "Disastrous Tories pose a threat to democracy", May 11, 2003.
72. *Daily Express*, "Vote for a fair Britain", May 4, 2005.
73. *Daily Star*, "Vital you take part", May 1, 2005.
74. *Guardian*, "Once more with feeling", May 3, 2005.
75. *Independent*, "It is vital that the forces of liberalism prevail in this complex election", May 4, 2005.
76. *Daily Telegraph*, "Small government + freedom + low tax = vote Tory", May 5, 2005.
77. *The Times*, "Governing and choosing", May 3, 2005.
78. Andrew Sparrow, "Sept 11: 'a good day to bury bad news'", *Daily Telegraph*, October 10, 2001.
79. Nicholas Watt, "Byers resignation", *Guardian*, May 29, 2002.
80. The Hutton Inquiry, http://www.the-hutton-inquiry.org.uk/content/report/chapter02.htm#a9.
81. Andrew Gilligan, "I asked my intelligence source why Blair misled us all over Saddam's weapons. His reply? One word . . . CAMPBELL", *Mail on Sunday*, June 1, 2003.
82. See the Hutton Inquiry, p. 179, http://www.the-hutton-inquiry.org.uk/content/report.
83. Greg Dyke, *Inside Story* (London: Harper Perennial, 2005), p. 272.
84. See the Hutton Inquiry, p. 279, http://www.the-hutton-inquiry.org.uk/content/report.
85. *Guardian*, "Hutton aftermath", February 2, 2004.
86. Ronald Neil, "The BBC's journalism after Hutton", http://www.bbc.co.uk/info/policies/pdf/neil_report.pdf; and Dominic Timms, "BBC tightens editorial rules", *Guardian*, July 15, 2004.

87. See John Bartle, "The Press, Television and Internet", in Pippa Norris and Chris Wlezien, eds, *Britain Votes, 2005* (Oxford: Oxford University Press, 2005).
88. ICM Polls, http://www.icmresearch.co.uk/reviews/2004/guardian-hutton-jan-2004.asp.
89. Prime minister's press conference, http://www.number10.gov.uk/output/Page7215.asp.
90. Timms, "BBC tightens editorial rules".
91. Toynbee, "Breaking news".
92. *Independent,* "A move to end the worst excess of spin", January 20, 2004.
93. Bruce Andersen, "Alastair Campbell's return to politics signals a campaign of dirty tricks and cynicism", *Independent,* February 7, 2005.
94. Andrew Neil, "You can cuddle up to Rupert, but it's not worth it", *Observer,* March 29, 1998.
95. Polly Toynbee and David Walker, *Did Things Get Better? An Audit of Labour's Successes and Failures* (London: Penguin, 2001), p. 69.
96. Lucy Ward, "Murdoch paper says Blair played vital role in talks with Italian media tycoon's network", *Guardian,* March 27, 1998.
97. Martin Kettle, "Rupert Murdoch may be the man who saved Europe", *Guardian,* June 14, 2005.
98. Rentoul, *Tony Blair,* p. 376.
99. Kamal Ahmed, "Nightmare at No.10", *Observer,* July 9, 2000.
100. Short, "The corrosion of integrity".
101. Anthony King, "Swing to Tories will not be enough to topple Blair", *Daily Telegraph,* March 25, 2005.

7

Why Labour Won—Yet Again

Anthony King

The outcome of the 1997 general election was easy to explain—a "no-brainer" as the Americans say. The Conservative government of John Major was divided and inept and in the early 1990s found itself presiding over a period of unprecedented financial turmoil (at least unprecedented under a Conservative administration). Meanwhile, the Labour Party under Tony Blair—now rebranded "New Labour"—had jettisoned unpopular policies, abandoned its historic commitment to state-centred socialism, distanced itself from the trade unions and persuaded millions of voters that, while a Labour government might not manage the British economy any better than the Conservatives, it was unlikely to manage it any worse. A despised Conservative government thus confronted a plausible Labour opposition. Labour won. No one was surprised, though many were taken aback by the sheer scale of Labour's victory.

The outcome of the 2001 general election was just as easy to explain. The Conservatives, now led by William Hague, were still saddled with blame for the financial turmoil of a decade before and seemed, in addition, to have lost any sense of direction. All that voters knew was that, if they elected the Conservatives, Britain would refuse to sign up to the single European currency, the euro. But, by promising a popular referendum on the euro issue, Tony Blair made it possible for voters opposed to the single currency to vote Labour anyway: the single-currency issue would be decided later—and separately. Meanwhile, the Blair government as a whole proved itself moderate, sensible and, above all, economically competent. Nothing went brilliantly right, but nothing on the domestic front went desperately wrong. Unsurprisingly, Labour won again—on almost the same scale as four years before.

The outcome of the 2005 general election is a little harder to explain. By May 5, 2005, the date of the election, Tony Blair as prime minister was ill regarded by a large majority of voters and so was his administration. The Parliamentary Labour Party was increasingly divided. There were ministerial resignations. The Iraq invasion, although successful in purely military terms, was proving a costly, messy and protracted embarrassment. Neither Blair nor those around him were trusted. Yet Labour won anyway—by a reduced but still substantial margin. This chapter sets out to explain why.

Disenchantment with New Labour

Someone monitoring voters' responses to Tony Blair and his government between 2001 and 2005 while at the same time ignoring their responses to the Conservative opposition would have concluded that Labour was in real trouble. Practically every indicator of respect for the Labour government trended downwards, and millions of voters, who had shown every sign of being genuinely enchanted with New Labour in its early days, were thoroughly disenchanted by May 2005. By the time of the general election, Tony Blair's personal ratings were also a shadow of their former selves. A hero in the United States because of his steadfast support for America following 9/11 and subsequently during the Iraq conflict, Blair never became a villain in Britain but he was certainly the subject of widespread head-shaking, some of it angry, some of it merely dismissive. There was a striking parallel in this respect between Tony Blair and Margaret Thatcher. In the United States, Thatcher was almost universally regarded as a *Great* Woman, but in Britain she was increasingly regarded as *That* Woman. So it was with Blair.

The data on the decline in popular respect for Tony Blair's New Labour administration tell a story that, if not quite tragic, is nevertheless pretty grim. Opinion polls in Britain have asked for more than half a century: "Do you approve or disapprove of the government's record to date?" In response to this question, Tony Blair's government never plunged as far into the depths as

Figure 7.1 Approval of "the Government's Record to Date"

Q. Do you approve or disapprove of the government's record to date?

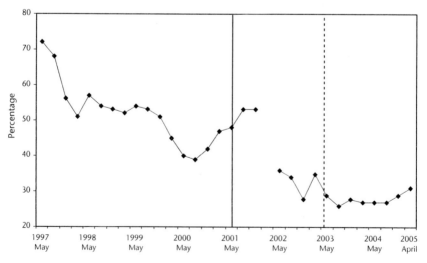

Sources: Gallup Political and Economic Index. 1997–January 2002; assorted NOP surveys conducted for the *Daily Telegraph,* 2002; YouGov, "Political Trackers, 2003–2005". http://www.yougov.com.

Note: The graph sets out the average percentage of those replying "Approve" to the question for each quarter. The question was asked in most months but not all. There is a gap in the data for February–April 2002.

John Major's government between 1990 and 1997; the Blair government's worst-ever approval rating was 25 per cent compared the Major government's worst-ever rating of only 10 per cent.[1] Nevertheless, as Figure 7.1 shows clearly, the proportion of people apparently content with the government's overall performance fell sharply in New Labour's second term compared with its first, especially from the latter half of 2002 onwards. In the year and a half prior to the 2005 election, the government's approval rating seldom rose above 30 per cent and more than once fell to 25 per cent. The proportion of voters unhappy with the government—not shown in the figure—sometimes exceeded 60 per cent. The Blair government, whatever else it was, was *not* popular.

Neither was Blair himself. One of Britain's leading market-research organizations, MORI, asks in most months: "Are you satisfied or dissatisfied with the way Mr Blair is doing his job as Prime Minister?" To begin with, as the trend line in Figure 7.2 shows, more than 60 per cent of MORI's respondents typically expressed satisfaction with Blair as prime minister and that proportion seldom fell below 45–50 per cent until well after the 2001 general election. But then, beginning in the late spring and early summer of 2003, it descended into the 30–35 per cent range and remained there till polling day in 2005. A man once numbered among those postwar British prime ministers deemed worthy of the highest esteem now found himself languishing among those deemed little more than mediocre.[2] By the time of the election, Tony

Figure 7.2 Satisfaction with Tony Blair as Prime Minister

Q. Are you satisfied or dissatisfied with the way Mr Blair is doing his job as Prime Minister?

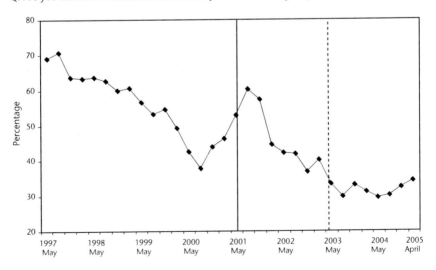

Source: MORI, http://www.mori.com/polls/trends/satisfac.shtml.

Note: The graph sets out the average percentage of those replying "Satisfied" to the question for each quarter. The question was asked almost every month.

Blair's personal standing as prime minister was actually lower than that of all three of his postwar Labour predecessors in the office, Clement Attlee, Harold Wilson and James Callaghan.[3]

Voters not only voiced their dissatisfaction with the Blair government to anonymous pollsters: they seized every other available opportunity to give Tony Blair and his colleagues what Britons like to call "a good kicking". During Blair's first term, Labour had defended seven seats in parliamentary by-elections and lost none of them. During its second term, Labour defended only six seats but lost two of them (both to the Liberal Democrats) and nearly lost a third (also to the Liberal Democrats). In four of the six seats Labour's share of the vote fell sharply. In the June 2004 elections to the European Parliament, Labour was humiliated, losing seats, struggling to finish second behind the Conservatives and contriving to win a mere 22.6 per cent—less than a quarter—of the popular vote. Labour also took a drubbing in the annual rounds of local elections, losing hundreds of council seats and control of dozens of councils. One commentator described Labour's performance in the 2004 local elections, held less than a year before the 2005 general election, as "among the worst suffered by either major party in local elections since the Second World War".[4]

Voters, including erstwhile Labour voters, were thus dismissive of the Blair government, the prime minister in charge of it and the Labour Party that supported it in parliament and the country. Why? What accounts for this high level of alienation, for such a volume of "switching off"? There are almost too many answers. The most important factors reinforced one another, together contributing to the widespread mood of disenchantment among voters that undoubtedly existed by 2005. At the beginning of the previous decade, a single episode—Britain's enforced departure from the European Exchange Rate Mechanism on September 16, 1992, "Black Wednesday"—had finally destroyed the credibility of John Major's government. No such single episode occurred between 2001 and 2005 to mark the falling out of favour of Tony Blair's government. Rather, a combination of decisions, events, circumstances—and also, to some extent, the sheer efflux of time—conspired against the prime minister and his administration.[5]

The invasion of Iraq was undoubtedly of major importance. Whatever its rights or wrongs as an act of public policy, the decision to go to war in Iraq did the government and the Labour Party no good at all in electoral terms. Although, of course, most Britons wished the Anglo-American forces every success once they were engaged in combat, in Britain there was virtually no US-style rallying to the flag. The military phase of the war, as distinct from the unrest and the insurgency that followed, took place in March and April 2003. As a glance back at Figures 7.1 and 7.2 will show, it was in the months immediately following the war that approval of the government and satisfaction with the prime minister, both of which were already declining, fell away sharply, never wholly to recover. It was also in the aftermath of the war that

Labour suffered its two losses in by-elections: the London seat of Brent East in September 2003 and Leicester South in July 2004.

Iraq damaged the government in three distinct ways. In the first place, it produced divisions bordering on turmoil within the Labour Party. Robin Cook, the leader of the House of Commons, and John Denham, a middle-ranking Home Office minister, both resigned from the government. Cook, in particular, was no run-of-the-mill politician: he had served as foreign secretary during Blair's first term and was a man of genuine intellectual and political stature. Cook resigned on principle—he believed that the case for war had simply not been made out—and his resignation won him many admirers, even among those who disagreed with him.[6] Another member of the cabinet, Clare Short, also dissented publicly from the government's decision to invade and eventually tendered her resignation. The revolt on the Labour back-benches in parliament against the impending invasion was on a massive scale, with 139 Labour MPs (out of 412) registering their opposition. Over Iraq, a government that had prided itself on its unity and discipline was suddenly made to look ill-disciplined and ragged.

Iraq also damaged Labour and the government in a more direct way. It is a myth that the Iraq invasion never enjoyed popular support in Britain. Initially it did. Immediately before the war, then during the fighting and then for some months afterwards, substantial majorities believed Britain and the United States were right to take military action against Saddam Hussein. However, even at that early stage, opinion was divided, with roughly a third of respondents in most opinion polls agreeing with Robin Cook that the invasion was, at best, ill advised or, at worst, immoral. Moreover, as much of newly liberated Iraq descended into chaos, the balance of opinion in Britain gradually shifted until, by the summer of 2004, a clear majority believed that, looking back, the war had never really been justified.[7] Needless to say, the Iraq War was not at the top of every voter's personal agenda, and there is no way of knowing how many people would have continued to support Tony Blair and his government but for the war. However, it is certain that millions were opposed to the war, that a large proportion of those millions had backed Labour in 1997 and again in 2001 and that for many of these erstwhile Labour supporters the Iraq invasion was the last straw: they were not going to vote Labour again, at least so long as Tony Blair remained prime minister and party leader. Among those who felt most strongly on the issue were a large proportion of Britain's 1.6 million Muslims, who took exception to the Anglo-American attack on a Muslim country. It was no accident that Labour's worst post-Iraq by-election reverses all came in seats with substantial Muslim minorities.

Finally, but far from least, the war in Iraq damaged Blair and his government by calling into question their honesty and integrity. George W. Bush in the United States had rested the case for war heavily on the fact that Saddam Hussein was a tyrant and on the desirability therefore of ousting him, but Tony Blair in Britain had rested the case almost exclusively on the fact that Saddam possessed weapons of mass destruction and that he was prepared to use them, as he had done in the past against his fellow countrymen. But no such weapons were ever found and, while some Britons were prepared to give Blair the benefit of the doubt and to suppose that he had sincerely believed in the existence of such weapons, many were not. For example, a survey in October 2004 by the online polling organization YouGov reminded respondents that before the war Blair had insisted that Saddam's weapons of mass destruction posed "a serious and current threat" to the outside world and asked them whether they believed him or not. Roughly one-third, 32 per cent, replied that they genuinely thought he believed in the existence of such a threat and that he had told the truth as he saw it, but even more, 39 per cent, reckoned that, although he believed in the threat, he had "exaggerated it in order to justify the invasion" and a substantial minority, 25 per cent, claimed that he had known all along that no such weapons existed and that "he was lying".[8] In other words, nearly two-thirds of the electorate thought that, at least on Iraq, the prime minister of the United Kingdom was capable of gross exaggeration or even downright deceit.

The belief that Blair and his colleagues were capable of exaggeration and deceit would have been damaging in any case, but in the case of Iraq it merely served to reinforce an impression that had already gained widespread credence: namely, that, as John Bartle has shown in Chapter 6, the Blair government was at bottom a dodgy affair, prone to point-scoring, credit-claiming, the telling of half-truths and the endless exaggeration of its achievements—in short, a government pious without but, in the eyes of many, including many Labour supporters, rotten within. This notion, that the Blair government was inherently untrustworthy, had become the majority view even before the 2001 general election. A journalist at that time was quoted as saying, "If the government announced that the sun was going to rise in the east tomorrow, I would get out of bed in the morning and instinctively face west"; but following the Iraq War the proportion of opinion-poll respondents saying they believed that the government was, on balance, "dishonest and untrustworthy" reached 71 per cent and seldom fell below that figure until shortly before the 2005 election.[9] The s-word associated with the Major government had been "sleaze". By the time of the 2005 election, the s-word indelibly associated with the Blair government was "spin". It is impossible to measure accurately the amount of harm done, but it must have been considerable.

Another source of difficulty for the government had less to do with style and more to do with substance. From its beginning, one of the central determinations of the Blair government was to focus less than previous governments on inputs of resources and more on outputs, less on the amounts of money spent and more on the quantity and quality of the services delivered. "Delivery" was to be a key concept in the New Labour lexicon. Services such as the National Health Service, the state school system, the police and fire services and the personal social services were to be reformed, made more efficient and effective and also made more responsive to the interests of consumers and less to the interests of producers. Ministers wished to cut or contain costs, but they also wanted to make, say, the local general practitioner's surgery as welcoming, flexible and customer-friendly as the local supermarket.

There were, however, political difficulties inherent in this project. Powerful producer groups had to be negotiated with and frequently bought off and placated. The details of the changes to be introduced in each service were often complicated, and it was hard to find vivid and intelligible language in which to explain to ordinary voters what the government was trying to achieve. Words such as "reform" and "modernization" and concepts such as "public–private partnerships" and "purchaser–provider splits" had little or no hold on the public imagination. Not least, it was hard for voters to discern the connections between government pronouncements and decisions and what, if anything, was actually happening on the ground. The inevitable delays in instituting reforms and in completing capital projects meant that improved services were often a long time in coming, and in any case it was often unclear who was responsible for what. The central government in London tended to attract blame for the things that went wrong, or did not happen at all, but to receive little or no credit for the things that went right. Citizens paid more in taxes, and the frequent tax increases imposed by the New Labour government were in most cases highly visible and immediately felt, but any benefits in improved services that accrued were more often than not only semi-visible, if visible at all, and felt by only scattered minorities of the population: patients at this or that local hospital, the parents of children at this or that local school. Change was inevitably slow. In connection with the public services, there was not—and could never be—a Big Bang. Unsurprisingly, portions of the electorate grew restless. The disjunction between perceived costs and perceived benefits was simply too great.

Evidence bearing on this point abounds. A 2002 survey noted that "there is a lot of talk at the moment about whether the present government is or is not 'delivering'" and asked respondents for their views on the issue. The results were discouraging. Only 27 per cent thought the government was improving the National Health Service (NHS), only the same proportion thought it was improving the quality of education in schools, only 20 per cent thought that (echoing an earlier Blair slogan) it was proving "tough on crime and tough on the causes of crime", and a mere 9 per cent thought it was improving the quality of public transport.[10] A year later the same polling organization, YouGov, set out a list of "some reasons people give for not wanting to vote Labour at the moment" and asked respondents which they themselves sympathized with. A formidable 71 per cent said they sympathized with the view that "Labour is failing to deliver on the major public services, like the NHS and education" (exactly the same proportion as sympathized with the view that "there is a culture of deceit and spin at the heart of this government").[11] A year after that, only seven months before the general election, nearly half of all voters, 46 per cent, said they thought that Britain's public services—things like the NHS, education and public transport—had actually "got worse" under New Labour. Fewer than half that proportion, 22 per cent, thought they had "got better", with most of the remainder, 29 per cent, reckoning they had "stayed about the same".[12]

This combination of taxes which were undoubtedly higher and widespread doubts about whether those higher taxes had actually led to improvements in public services resulted, as might well have been expected, in something of a tax revolt. People did not take to the streets or refuse to pay their taxes, but they showed an increasing reluctance to pay more. One wide-ranging survey on the twin issues of taxation and government spending found that more than two-thirds of Britons, 69 per cent, thought that they personally paid too much in taxes each year. Roughly the same proportion, 67 per cent, believed—wrongly—that they paid higher taxes than people in other European countries. And only one voter in four, 27 per cent, professed a willingness to pay higher taxes themselves in the interests of increasing spending on the public services. Perhaps most damaging from the government's point of view were the large proportions of those responding to the survey who believed a considerable amount of taxpayers' money was already wasted (79 per cent) and that, if taxes were further increased to extend public services, "much of the [additional] money would be wasted" (also 79 per cent).[13]

As in the case of every government, there were other concerns which alienated voters from the government of the day. Three that stood out in the 2001–2005 period, as Thomas Quinn has indicated in Chapter 1, were crime, anti-social behaviour (notably, but not exclusively, binge drinking and the fighting and raucous behaviour that often accompanied it outside city-centre pubs) and the influx into Britain of both legal immigrants, many of them from the European Union's new "accession states" such as Poland and Slovakia, and asylum-seekers, many of them legitimate, many of them not. Britain had never been a classic immigration society along the lines of the United States, Canada and Australia, but it was rapidly becoming one. Many people did not mind. Many people did. Fortunately for the government, most of those who minded the most were Conservative supporters already.

Much of the national press both responded to and played upon discontents of this kind. In particular, the *Sun* (daily readership 8.6 million), the *Daily Mail* (daily readership 5.8 million) and the *Daily Express* (daily readership 2.1 million), along with their Sunday equivalents, filled their pages with horror stories of one kind and another and directed an unremitting flow of criticism—some of it fair, some of it not, a great deal of it highly personal—at the prime minister, his government and, for good measure, his wife.[14] This topic has already been discussed in the previous chapter, and there is no need to go into detail here; but the central point is that millions of voters—approaching half the entire electorate—read every day a newspaper that was either cool towards the government, or often critical of it, or else unremittingly hostile towards it. The Blair government had few friends in the press and many enemies. Social scientists mostly despair of estimating the cumulative effect on voting behaviour and election outcomes of any nation's "press environment", but it is hard to believe that in the Britain of 2005 Labour was not handicapped, at least to some extent, by the almost audible drumbeat of newspaper criticism and contempt that was directed at it.

Finally, what role, if any, did Tony Blair as an individual play in Labour and the government's fall from grace? In so far as he was personally responsible for the invasion of Iraq and its aftermath—in the sense that another Labour prime minister would not have allied himself so closely with the United States—then he must bear a great deal of the responsibility for Labour's difficulties. And the same goes *mutatis mutandis* for New Labour's "culture of spin" and the government's emphasis on delivery and its determination to press ahead with reform of the public services. Blair was, as the world goes, a strong prime minister. The policies of the government were largely *his* policies. It follows that, to the extent that those policies became unpopular, their unpopularity must be laid at his door. They cannot be laid anywhere else. With one exception, Blair's personal characteristics—his physical appearance, his rhetorical style, his smile, his speech mannerisms—seem to have mattered less. MORI asks respondents annually whether they think each of a variety of statements about politicians does or does not "fit" Tony Blair. It is striking that MORI's findings in connection with most of the statements were virtually identical on the eve of the 2005 election to what they had been four years earlier on the eve of the 2001 election when both he and his government were in a much stronger political position. By 2005, in other words, most people had long since made up their minds about the prime minister. The one exception, however, is telling. Already in April 2001 only 17 per cent of MORI's respondents reckoned that Blair was "more honest than most politicians", but by April 2005, only weeks before the general election, that already modest proportion had shrunk further to only 10 per cent.[15] The failure of the anti-Saddam coalition to find weapons of mass destruction in Iraq undoubtedly inflicted substantial, probably irreparable, damage on Blair's reputation.

Going into the 2005 election campaign, the Labour Party was thus extremely vulnerable, far more vulnerable than it had been in either 1997 or 2001. New Labour no longer looked new. On the contrary, it looked old and scruffy, even a little shifty, like a dog that has been caught raiding the pantry. But at this point we have to deal with a paradox. Labour was certainly vulnerable—no one denied that—but at the same time no one apart from a small minority of over-optimistic Conservatives thought that Labour could possibly lose the coming election. Blair himself was certainly confident of winning. That was why he had no hesitation in calling the election for May 2005, fully a year earlier than, by law, he needed to.

The truth is that throughout the 2001–2005 period there were two factors—so far not mentioned at all in this chapter or mentioned only in passing—that were working powerfully in the Labour Party's favour. Between them, they made all the difference between an outright Labour victory, such as the one Labour actually secured on May 5, and either crushing defeat at the opposition's hands or else victory by such a narrow margin that governing as New Labour, or even as Old Labour, would have become difficult if not impossible. One of those two factors was the economy.

Labour, the Electorate and the Economy

The history of successive Labour governments' attempts to manage the British economy during the past hundred years makes depressing reading. The minority Labour administration of James Ramsay MacDonald between 1929 and 1931 coincided with the onset of the Great Depression. The Labour government of Clement Attlee between 1945 and 1951 presided over a period of full employment but struggled to overcome acute shortages of food, fuel and essential raw materials. Harold Wilson's Labour administration between 1964 and 1970 witnessed slow growth, gradually rising unemployment, constant inflationary pressures and recurrent balance-of-payments crises. Under the Labour governments of Harold Wilson and James Callaghan between 1974 and 1979, growth remained slow, unemployment rose higher, inflation climbed at one point to an annual rate of 26 per cent and the number of working days lost through industrial stoppages stayed high, culminating in the chaotic "winter of discontent" of 1978–79. For obvious reasons, British voters did not instinctively associate Labour governments with good times.

Worse in some ways, because more symbolic, there was an almost perfect correlation between periods of Labour government and major financial crises. When Labour was in power, there was invariably a world-class financial crisis; when Labour was not in power, there invariably was none. It was as simple as that. The only exception was the short-lived—it survived for only nine months—first Labour government of 1924. Britain was forced off the gold standard immediately following the break-up of Ramsay MacDonald's Labour government in 1931.[16] Sharp falls in Britain's gold and dollar reserves forced the Attlee government in 1949 to devalue sterling drastically from $4.03 to $2.80. Another run on the pound in 1967 forced the Wilson government to devalue the pound again from $2.80 to $2.40. Yet more selling of sterling in 1976 still further depressed the international value of the currency and forced the Callaghan government to borrow heavily from the International Monetary Fund. It was not a happy history. Few in Britain remembered the details, but probably most had a vague sense that Labour governments spelt trouble, potentially Big Trouble.

It was against that background that New Labour under Tony Blair in the mid 1990s set out to convince swing voters that under the next Labour government things would be different. The bulk of Margaret Thatcher's laws limiting the power of trade unions would remain on the statute books. Full employment would remain a goal, but not one to be striven for if achieving it would mean any reduction in productivity or runaway inflation. Keeping inflation under control would, indeed, be given the highest priority. Gordon

Brown, the shadow chancellor of the exchequer, announced that during the first term of a Labour government the Conservative administration's forward spending plans would be rigidly adhered to. There would be no increase in either the standard or the higher rates of income tax. Labour spokesmen happily admitted that the name of the game, so far as the electorate was concerned, was "reassurance, reassurance, reassurance". Blair and Brown were determined to reassure voters and also to campaign in such a way that, once Labour was returned to power, the entire labour movement would be committed, and be seen to be committed, to a fundamentally conservative economic strategy. And it worked. Voters were reassured, and Labour won.

More to the point, Labour's economic management, at least between 1997 and the mid 2000s, was as conservative as Blair and Brown pledged it would be. Thatcher's union-restricting legislation remained on the books. The Blair government, more than any of its Labour predecessors, pursued free-market and business-friendly policies. The standard and higher rates of income tax remained unchanged. A lid was kept on government spending (though a tighter lid during the first term than during the second). Above all, the newly independent Monetary Policy Committee of the Bank of England manipulated interest rates to ensure that inflation was kept under control. Partly as a consequence, Britain in the period leading up to the 2005 election—as Thomas Quinn has shown in Chapter 1—enjoyed low interest rates, low inflation, low unemployment and, by British standards, remarkably high rates of economic growth. The sick man of Europe had risen from his sick bed. He was well again. He was, in fact, enjoying robust good health.

The political benefits that accrued to the Blair government and the Labour Party were enormous. Survey after survey testified to New Labour's success on virtually the whole range of economic and financial issues. For example, we noted earlier under the heading of "delivery" that large majorities believed that Labour was failing to deliver improvements in the NHS, education and public transport, but majorities in the same survey said they thought the government was successfully "getting people back to work" (54 per cent) and was also succeeding in "putting an end to the old stop-go, boom-and-bust economic cycle" (51 per cent).[17] That survey was conducted in 2002. A year later an even larger proportion, 62 per cent, said they were "satisfied with the strength of Britain's economy at the moment".[18] Even closer to the election, in the autumn of 2004, a majority, 51 per cent, rejected the view that "the British economy—things like inflation and unemployment—have been badly managed under Labour."[19] Another sign of the government's success was the fact that economic problems that had plagued Britain for decades, notably inflation and unemployment, simply slid off the lists of things that people numbered among the most serious problems facing the country. For example, in October 1994 fully 52 per cent of voters cited unemployment as being among the most urgent problems facing Britain. Exactly a decade later, in October 2004, that figure had fallen to a paltry 9 per cent.[20] Labour's success lay, not least, in largely pushing economic issues off the political agenda. The economy by 2005 had become Labour's silent ally.

The contrast with the past, with the whole of Labour's previous history, cannot be overemphasized. Nearly half a century before, during the era of Harold Macmillan, the Conservatives' election posters in 1959 had proclaimed "Life's better with the Conservatives: Don't let Labour ruin it." Now the tables were turned. In January 2005, five months before the general election, Labour unveiled a poster emblazoned with the words, "Britain is working: Don't let the Tories wreck it again." Labour's manifesto for the election, when it came in May, asserted proudly: "Our economic record has finally laid to rest the view that Labour could not be trusted with the economy."[21] Remarkably few voters were disposed to disagree.

The Conservatives: A Hopeless Opposition

The economy was thus one of the two factors working powerfully in Labour's favour. As most readers will already have guessed, the other factor was the Conservative Party. Seldom can an unlucky government have been so lucky in its opposition. Had the 2005 general election been nothing more than a popular referendum on the Blair government's record, the result, despite the government's economic record, would almost certainly have been a resounding negative. But of course it was not a referendum: it was a competitive election, and there was another party in play, the Conservatives led by Michael Howard. Actually there were two other parties in play, the Conservatives and also the Liberal Democrats under Charles Kennedy. However, not even the most starry-eyed Liberal Democrats believed their party could form a government after the election. Only about a dozen Labour-held marginal constituencies were vulnerable to the Liberal Democrats. If Labour was to be ousted from power or even deprived of its overall parliamentary majority, it was the Conservatives—the runners-up in the great majority of Labour-held marginal seats—who were going to have to do the heavy lifting. And they were just not up to the job.

They were multiply handicapped. As Philip Norton observes in Chapter 2, the economic and financial turmoil of the early 1990s deprived the Conservatives of their reputation for economic competence. No longer were they regarded as a safe pair of hands. On the contrary, the events of the 1990s—especially the manner in which Britain was bundled out of the Exchange Rate Mechanism—made the Conservatives seem cack-handed and clumsy. More than a decade later, Labour in its poster could confidently warn voters not to "let the Tories wreck it *again*". The trouble with reputations is that, once lost, they can be hard, sometimes impossible, to regain. During the nearly three decades from the mid 1960s until the early 1990s, the Conservatives almost invariably led Labour on the crucial issue of economic competence. From 1992 onwards, they almost never did. As Quinn points out in Chapter 1, the opinion-poll evidence gathered between 2001 and 2005 consistently showed Labour ahead. The past thus lived on in the present to drag the Tories down.[22]

The Conservatives were also handicapped by the widespread public suspicion that, whatever they might say, they were not in the end desperately interested in maintaining and improving the quality of Britain's public services. At a private conference held shortly after the Tories' crushing defeat in 1997, a former party official neatly summed up the reasons for that defeat: "In 1992 we were thought to be uncaring but competent—and we won. In 1997 we were thought to be uncaring and also incompetent—and we were done for." By 2005 the party had still not succeeded in convincing voters that it was a "caring" party, that the National Heath Service, the state education service and other public services would prosper under a Conservative administration. Month after month, when the opinion polls asked voters which party they thought would best handle a variety of problems facing the country, Labour led the Conservatives not only on the economy but on every issue relating to public services and public welfare.[23] Labour might not be delivering, but only a minority of voters believed that the Conservatives, if they were returned to power, would deliver—or even that they wanted to deliver. During the election campaign, YouGov asked respondents what they thought would happen to the quality of public services such as the NHS and education if the Conservatives won and then, separately, if Labour won. The central thrust of the responses was pessimistic. Only 30 per cent thought services would improve if Labour won again, and only 26 per cent thought they would improve under a Tory government. However, it was, as usual, the Conservatives who evoked the greater pessimism. Whereas a gloomy 30 per cent of YouGov's respondents thought the quality of public services would deteriorate even under Labour, the proportion believing they would deteriorate under the Conservatives was substantially higher: 44 per cent.[24] Unfortunately for the Tories, the quality of public services was not some kind of side issue. It remained near the top of millions of voters' personal agendas.[25]

An additional problem for the Conservatives—one they had not even begun to solve by 2005—was that New Labour really was new. The Labour Party under Tony Blair was a completely different political formation from the one that the Conservatives had been used to confronting for more than three-quarters of a century, ever since the early 1920s. Old Labour had been, in some meaningful sense, a socialist party. It believed in public ownership: Labour governments progressively extended the boundaries of the state-owned sector of the economy. It believed in at least some degree of state economic planning, and in 1965 Harold Wilson's first government published a comprehensive National Plan. It believed it was part of something called "the labour movement" and, as such, took for granted—and positively valued—its close ties with the trade unions. Its ties with the unions meant that in practice its relations with City financial institutions and the rest of the business community were sometimes hostile and invariably less than cordial.

A Labour Party constructed along those lines provided the Conservatives with an ideal target. Conservatives knew *who* the enemy was, and they knew *what* it was. Their own ideology, however loosely defined, stood in stark contrast to Labour's, and, because the Labour Party based itself on the working classes (as its very name implied), the Conservatives knew that they could count on the organizational, financial and electoral support of the bulk of the middle classes. Moreover, as time went on, the Conservatives benefited from the fact that more and more of Labour's causes and associations became increasingly unpopular with larger and larger sections of the electorate. Majorities of voters were opposed to the further extension of public ownership, not least because most of the nationalized industries, as they were called, proved in practice to be top-heavy, overmanned, over-centralized, slow-moving, glum, grim and generally inefficient. State planning likewise proved a failure and fell into desuetude. For their part, the trade unions became increasingly unpopular during the strike-prone 1970s and 1980s, and their unpopularity inevitably rubbed off on the Labour Party. Old Labour's share of the popular vote fell below 40 per cent in the mid 1970s and stayed there for the next thirty years. Between 1979 and 1992 Old Labour lost four general elections in a row. With an enemy like Old Labour, Conservatives must occasionally have asked themselves, who needed friends?

But Tony Blair, taking up where his predecessor but one as Labour leader, Neil Kinnock, had left off, changed all that. He re-made the party and, in the course of re-making it, re-branded it. Under his leadership, Labour effectively ceased to be a socialist party (though still counting many socialists among its members). Public ownership and nationalization gave way to privatization and public–private partnerships. "Planning" was a word seldom, if ever, used. The trade unions were treated as just one pressure group among many. Leading Labour politicians courted individual businessmen and frequently appeared at gatherings of business organizations. New Labour not merely accepted capitalism, the market economy, private enterprise and free trade: it enthusiastically embraced the whole lot.

The result on the Conservative side was, and remains, total confusion. The big Old Labour target, the socialist target, so easy to aim at and hit, had vanished. The Tories no longer instinctively knew where to aim their fire or what they were supposed to hit—apart, of course, from the New Labour government, which, like any other incumbent government, they were bound, as the official opposition, to oppose. Hence the party's ideological fragmentation. Hence, in part, its frequent changes of leader. Hence, not least, the starts, stops, changes of direction, inconsistencies and lurches in policy described so vividly by Philip Norton in Chapter 2. As Norton says, the party between 2001 and 2005 "kept thrashing about for new policies, but without creating a clear, consistent and innovative vision for the future."[26] Millions of voters, including millions of potential Conservative voters, noticed.

The party's difficulties were further compounded by the fact, too seldom acknowledged, that Blair had not merely thrown overboard most of Old

Labour's ideological and policy baggage: he had invented a new type of politics. Blair woke up to the fact that most voters were simply not interested in the old battles between left and right, between nationalization and privatization and between the rival claims of the public and private sectors. What concerned most voters was jobs, the cost of living, education, housing, pensions, the state of the health service, crime, immigration and so forth. And what most voters wanted was that these issues should be effectively addressed. They cared much less, if they cared at all, about *how* these issues were addressed. In other words, most voters in Britain broadly agreed on the desirable ends of public policy but at the same time were largely unconcerned about how those ends were achieved. In the language of political science, politics for most ordinary voters was principally "valence" politics—in effect, the politics of delivery—rather than "position" politics—the politics of taking up fixed ideological and policy positions.[27] Blair probably did not read much academic political science, but he seems instinctively to have grasped that New Labour should be, and could afford to be, almost infinitely flexible in policy terms provided it addressed the issues that were uppermost in voters' minds. Blair was often said to have moved the Labour Party onto the political "centre" ground. That formulation was true as far as it went—Blair had certainly, following Kinnock, distanced the party from its traditional left-wing brand of socialism—but it was also misleading. In opposition, and then in government from 1997 onwards, Blair and those around him pursued some policies that were left-wing (their efforts to reduce childhood poverty, for example), some policies that were right-wing (the steps they took to combat terrorism, for example) and many policies that were no-wing (their attempts to encourage the unemployed back into work, for example). Blair was thus a centrist politician only in the impoverished sense that he was neither consistently left-wing nor consistently right-wing. Blair was, in fact, not a centrist at all: he was a pragmatist.[28]

That simple fact further discomfited the Tories. As the main party of opposition, they were supposed to oppose and mostly did. But the Blair government frequently adopted right-wing policies (or policies that could be construed as right-wing) and that were therefore hard or impossible for the Tories to take exception to, the most notable (and most important) being the government's decision to join with the Bush administration in invading Iraq. Often the Conservatives did not know what to do. Oppose, simply because the government's policy was, indeed, the government's? Or acquiesce, knowing that, if the truth be told, a Conservative administration would probably have behaved in much the same way? Norton in Chapter 2 cites example after example of Conservative indecision and flip-flops. Generations of Conservative politicians had confronted a Labour party that resembled a slow-moving—and increasingly elderly—heavyweight boxer. Now the Tory leadership found itself confronting an agile, supple and youthful exponent of the political martial arts. Traditional Labour leaders in policy terms had tended to be uptight. Blair hung loose. It was all terribly disorienting.

Another problem facing the Conservatives was the sense that many voters seem to have developed over a period of years that the Tories were somehow an alien party, disconnected to a considerable degree from the society around them. A traditional, and in former times well-attested, view of voting behaviour held that large numbers of voters, possibly a majority, identified closely with one or other social group (say, the working class), that they perceived a particular political party as being the party of that group and that they therefore identified, possibly closely, with that party. What has happened in recent decades, however, is that fewer and fewer voters identify themselves with a single social group and that, partly for that reason, fewer and fewer voters identify themselves with any single party. The individual–group–party nexus has been, if not quite broken, then at least substantially frayed. Nevertheless, it may be that many voters in the 2000s still have a sense that, even if no party is especially close to themselves, one or more parties are especially distant from themselves. Positive "we-feeling" has undoubtedly declined, but "nothing to do with us" feeling may well have survived. If it has, the Conservatives in Britain have disproportionately suffered.

YouGov in September 2004 asked voters how close they saw the Conservative Party as being to each of a number of different kinds of people. The findings are set out in Table 7.1, with the "Proximity index" being simply the proportion who saw the Conservatives as being either "very" or "fairly" close to each group minus the proportion who saw them as being "not very" or "not at all" close to each. The percentages in the table point to a highly probable source of the Tory Party's electoral difficulties. Large majorities of YouGov's respondents identified the Conservatives only with the rich, professional and business people and "people who live in the country" (the question having been asked at a time when large numbers of people probably associated people who live in the country with the unpopular cause of fox-hunting). Large majorities saw the Conservatives as *not* being close to such large social groups as trade-union members, the poor, the working classes, members of ethnic minorities and—especially damaging from the Tories' point of view—women. The Conservatives were thus seen overall as an old-fashioned and socially exclusive party, not one in touch with the Britain of 2005. Such an image cannot have done the Conservatives any good. The proximity indices for Labour, not shown in the table, were consistently more favourable.[29]

The idea of the Conservatives' "image" is worth broadening out. By the time of the 2005 election, it was clear that, while large numbers of voters responded favourably to specific Conservative policies, notably those on law and order and immigration, a large majority did not respond at all favourably to the Conservatives as a party. It was not Tory policies that were disliked: it was the Tories. A few days before polling day on May 5, YouGov asked a sample of electors to say, irrespective of how they themselves intended to vote, which of a number of statements they thought applied more to the Conservative Party and which they thought applied more to Labour. The results,

Table 7.1 How "Close" Voters Felt To the Conservative Party

Q. "People often see political parties as being close, or not close, to various sections of society. How close do you see the Conservatives as being to each of these kinds of people?"

	Very, fairly close	Not very, not at all close	Proximity index
Trade union members	8	82	-74
The poor	11	80	-69
Gay people	16	66	-50
Working-class people	19	75	-56
Members of ethnic minorities	21	68	-47
Women	31	57	-26
People who live in the country	69	21	+48
Professional and business people	87	7	+80
The rich	89	5	+84

Source: Anthony King, "Can Howard rally his party and steer it out of the doldrums?" Daily Telegraph, October 4, 2005.

set out in Table 7.2, were devastating for the Conservatives (and, to a large extent, for both major parties simultaneously). Above the line are listed a total of nine statements that either an absolute majority or—in American parlance—a plurality of respondents thought applied more to the Conservatives than to Labour. Of the nine, eight, as can be seen, are indubitably negative. Forty per cent or more of voters regarded the Conservative Party in the spring of 2005 not only as having no chance of winning the coming election but as appealing only to one section of society, as seeming stuck in the past, as seeming old and tired and as wanting to divide people instead of uniting them. Below the line are six additional statements that a plurality of respondents thought applied more to Labour than to the Conservatives. Of these six statements, as can also be seen, five are actually positive, with the sixth being more or less neutral. In other words, offered negative statements, people associated them with the Tories. Offered positive statements, they were much more likely to associate them with Labour. No wonder Labour, despite its unpopularity, was ahead.

Labour was also ahead in another sense. One of Britain's polling organizations asks from time to time a forced-choice question: "If you had to choose, which would you prefer, a Conservative government led by Michael Howard [previously, Iain Duncan Smith] or a Labour government led by Tony Blair?" Roughly one-fifth of voters typically responded "Don't know" either because they refused to choose or because they genuinely had no view, but a large majority were always prepared to say which party they preferred, and in the year prior to the general election that party was always Labour. In one month, June 2004, Labour's lead over the Conservatives fell to 2 points, but it rose steadily until, on the eve of polling day, it stood at 17 points, with 52 per cent saying they would prefer a Blair-led government and only 35 per cent saying they would prefer to see Howard installed in Number 10.[30] The findings were significant as well as consistent. They indicated that, while a

Table 7.2 The Two Major Parties' Images

Q. "For better or worse, only two of the political parties—the Conservatives and Labour—have a real chance of forming a government after this election. Irrespective of how you intend to vote, which of the following statements do you think apply more to the Conservatives and which apply more to the Labour Party?"

	Con	Lab	Neither, both, don't know
It has very little chance of winning this election	63	6	31
It seems to appeal to one section of society rather than to the whole country	48	20	32
It seems stuck in the past	45	11	44
It seems rather old and tired	44	18	37
It seems to want to divide people instead of bringing them together	41	20	39
It seems to chop and change all the time: you can never be quite sure what it stands for	35	26	38
It is too extreme	29	16	55
Its leaders tell people what they think they want to hear instead of doing what they believe to be right	29	26	45
Its leaders are by and large pretty honest	23	22	55
It seems to have succeeded in moving on and left its past behind it	17	42	41
Its leaders are prepared to take tough and unpopular decisions	19	42	39
Even if I don't agree with them, at least its heart is in the right place	22	40	39
The kind of society it wants is broadly the kind of society I want	33	40	27
It is led by people of real ability	19	36	46
Its outlook on the world outside Britain is similar to mine	27	29	44

Source: YouGov General Election Survey 8, for the *Daily Telegraph* May 3, 2005, www.yougov.com

Note: The table as published in the *Daily Telegraph* contained several errors. These have been corrected above.

majority of voters took a dim view of Tony Blair and his government, they took an even dimmer view of Michael Howard and his party. They also suggested that third-party supporters who knew that their preferred party's candidate had no chance of winning in their own constituency would vote tactically to keep the Conservatives out as they had done in large numbers in both 1997 and 2001.[31] In other words, despite Labour's unpopularity, the evidence suggested that an informal, unorganized anti-Conservative voter coalition still existed on the ground.

Campaigning, Voting and the Outcome

Almost everyone in the political world had long assumed that the next general election would take place in the late spring or early summer of 2005, and by the time the date of the election was formally announced in early April campaigning was already under way. Of the campaign itself, little need be said.[32] Labour, after some initial hesitation, focused on the public services and the economy, assigning a prominent role to Gordon Brown, the chancellor. The Conservatives chose to focus on five assorted issues—tax cuts, school discipline, controlled immigration, clean hospitals and an increase in police

numbers—and persisted in plugging away at all five, though with the heaviest emphasis on immigration. As always in British campaigns, both the broadcasters and the press focused on the three main party leaders, Charles
Kennedy as well as Tony Blair and Michael Howard. Howard accused Blair
of being "a liar" (he actually used the word). Blair looked pained. Kennedy,
declining to take part in the two-party slugging match, looked relaxed and
cheerful throughout—and also faintly disapproving.

The campaign as a whole was unedifying, and it is doubtful whether
more than a small minority of voters paid much attention to it. Even before
the election date was announced, more than a quarter of those questioned in
one poll complained that they found the pre-campaign skirmishing infantile,
negative, boring, dishonest and unpleasant. Almost no one—fewer than 5 per
cent—said they found the parties' electioneering grown-up, intelligent, honest and/or a credit to democracy.[33] It is also doubtful whether the campaign
made much difference to the outcome. None of the dozens of polls conducted
during the four weeks of the campaign proper put the Conservatives ahead.[34]
Most showed Labour with a lead of between 3 and 7 points. Labour's campaign seems to have been broadly neutral in its effects, the Conservative campaign to have done that party, on balance, somewhat more harm than good.[35]
Only the Liberal Democrats gained ground. The fact that a campaign was
being fought at all had, as usual, the beneficial effect from the Liberal Democrats' point of view of reminding voters that they existed. In addition, Charles
Kennedy's laid-back style undoubtedly attracted some support—he topped
voters' list of the political leaders who had done the best job of presenting
their party and its policies—and considerable numbers of voters almost certainly switched to the Liberal Democrats when they realized that Labour was
going to win anyway and that they could therefore vent their displeasure at
the Blair government and vote Lib Dem without running any risk of letting in
the Tories.[36]

Labour won, and it is more than a cliché to describe Labour's victory as
"historic". The Labour Party had never before won two general elections in
a row with overall House of Commons majorities. Now they had won
three—and all under the same leader. Having first been elected in 1997, New
Labour could now count on governing continuously until 2009 or 2010
(though Tony Blair would no longer be prime minister, having announced
before the election that, while he would serve for most of a third term, he
would retire before the next election). Blair had now, among many other
things, seen off no fewer than four Conservative leaders: John Major, William
Hague, Iain Duncan Smith and Michael Howard. He was, and remained, *the*
dominant figure on the British political scene.

Yet New Labour's third successive victory was a subdued affair, and on
the night itself and again the next day Tony Blair, far from appearing elated,
looked tired, forlorn and deeply depressed, not at all like a victor, more like
a person who has just been vanquished. The magician had lost his magic—
and he knew it. Although Labour had won, its victory was on a scale much

reduced compared with that of both 1997 and 2001. Moreover, it was on a scale far smaller than the opinion polls had led almost all onlookers to expect. The results thus came as a surprise as well as a shock. On a turnout of only 61.3 per cent, the Labour Party secured 35.2 per cent of the popular vote, more than any other single party but considerably less than the 43.2 per cent of 1997 or the 40.7 per cent of 2001. Labour had lost no less than a fifth of its share of the vote since the landslide victory of 1997. Not since 1924 had any party formed a government with such a narrow electoral base. Never before in British history had a party won an overall majority in the House of Commons with the backing of such a small proportion of the eligible electorate.[37] Because of the low turnout, the Blair government had been returned to office with the support of not much more than 20 per cent of the electorate. New Labour remained in power but with nothing that could be described, even remotely, as an electoral mandate.

Labour's loss of votes was bad enough. In terms of the government's ability to govern—in particular, its ability to command a majority in the House of Commons for controversial legislation—its loss of seats was even worse. Labour suffered a total loss of forty-seven seats, thereby cutting its parliamentary majority by nearly two-thirds from the 167 of 2001 to the much more modest (though still respectable by historical standards) sixty-six of 2005. Thirty-one of the losses went to the Conservatives, twelve to the Liberal Democrats, two to the Scottish National Party and two to candidates who were more or less independent.[38] New Labour under Blair had been on a roll for the better part of a decade. Now, for the first time, it was on a roll backwards. Many, perhaps most, on the Labour side blamed Blair. His personal authority, which had rested so largely on his ability to win votes and seats for the Labour Party, was substantially undermined.

Not that the Conservatives could take much comfort from the day's developments. To be sure, they made a net gain of thirty-three seats, increasing their parliamentary representation from 166 MPs to 198.[39] They took thirty-one seats from Labour and five from the Liberal Democrats while at the same time losing three seats to the Lib Dems. It was the first time for a generation that the Tories had gained a significant number of seats at any general election. However, the Conservatives were lucky to gain a considerable number of seats that Labour had held by the narrowest of margins, because the Conservative share of the vote increased by a minuscule 0.7 percentage points, from 31.7 per cent in 2001 to 32.4 per cent in 2005. The Tories had now secured less than one-third of the popular vote at three successive elections. Apart from 1997 and 2001, their 32.3 per cent share of the vote represented their worst showing since their rout following the passage of the 1832 Great Reform Act. The Tory leader at that time was the Duke of Wellington, the British victor over Napoleon at Waterloo. One wag calculated that at their current rate of progress the Conservatives might hope to regain power sometime during the 2030s—i.e., in about thirty years' time. Michael

Howard announced on May 6 that he would step down as party leader as soon as new rules for the election of his successor could be agreed.

Labour's vote had fallen sharply, but the Conservatives' had scarcely risen. The explanation lies in the fact that British electoral politics was no longer strictly two-party politics and that in 2005 the total vote for the Liberal Democrats and a range of smaller parties increased substantially. The Liberal Democrats, benefiting from millions of voters' almost equally balanced dislike of the two major parties, won 22.1 per cent of the popular vote, an increase of 3.8 percentage points compared with 2001. Because their vote was more concentrated geographically than in the past, the Lib Dems found that this relatively modest increase in their share of the vote translated into a net gain of eleven seats, giving them sixty-two seats in the House of Commons, nearly a tenth of the total and the largest number won by the Liberal Democrats or their predecessor party, the Liberals, since 1923. The Lib Dems lost five seats to the Conservatives but gained three from the Tories, one from the Party of Wales (Plaid Cymru) and fully a dozen from Labour. One of the most striking features of the election was the Liberal Democrats' success in wresting seats from the Labour Party. Hitherto the Lib Dems had reckoned to make most of their gains, and potentially to suffer most of their losses, in Conservative–Liberal Democrat marginal seats. Now they were making inroads into previously Labour-held territory. Disgruntled Labour voters who were evidently not prepared to switch to the Tories were, it seemed, prepared to switch to the Lib Dems. The Labour Party in the future, far more than in the past, would find itself fighting on two fronts.

The Liberal Democrats were the main beneficiaries of voters' reluctance to back either of the two major parties, but not the only ones. As Nicholas Allen reports in Chapter 3, no fewer than 8.2 per cent of those who went to the polls in 2005—the highest proportion since the Second World War—voted for independent candidates or candidates of parties other than Labour, the Conservatives, the Liberal Democrats and the Scottish and Welsh nationalist parties. This discontented minority went off in all directions: to the United Kingdom Independence Party (opposed to Britain's continued membership of the European Union), George Galloway's Respect (opposed to both the Iraq War and Blair personally), the Greens (opposed to man's despoliation of Planet Earth), the British National Party (opposed to immigrants and immigration) and Veritas (opposed to anyone less than wholly respectful of its megalomaniac leader, Robert Kilroy-Silk). What the vast majority of these disparate voters had in common was that they were voting—and knew that they were voting—for candidates or parties that had no chance of winning in their own constituency, let alone of forming a government. In effect, they were thumbing their noses—or emitting cries of pain. That said, independents and quasi-independents did, as Allen reports, contrive to win three seats out of the 628 on the British mainland: Bethnal Green and Bow (won by Galloway on the strength of widespread Muslim anger at the invasion of

Iraq), Blaenau Gwent (where an anti-Blair Labour maverick savaged the official Labour candidate) and Wyre Forest (held by the same local doctor who had captured the seat four years earlier on the strength of his campaign to prevent the downgrading of a local hospital).

The Scottish and Welsh nationalist parties might have been expected to profit from voters' lack of enthusiasm for both of the major parties, as the Scottish National Party, in particular, had done in the 1970s. But they did not. The devolving of substantial powers to the Scottish Parliament and the Welsh Assembly appears to have reduced the appeal of parties campaigning for full independence. In addition, both the SNP and Plaid Cymru, formerly parties of radical protest, had by 2005 become part of their country's political establishment. The SNP's share of the Scottish vote fell from 20.1 per cent in 2001 to 17.7 per cent in 2005 (it had been 30.4 per cent in October 1974), and, having finished second in Scotland at the two previous elections, the SNP in 2005 dropped into third place behind the Liberal Democrats. Tactical voting and intensive local campaigning, however, enabled the SNP to increase its representation at Westminster from five seats to six (and the hapless Scottish Conservatives again came in fourth, winning only a single seat). In Wales, Plaid Cymru's share of the vote fell from a modest 14.3 per cent in 2001 to an even more modest 12.6 per cent in 2005, and Plaid lost one of its four seats to the Liberal Democrats. (The Welsh Conservatives fared considerably better than their Scottish comrades, finishing second and increasing their Westminster representation from zero in 2001 to three.)

The electorate's restlessness and discontent manifested themselves in a variety of ways, not just in the low turnout and the unwillingness of millions of voters to back either of the major parties. One of the most remarkable features of the 2005 election was the sheer variety of the national, regional and constituency-by-constituency results. Half a century before, the whole of the United Kingdom had constituted, so to speak, a single weather system. When the political winds blew, they blew from the same quarter and at much the same speed across the whole country. Political scientists and pundits referred to the phenomenon of "uniform national swing". By 2005, however, Scotland, Wales and Northern Ireland had become, as we saw in Chapter 5, distinct climatic zones. Moreover, by 2005 large parts of the country had also become dotted with what amounted to political micro-climates. The American politician Tip O'Neill famously proclaimed that "all politics is local", but that had not been true of Britain during most of the postwar period. It was still not true in 2005, but it was certainly much truer than it had been before.

A few examples will illustrate the point. Cheadle, a suburb of Manchester in the north of England, and Guildford, a suburb of London in the south of England, are almost identical in their social make-up. Both are affluent, both are mostly white, and both have large commuter populations. Both are natural Conservative territory and were once safe Conservative seats. Both remained Conservative even in the midst of the Labour landslide of 1997. However, both fell to the Liberal Democrats in 2001, Cheadle by a minuscule

33 votes, Guildford by only 538. Given their demography and history, most observers imagined that in 2005 they would behave in much the same fashion, whatever that fashion was. But they did not. The Liberal Democrat in Cheadle increased her majority from 33 to 4,020 on a Conservative-to-Lib Dem swing of 4.2 per cent, but Guildford went the other way, with the Liberal Democrat majority of 538 being turned into a Conservative majority of 347 on a Lib Dem-to-Conservative swing of 0.9 per cent.[40] Like did not behave like like.

Like Cheadle and Guildford, the county of Dorset was once solid Tory territory, and, also like Cheadle and Guildford, the Conservatives held on to all eight Dorset seats even as Labour was sweeping the country in 1997. In 2001, however, Labour gained Dorset South from the Conservatives, and the Liberal Democrats gained Mid Dorset and Poole. A one-party county, at least in terms of seats, was now a three-party county. In 2005 Labour and the Liberal Democrats held on to their two gains of four years before, but what is striking is the extent to which the county's seats, once relatively uniform in their behaviour, diverged from one another. In 2005, three of the county's seats, already Conservative, swung further to the Conservatives, but the three other Conservative-held seats, while remaining in Conservative hands, nevertheless swung to the Liberal Democrats. The one Lib Dem seat became more Liberal Democrat. The one Labour seat became more Labour. Not every city and county exhibited such diversity—every one of Kent's seventeen seats, for instance, swung in the Conservatives' favour—but many did.

The pattern—or, rather, lack of pattern—of the Liberal Democrats' gains and losses helps to make the same point. The Liberal Democrats' net gain of eleven seats represented a compound of sixteen gains and five losses. The Lib Dems lost Torridge and West Devon to the Conservatives while retaining North Devon next-door with an increased majority and a swing in their favour. They lost Newbury in Berkshire, also to the Conservatives, while retaining nearby Oxford West and Abingdon with only a small swing against them. Their gains in urban Britain were scattered widely across the landscape, as the names of some of the seats they gained attest: Solihull in the West Midlands (described in one pre-election reference book as "ultra-safe" for the Conservatives), Cardiff Central, Bristol West, Leeds North West, Cambridge, Birmingham Yardley, Hornsey and Wood Green (in London), Brent East (also in London) and Manchester Withington. In Scotland they gained Dunbartonshire East on the outskirts of Glasgow and the deliciously named Inverness, Nairn, Badenoch and Strathspey in the northern Highlands. Some of the Lib Dem gains abutted on seats already held by the party or else had long, if latterly suppressed, Liberal traditions, but many did not. One factor that a number of them had in common was the presence of substantial numbers of students, university teachers and other members of the liberal professions in their electorates. Cambridge, Bristol West, Cardiff Central, Leeds North West and Dunbartonshire East fell broadly into this category. Almost all these gains were from Labour. Significant numbers of voters clearly intended to punish

Labour as a party for the Blair government's invasion of Iraq and its decision to raise university tuition fees.[41]

Among those determined to punish the government for the Iraq invasion were large numbers of British Muslims. The 2005 election was the first election in British history at which large sections of a minority ethnic group abandoned their traditional partisan attachments in response to a specific event. Most British Muslims, like a majority of all British Asians, had traditionally been Labour supporters, partly because they were disproportionately working-class and partly because Labour seemed more welcoming to members of ethnic minorities than the other main parties, certainly than the Conservatives. However, the invasion of Iraq was construed by many British Muslims as an attack on fellow Muslims. They were angered by it, and many of them took it personally, almost as though they themselves had been attacked. One result was that on polling day Muslim voters deserted Labour in substantial numbers, most of them, if they voted at all, switching to the Liberal Democrats, who had consistently opposed the war, and some of them to George Galloway's Respect.

Table 7.3 lists the seventeen parliamentary constituencies in which, according to the 2001 census, the Muslim proportion of the local population exceeded 15 per cent (a proportion that had probably increased in several constituencies by 2005 but that also included children and teenagers too young to vote). Census data are not available for an eighteenth constituency listed in the table, Birmingham Sparkbrook and Small Heath, but it, too, almost certainly by 2005 contained a Muslim minority in excess of 15 per cent. The table also shows for each constituency the extent of the drop in Labour's share of the vote in 2005 as compared with 2001 and the name of the party that won the seat. The table tells its own story. On the one hand, with only one exception Labour's vote fell far more sharply in these eighteen seats than in the country as a whole; Labour's vote fell nationally by 5.5 percentage points but in these eighteen seats it fell by an average of 12.7 points, more than twice as much. On the other hand, Muslim defections can have cost Labour only two seats—Bethnal Green and Bow, and Rochdale—because Labour held on to all the others. Not shown in the table are the shares of the vote obtained by the anti-war Respect party. Respect won 39.2 per cent of the vote in Bethnal Green and Bow, 27.5 per cent in Birmingham Sparkbrook and Small Heath, 20.6 per cent in East Ham, 19.5 per cent in West Ham and 17.2 per cent in Poplar and Canning Town—all, apart from the Birmingham seat, constituencies in the East End of London with large Pakistani and Bangladeshi populations. Labour's share of the vote may have fallen so little in Oldham West and Royton because of Muslim fears of the British National Party in that constituency, where the BNP's leader had finished a strong third in 2001.[42] The extent of Muslim alienation from New Labour revealed by the table may possibly provide a sinister pre-echo of the suicide bombings in London that took place only nine weeks later.

The broader demographics of the election differed relatively little from those of 2001, but they tended to confirm longer-term changes that were

Table 7.3 Voting in Constituencies with Large Muslim Minorities

	Percentage Muslim	Percentage point change in Labour's share of vote	Winning party
Bethnal Green and Bow	39	-16.5	Respect
Bradford West	38	-7.9	Labour
East Ham	30	-19.2	Labour
Blackburn	26	-12.1	Labour
Poplar and Canning Town	25	-21.1	Labour
West Ham	24	-18.7	Labour
Bradford North	21	-7.2	Labour
Ilford South	20	-10.8	Labour
Leicester South	19	-15.1	Labour
Oldham West and Royton	19	-2.1	Labour
Walthamstow	18	-11.9	Labour
Rochdale	18	-9.2	Lib Dem
Luton South	17	-12.5	Labour
Leyton and Wanstead	17	-12.2	Labour
Dewsbury	17	-9.5	Labour
Holborn and St Pancras	16	-10.7	Labour
Tottenham	15	-9.6	Labour
Birmingham Sparkbrook and Small Heath	n.a.	-21.4	Labour

Source: The census data are from the British Parliamentary Consituency Database, 1992–2005.

already in train. The Conservatives have long since lost their hold on the hearts and minds of the posh end of British society. As the figures in Table 7.4 show, only about a third of the country's professional and managerial classes voted Conservative in 2005, with more than a quarter voting Labour and roughly the same proportion backing the Lib Dems. Both the Conservatives and Labour failed to increase their share of the middle-class vote. Only the Liberal Democrats enjoyed a modest swing in their favour. But more significant changes were occurring further down the social scale. Labour suffered its heaviest losses among working-class voters and their families—that is, among their own traditional supporters. According to MORI, which provided the data reported in Table 7.4, Labour's share of the vote fell between 2001 and 2005 by nearly one-fifth among skilled manual workers and by roughly one-eighth among unskilled workers. Moreover, manual workers showed themselves considerably readier than professional and managerial people to switch to the Conservatives and not just to the Liberal Democrats. Some Labour supporters, not only on the left, have worried for years that Labour's working-class base may be crumbling gradually, with potentially devastating long-term consequences. Demographic analyses of recent elections suggest that they may be right.[43]

Apart from this changing demographic pattern and the increased local-centredness of British electoral politics, the most striking single feature of the results of the 2005 election was the gross disparity they revealed between the percentages of votes cast for each party and the percentages of seats in the House of Commons won by each party. Earlier we suggested that New

Table 7.4 Voting by Social Group

	Labour		Conservative		Liberal Democrat		Swing Lab to Con	Swing Lab to Lib Dem
	2001	2005	2001	2005	2001	2005		
Social class								
Professional and managerial (AB)	30	28	39	37	25	29	0	3
Routine white collar (C1)	38	32	36	37	20	23	4	5
Skilled manual (C2)	49	40	29	33	15	19	7	7
Unskilled manual (DE)	55	48	24	25	13	18	4	6
Gender								
Male	42	34	32	34	18	22	5	6
Female	42	38	33	32	19	23	2	4
Age								
18–24	41	38	27	28	24	26	2	3
25–34	51	38	24	25	19	27	7	11
35–44	45	41	28	27	19	23	2	4
45–54	41	35	32	31	20	25	3	6
55–64	37	31	39	39	17	22	3	6
65+	39	35	40	41	17	18	3	3

Sources: MORI's "How Britain Voted in 2001", and "Final Aggregate Analysis", 2005, http://www.mori.com.

Note: The estimated figures are based on the aggregate of all MORI's surveys during the 2001 (N=18,657) and 2005 (N=17,959) election campaigns. It is assumed that all those who said they were "certain to vote" voted in line with their intentions and the remainder did not vote.

Labour had two factors working powerfully in its favour: the economy and the Conservative Party. But there was actually a third: the electoral system, or at least the electoral system as it operated in the specific circumstances of the late 1990s and early 2000s.

Table 7.5 shows all the general elections since the Second World War and sets out the proportions of the popular vote that each of the main parties has won, the proportions of seats in the House of Commons seats it has won and the difference between the two. The table makes clear the extent to which the British simple-plurality electoral system punishes a party like the Liberals, now the Liberal Democrats, that finds its vote spread more or less evenly across the country—and, of course, the extent to which, in punishing the third party, it benefits one or both of the two main parties. It also shows how the system disadvantaged the Labour Party to some degree in the 1950s and advantaged the Conservatives to a considerably greater degree between 1979 and 1992. But for our purposes the significance of the table lies in the bottom three rows, those relating to the last three elections. As can be seen, the electoral system since 1997 has awarded Labour an enormous bonus in terms of its share of seats in the House of Commons and—to a greater extent than at any time in the postwar period—deprived one of the major parties, the Conservative Party, of its "fair" share of Commons seats. In other words, the electoral system in recent times has been heavily biased in favour of the Labour Party and against the Conservatives.[44]

Table 7.5 Votes and Seats Since 1950

	Labour			Conservatives			Liberals/Liberal Democrats		
	Vote (%)	Seats (%)	Difference	Vote (%)	Seats (%)	Difference	Vote (%)	Seats (%)	Difference
1950	46.1	50.4	+4.3	43.3	47.8	+4.5	9.1	1.4	-7.7
1951	48.8	47.2	-1.6	48.0	51.4	+3.4	2.6	1.0	-1.6
1955	46.4	44.0	-2.4	49.6	54.6	+5.0	2.7	1.0	-1.7
1959	43.8	41.0	-2.8	49.4	57.9	+8.5	5.9	1.0	-4.9
1964	44.1	50.3	+6.2	43.3	48.1	+4.8	11.2	1.4	-9.8
1966	47.9	57.6	+9.7	41.9	40.2	-1.7	8.5	1.9	-6.6
1970	43.0	45.6	+2.6	46.4	52.4	+6.0	7.5	1.0	-6.5
F1974	37.2	47.4	+10.2	37.8	46.8	+9.0	19.3	2.2	-17.1
O1974	39.3	50.2	+10.9	35.7	43.5	+7.8	18.3	2.0	-16.3
1979	36.9	42.2	+5.3	43.9	53.4	+9.5	13.8	1.7	-12.1
1983	27.6	32.2	+4.6	42.4	61.1	+18.7	25.4	3.5	-21.9
1987	30.8	35.2	+4.4	42.2	57.7	+15.5	22.6	3.4	-19.2
1992	34.4	41.6	+7.2	41.9	51.6	+9.7	17.8	3.1	-14.7
1997	43.2	63.4	+20.2	30.7	25.0	-5.7	16.8	7.0	-9.8
2001	40.7	62.5	+21.8	31.7	25.2	-6.5	18.3	7.9	-10.4
2005	35.2	55.1	+19.9	32.4	30.7	-1.7	22.1	9.6	-12.5

Source: House of Commons Library, Research Papers, 04/61 and 05/33.

Note: The Liberal/Liberal Democrat column includes the Liberal/Social Democratic Alliance in 1983 and 1987. The 2005 figures include the result of the delayed election in the constituency of South Staffordshire.

Why? The bias has certainly not been deliberately introduced, by the Labour Party or anyone else. In Britain, unlike in some countries, a wholly independent, non-partisan body determines the boundaries of parliamentary constituencies. To a small extent, the bias has been caused by the persistence during the last three elections, including the 2005 election, of anti-Conservative tactical voting, with voters who would probably otherwise have voted Liberal Democrat swinging behind Labour and enabling Labour to hold on to a handful of highly marginal seats. But far more important have been demographic shifts with far-reaching political implications. The constituency boundaries on which the 2005 election was fought were drawn up on the basis of census data dating from the early 1990s.[45] In other words, by the time of the 2005 election the boundaries still in use were already more than a decade out of date. That would not have mattered if either the country's population had remained largely immobile or any movements of population that did occur had been neutral in their political effects. But neither of these conditions was fulfilled. Massive shifts of population took place between the early 1990s and the mid 2000s, the bulk of them from inner cities into the countryside and suburbs and from Scotland and the north of England to the south of England.

The effects on the outcome of the last three elections have been immense. The size of the electorates in Labour-held seats in big cities and the north has been falling while in Conservative-held suburban, rural and southern seats it has been rising steadily. To take admittedly extreme examples, by 2005 the size of the electorate in the safe Labour-held seat of Newcastle upon Tyne and Wallsend in the north east of England had fallen to 56,900 while the size of the electorate in the Conservative-held Isle of Wight constituency had risen to 109,046—a difference between the two seats of over 45 per cent. Even if no other factors had been in play, the immediate effect of this development, repeated widely across the country, would have been to tilt the electoral system in Labour's favour.

There was, however, another important factor in play. Not only were the electorates in Labour-held seats typically smaller than those in Conservative-held seats, but, in addition, the smaller number of voters resident in Labour-held seats typically turned out to vote in smaller numbers than voters elsewhere. As in other countries, blue-collar workers and the poor tend to vote less often than the better off, and there is evidence that in the three most recent elections some Labour voters, living in safe Labour seats and confident that the Labour Party was bound to win in any case, have simply not bothered to cast their ballots. Whatever the causes of the lower turnout in safe Labour seats, this additional downward ratchet—lower turnout added to smaller electorates—meant in 2005, as it had in 1997 and 2001, that Labour MPs on average were elected by smaller numbers of individual voters than were Conservative MPs, let alone Liberal Democrats. Again to take extreme examples, in 2005 the Labour member for Sunderland North was elected, on a turnout of 49.7 per cent, by just 15,719 individual voters while the Conservative member for South West Norfolk was elected, on a turnout of 62.5 per cent, by 25,881 individual voters—a difference in the order of 40 per cent. This pattern was repeated, though not always on such a large scale, over much of the country, further tilting the balance of the system in the Labour Party's favour.[46]

A set of election results so unfair on the face of it as to give one party fully 55.1 per cent of the seats on the back of only 35.2 per cent of the vote, another party only 30.7 per cent of the seats on the back of 32.4 per cent of the vote and—worst of all—yet another party a mere 9.6 per cent of the seats on the back of a respectable 22.1 per cent of the vote might have been expected to elicit howls of moral outrage as well as renewed calls for electoral reform. But there were no such howls and few such calls. Remarkably little was said. The reasons are probably very simple. A majority of voters, as we saw earlier, whatever their personal feelings about Tony Blair and his government, wanted Labour rather than the Conservatives to win. And Labour did win. Undoubtedly a majority also wanted Labour, if it won at all, to win with a substantially reduced parliamentary majority. And that outcome, too, the electoral system produced. For their part, the Liberal Democrats, who might have been expected to howl the loudest, were probably not wholly displeased when they made a net gain of eleven seats, won a total of sixty-two seats and found themselves occupying more space on the green benches in the House of Commons than any group of Liberal or Liberal Democrat MPs since the days of Herbert Henry Asquith and David Lloyd George. Only the

Conservatives were desperately unhappy about the outcome of the 2005 election. And the electoral system itself had not done all that badly by them. If the Conservatives were now the underlings of British politics, their fault was not in their stars but in themselves.

Notes

1. The Major government's approval rating plunged to 9.7 per cent in December 1994. Between 1993 and 1995 it frequently hovered around 10–11 per cent. See Anthony King, ed., *British Public Opinion 1937–2000: The Gallup Polls* (London: Politico's, 2001), p. 176.

2. The three postwar British prime ministers who, if their Gallup Poll satisfaction ratings are averaged over their whole time in office, were held in the lowest esteem were, in chronological order, Edward Heath (average satisfaction rating 38 per cent), Margaret Thatcher (40 per cent) and John Major (32 per cent). According to MORI, Blair's rating in the twelve months before the start of the 2005 election campaign was 32 per cent, putting him on a par with Major. Of course, these average ratings in some cases conceal substantial fluctuations. Heath's ratings were the steadiest, seldom rising above 40 per cent and never falling below 30 per cent. Thatcher's ranged from 53 per cent (never as high as Blair's highest) to 23 per cent (considerably lower than Blair's lowest). Major's ratings were consistently high until the late summer of 1992 when Britain was unceremoniously bundled out of the European Exchange Rate Mechanism. Major's satisfaction rating plummeted in a matter of weeks from 47 per cent to 22 per cent. The Gallup findings for prime ministers between 1938 and 2000 can be found in King, *British Public Opinion*, chap. 7. For Blair's ratings throughout his time in office until the spring of 2005, see MORI's website, http://www.mori.com/polls/trends/satisfac.shtml.

3. In their last month in office as prime minister, Attlee's satisfaction rating was 43 per cent, Wilson's 46 per cent and Callaghan's 48 per cent. In March 2005, shortly before the start of the election campaign opened, Blair's personal rating, according to MORI, was 34 per cent. See n. 2.

4. Anthony King, "Labour expected a drubbing, but where were the Tories?" *Daily Telegraph*, June 12, 2004.

5. As regards "the sheer efflux of time", Martin Paldam argues for the existence in most democratic countries of a time-related cost of governing in "The Distribution of Election Results and the Two Explanations of the Cost of Governing", *European Journal of Political Economy*, 2 (1986), 5–24. He does not, however, discuss in detail why this should be so, and he does not relate his findings specifically to Britain. Election results in the United Kingdom over the postwar period would seem, on the face of it, to be hard to interpret in cost-of-ruling terms.

6. Cook made clear why he had resigned and continued to oppose the government's policies in Iraq, but he did not attack Blair or his erstwhile cabinet colleagues personally and, apart from undertaking a regular newspaper column, he did not use his opposition to the war as a means of personal political advancement. Cook died suddenly on a walking holiday in August 2005.

7. For details of the changes in public opinion concerning the war, see YouGov, "Iraq War Right or Wrong? Tracker", http://www.yougov.com.

8. Findings of YouGov poll reported in the *Daily Telegraph*, October 29, 2004. The present writer commissions and analyses YouGov polls for the *Daily Telegraph*, and for the sake of convenience the findings of YouGov surveys are the poll findings mainly quoted in this chapter. Between 2001 and 2005 there were seldom wide divergences between YouGov's findings and those of other polling organizations that asked the same or similar questions.

9. The anonymous journalist is quoted in Anthony King, ed., *Britain at the Polls, 2001* (New York: Chatham House, 2002), p. 33. For details of voters' responses to the question "Do you think that the government has, on balance, been honest and trustworthy or not?", see YouGov, "Political Trackers 2003–2005", http://www.yougov.com.

10. Findings of YouGov survey reported in the *Daily Telegraph*, September 30, 2002.

11. Findings of YouGov survey reported in the *Daily Telegraph*, September 29, 2003.

12. Supplement, "What Labour needs to do to keep its grip on power", published in conjunction with the *Daily Telegraph*, September 28, 2004. The data from this survey can also be found at "Labour Party Conference Poll", http://www.yougov.com.

13. Anthony King, "Angry voters check their pay slips and say: 'You're wasting our money, Mr Brown'", *Daily Telegraph*, December 8, 2003.

14. The readership data cited in the text cover the period April 2004–March 2005 and can be found at the National Readership Survey website, http://www.nrs.co.uk. Readers are defined as people aged 15 and over.

15. MORI offered respondents a list of fourteen statements about politicians—some of them favourable, some of them unfavourable—and asked which of them people thought fitted Tony Blair. The findings are available at http://www.mori.com/polls/trends/leader-image-lab.shtml.

16. Although the financial crisis of 1931 reached its climax shortly after the break-up of MacDonald's Labour government, it began and almost certainly became inescapable while that government was still in power. The statement in the text that "it was as simple as that" is therefore only a slight exaggeration.

17. See n. 10 above.

18. See YouGov, "Political Tracker (September)", poll for the *Daily Telegraph*, September 29, 2003, http://www.yougov.com.

19. Findings of YouGov survey reported in the *Daily Telegraph*, September 27, 2004. The same survey found that, even though the government remained unpopular overall, exactly half of those with a view on the matter said they sympathized with the proposition that "Labour has provided the country with a strong, stable economy".

20. See YouGov, "Domestic Political Issues", poll for the *Daily Telegraph*, October 29, 2004, http://www.yougov.com.

21. The Labour manifesto is reprinted in full in Tim Hames and Valerie Passmore, eds, *The Times Guide to the House of Commons, May 2005* (London: Times Books in association with Dod's Parliamentary Communications, 2005), pp. 316–39. The Labour Party's boast about the economy can be found on p. 316.

22. In a YouGov survey reported in the *Daily Telegraph* on May 2, 2005, only a few days before polling day, more than half of those polled, 52 per cent, agreed with the statement: "I still hold against the Conservatives the hardship and chaos of the early 1990s when interest rates went through the roof and John Major and Norman Lamont couldn't prevent Britain being forced out of the European Exchange Rate Mechanism." It is striking that so many respondents said they agreed with this statement even though the events referred to had occurred more than a decade before. Just as memories, including folk memories, of the Great Depression dogged the American Republican Party long after the depression was over, so memories of the events of the early 1990s seem destined to dog the British Conservative Party for some time to come.

23. MORI regularly asks respondents whether they think "the Conservative Party, the Labour Party or the Liberal Democrats" have the best policies on various issues. Links to the time-series figures can be found at http://www.mori.com/polls/trends.shtml.

24. Findings of YouGov survey reported in the *Daily Telegraph*, April 25, 2005.

25. For example, on polling day itself voters were offered a long list of issues and asked to say which two or three would be the most important to them in deciding which party to support in the election. Health came top, with 44 per cent citing it, and substantial proportions also cited education (28 per cent), pensions (22 per cent) and family life and childcare (16 per cent). See YouGov, "Sky News Election Day Survey", http://www.yougov.com.

26. See above p. 49.

27. The classic article that introduced the concept of valence politics is Donald E. Stokes, "Spatial Models of Party Competition", *American Political Science Review*, 57 (1963), 368–77.

28. Although, for the reasons given in the text, Blair is probably not best understood as a centrist in old-fashioned, left–right ideological terms, a majority of voters certainly thought of him as occupying the political centre (which was perhaps just as well because that is where a majority of voters located themselves). Gordon Brown, the chancellor, and the body of Labour MPs were seen as being considerably to the left of Blair. Michael Howard, the Conservative leader, was seen as being far to Blair's right. See Anthony King, "Blair is bang in the middle—but proves an impossible target", *Daily Telegraph*, September 27, 2004. The conjunction in the headline should, of course, have been "and". It is not clear from the survey what respondents understood by the terms left, centre and right. Many of them probably located Blair in the centre only because he obviously defied categorization as either a left-winger or a right-winger.

29. Majorities or pluralities of YouGov's respondents saw Labour as being close to professional and business people, members of ethnic minorities, trade-union members and gays, and far more of them saw Labour compared to the Conservatives as being close to the poor, working-class people and women. For the findings on Labour, see the *Daily* Telegraph article cited in n. 28.

30. The responses to this forced-choice question, which has been asked regularly since August 2003, can be found at You Gov, "Political Trackers 2003–2005", and "Telegraph Election Trends", http://www.yougov.com.

31. Anyone desperately anxious to know what happened during the campaign can consult Jon Smith, *Election 2005* (London: Politico's in association with the Press Association, 2005).

32. At the beginning of April 2005—that is, at the beginning of the campaign— YouGov asked respondents how they would vote in a variety of tactical situations. The pattern of responses suggested that the Labour Party rather than the Conservatives would benefit from any disposition to vote tactically and that such a disposition still existed on quite a large scale. For example, asked how they would vote if they believed that only Labour or the Conservatives had a chance of winning in their area, nearly half of Liberal Democrat voters, 44 per cent, said they would still vote Liberal Democrat, but 35 per cent said they would switch to Labour compared with fewer than half that proportion, 13 per cent, who said they would switch to the Conservatives. See YouGov, "General Election Survey 3", poll for the *Daily Telegraph*, April 15, http://www.yougov.com.

33. Findings of YouGov poll reported in the *Daily Telegraph*, March 4, 2005.

34. A few scattered polls suggested that the Conservatives might have a narrow lead, but only among those who claimed they were certain to vote. However, like their American counterparts, Britain's polling organizations have found it extraordinarily difficult to estimate in advance of any election how high or low turnout is likely to be or to identify which among those who say they are certain to vote will in the event not actually turn out (or which among those who say they are not certain whether or not they will vote will actually go to the polls).

35. During the campaign YouGov on several occasions asked respondents which party they thought could best handle each of eighteen "problems facing the coun-

try". Labour was consistently ahead of the Conservatives on fourteen of the eighteen and consistently behind on three, with the balance shifting from one party to the other on only one. During the course of the campaign, Labour improved its position vis-à-vis the Conservatives on seventeen of these eighteen problems. The Conservatives were always ahead on two of the issues on which they fought hardest—immigration and asylum, and law and order—but their lead was never great and tended to diminish as time went on. The proportion thinking Michael Howard would make the best prime minister also tended to decline. Findings of YouGov surveys reported in the *Daily Telegraph*, May 5, 2005.

36. A few days before polling day YouGov asked: "Irrespective of how you intend to vote, which of the three main leaders do you think has done the best job of presenting his party and its policies so far?" Even though the Liberal Democrats were trailing behind both Labour and the Conservatives, 30 per cent thought Charles Kennedy was proving the most effective campaigner. Only 25 per cent thought the same of Blair. A mere 16 per cent thought the same of Howard. In the course of the same survey, YouGov listed the names of ten prominent politicians in the three main parties and asked respondents to say whether they thought that each of them was an asset or a liability to his party. Only two of the ten were reckoned to be assets by more than 50 per cent of voters. The two were Gordon Brown (70 per cent) and Charles Kennedy (63 per cent). Blair was thought to be an asset by 41 per cent but a liability by 49 per cent. Howard was thought to be an asset by only 31 per cent and a liability by 52 per cent. See Anthony King, "The Tories are stuck with an image problem", *Daily Telegraph*, May 2, 2005.

37. The overall results for each general election between 1832 and 1997 are set out in Colin Rallings and Michael Thrasher, *British Electoral Facts, 1832–1999* (Aldershot, Hants.: Ashgate, 2000), pp. 67–8. In 1924 Labour succeeded in forming a (short-lived) minority government despite winning only 33.3 per cent of the popular vote. The lowest share of the vote previously won by a party able to form a majority government was the Conservatives' 38.2 per cent in 1922 when the party was led by Andrew Bonar Law.

38. The phrase "more or less" is meant to cover Respect, whose leader, George Galloway, won Bethnal Green and Bow almost entirely on his own. The reader should be alerted to the fact that the results of the 2005 election are made somewhat difficult to compare with those of the 2001 election because between the two elections the number of Scottish seats was reduced from 72 to 59. The creation of a Scottish parliament with a broad domestic jurisdiction meant that the previous over-representation of Scotland in the Westminster parliament could no longer be justified. The gains and losses reported in the text are, in the case of Scotland, based on estimates of how Scotland would have voted in 2001, and of how many Scottish MPs would have been returned to Westminster, if that election had been fought on the new 2005 constituency boundaries. For the detail of these estimates, see David Denver, Colin Rallings and Michael Thrasher, *Media Guide to the New Scottish Westminster Parliamentary Constituencies*, published in 2004 by a consortium of the main broadcasting organizations and the Press Association. The actual outcome in 2001 was Labour fifty-six seats (including the Speaker of the House of Commons), Liberal Democrats ten, SNP five and Conservatives one. Those who compiled the estimates calculated that the result in 2001 on the basis of the 2005 boundaries would have been Labour forty-six seats (including the Speaker), Liberal Democrats nine, SNP four and the Conservatives none. Among other things, that is why the Conservatives are credited with having made one gain in Scotland in 2005 even though they had one Scottish MP prior to that election and still had one and only one afterwards.

39. The numbers in the text obviously do not add up. The reason for the discrepancy is set out in n. 38 immediately above. According to Denver, Rallings and

Thrasher, the Conservatives would have held only 165 seats in the 2001 parliament had that parliament been elected on the 2005 boundaries.

40. The victorious Liberal Democrat in Cheadle, Patsy Calton, died shortly after the May election. Her successor as the Lib Dem candidate easily held the seat at the ensuing by-election.

41. According to census data (admittedly somewhat out of date), eight parliamentary constituencies in 2005 had student populations of 20 per cent or more. It is probably no coincidence that the Liberal Democrats, having previously held none of the eight, gained four of them on May 5, all four from Labour: Leeds North West, Cardiff Central, Cambridge and Bristol West. The swing from Labour to the Liberal Democrats in these four seats averaged 10.4 per cent (more than double the national average Labour-to-Liberal Democrat swing of 4.7 per cent). The other four seats—Nottingham South, Sheffield Central, Newcastle upon Tyne Central and Manchester Central—also witnessed well above average Labour-to-Liberal Democrat swings.

42. Oldham West and Royton was, and is, a safe Labour seat, and in 2001 the Conservatives, in second place, won only 17.7 per cent of the vote; but at that election Nick Griffin of the BNP nearly forced the Conservative candidate into third place, himself winning 16.4 per cent of the vote. In 2005 the BNP's share of the vote in the constituency fell by more than half to 6.9 per cent. Griffin had meanwhile switched his affections to the nearby constituency of Keighley, where, however, he fared less well, finishing fourth and winning only 9.2 per cent of the vote.

43. It is less clear how, if at all, an emerging British gender gap may have affected the outcome of the election. There has undoubtedly been a shift in the gender balance of British electoral politics. Women until at least the 1970s were somewhat more likely than men to vote Conservative and somewhat less likely to vote Labour (partly for reasons having to do with the relationship between gender and age rather than the relationship between gender and politics). At more recent elections, however, women and men have differed much less than in the past and sometimes—as in 1997 and 2001—have differed scarcely at all. The evidence relating to 2005 is conflicting. A headline in the *Observer* on May 8 proclaimed, "Women's support gave Blair the edge", and the MORI data set out in Table 7.4 certainly suggest that in 2005 women were considerably more likely than men to vote Labour and that the swing to the Conservatives among women was considerably lower than among men. However, other polling organizations' data did not point to such a wide divergence.

44. The origins and the scale of this bias have been studied in considerable detail. See, in particular, Ron Johnston, Charles Pattie, Danny Dorling and David Rossiter, *From Votes to Seats: The Operation of the UK Electoral System since 1945* (Manchester: Manchester University Press, 2001).

45. There was one exception. In the case of Scotland, the boundaries of that country's new constituencies were re-drawn using data from the 2001 electoral register.

46. Two other factors in 2005 probably cancelled each other out to a considerable extent and prevented the system from tilting even further in Labour's favour. On the one hand, large numbers of voters in safe Labour seats, people who would probably otherwise have voted Labour, chose instead to vote for candidates of other parties and even independents, either because they objected to the Iraq war, or because they felt New Labour was not doing enough for people like themselves, or for some other reason. In the safe Labour seat of Slough, for example, the sitting member, Fiona Mactaggart, won 58.3 per cent of the vote in 2001 but in 2005 only 47.2 per cent, a substantial drop of 11.1 points. However, the Tory vote scarcely changed between the two elections: it held steady at 26.2 per cent in 2001 and 26.1 per cent in 2005. Instead the Liberal Democrats and UKIP both increased their share of the vote (by 5.0 points and 1.9 points respectively) and

candidates for Respect and the Greens, standing for the first time, took between them 6.5 per cent. On its own, this sort of result, which was widely repeated across the country, would have enabled Labour to hold even more seats than in the past on the basis of relatively small numbers of votes. But, on the other hand, the drastic reduction in the number of Scottish seats (from 72 to 59) pulled in the opposite direction, because in Scotland the average Labour-held seat now had a much larger electorate than it had had in 2001. The mean size of electorates in Scottish constituencies in 2001 was 55,337. It rose in 2005 to 67,720, an increase of roughly one-fifth (see Denver, Rallings and Thrasher, *Media Guide to the New Scottish Westminster Constituencies,* p. 7). As a substantial majority of Scottish seats were still in Labour hands, the effect was to reduce the electoral system's bias in favour of Labour across Britain as a whole.

8

America's Other President:
The American Left, Right and Centre on
Tony Blair and the Election of 2005

E.J. Dionne Jr

At some point in the last eight years, almost every American has been an admirer of Tony Blair. His charms have eluded only the very furthest reaches of the right and the left, and a very small minority of Americans who take not a smidgen of interest in politics. At certain moments—notably in the weeks and months following the events of September 11, 2001—his appeal stretched clear across the American political spectrum. The right liked Blair for standing with the United States at a time of crisis. Americans on the centre-left liked that, too. But they also saw in Blair a spokesman for freedom far clearer and more eloquent than President Bush. Most Americans rallied to Bush after September 11, but many of his former (and future) opponents did so reluctantly and saw Blair as a more palatable spokesman for the battle against terror. "Tony Blair is *my* president", Brookings Institution scholar Ivo Daalder said rather famously after Blair's post-September 11 address. A Gallup poll in mid-October, 2001, found that 82 per cent of Americans had a favourable view of Blair.[1] Just 7 per cent viewed him negatively. Only elections held at gunpoint in Iraq have produced more positive numbers for a political leader. One of the few more lopsided ratings in the same Gallup survey was Osama bin Laden's—97:1 unfavourable.

Blair and Clinton: The Buddy Movie

Blair has had different American constituencies at different moments. In the years before his election through to the end of Bill Clinton's term, Blair was viewed among Democrats as part of a trans-Atlantic project aimed at revitalizing the centre-left. He was a friend, an ally and—though the word was almost never used—a "comrade".[2] He and Clinton were part of a "Third Way" that would transcend "the old Left and the new right", as Blair always put it—or "the brain dead politics of both parties", as Clinton liked to say. Reagan-Thatcherism would give way to Clinton-Blairism. Early on, Blair was seen as either a follower or an ally of Bill Clinton's, and sometimes both. Once Blair took office under a parliamentary system, he actually had more power than Clinton did under the United State's separated system.[3] So Blair seemed to have an easier time creating coherence out of the messy but excit-

185

ing politics of the Third Way. Blair never had to deal with anything like the 1994 Republican mid-term election victories. He never had to negotiate with Newt Gingrich. And of course there was no Monica Lewinsky to complicate the Blair project.

In light of Blair's later friendship with Bush, it is sometimes hard to remember just how close American and British progressives were in the 1990s. During Clinton's 1992 campaign, New Labour strategists flocked to Little Rock and then to Washington in search of clues to victory.[4] British and American centre-left politicians, think tankers and political consultants ran up record numbers of frequent-flyer miles crossing the Atlantic in search of new ideas and new policies, new strategies and new tactics. After Blair won, Clinton partisans were regular visitors at Numbers 10 and 11 Downing Street (the addresses of the prime minister and the chancellor of the exchequer) and Chequers (the prime minister's country retreat) for learned, lofty and policy-heavy discussions.

Washington and London—not Stockholm, Paris, Moscow or Havana—would be the capitals of a revitalized, if considerably more moderate, left. This charmed and charming circle steadily expanded to include Schroeder of Germany, Prodi of Italy and, eventually, social democrats from all over, including the Netherlands, Spain, Portugal and Bulgaria. Even the Democratic Party of Japan, an ideologically amorphous amalgam of political forces, declared itself "Blairite". In those heady days, it seemed that the Clinton–Blair approach to politics would change the world. They were, said Sidney Blumenthal—a journalist who became an aide to Clinton, who was close to Blair and found himself at the centre of the New Labour–New Democrat discussions—seeking "to create a new consensus".[5]

In this troubled and often cynical moment, it is difficult to remember the energy of those times. In those early years, Blair won popularity among moderate Democrats and many liberals in the United States because of a genuine optimism about political possibilities he and Clinton represented. On both sides of the Atlantic, politicians and intellectuals were debating what sort of politics should replace the traditional liberal and social democratic doctrines of the left and the free-market ideas of the right. The parties engaged in that quest were winning elections in the United States and Britain, but also in Italy and Portugal, the Netherlands and Germany.

The questions Blair and Clinton posed seemed like the right ones: how could democratic governments influence a global economy that increasingly ignored national boundaries and rules? How could the economic inequalities created by this bold new capitalism be redressed? How could individuals be equipped to keep up in a more competitive time? How could social welfare programmes constructed four to six decades ago be reconfigured? How could the dynamism of the market be balanced against the need to protect families and local communities from its inevitable disruptions?[6]

What did all this mean? You could look at the victories of Blair, Clinton and their allies and argue that at the moment of capitalism's high tide, voters supported those who proposed to put some limits on the free market and to offset some of the inequities it created. Or you could say that Clinton-Blairism made large accommodations to the marketplace and entrepreneurial capitalism. Or you could say—and this is probably most accurate—that both statements were true. Clinton and Blair were pioneers, even if imperfect ones, because they were among the first successful politicians on the centre-left to grapple openly with the problems of globalization. The regulatory state championed by America's New Deal and Great Society liberals and Europe's social democrats has great difficulty working its will in a global market. Companies and private investment are footloose. Labour and environmental regulation is difficult to enforce across national boundaries. That, increasingly, will be true of tax laws, too. Clinton and Blair may have offered incomplete answers, but they focused on the right problems and shared a great joy in their love of political victory and obsession with policy detail (otherwise known as "policy wonkishness").

The politics with which both Blair and Clinton were associated might be thought of as *sociological politics*. Both politicians, because they were in different ways influenced but not revolutionized by the 1960s, were acutely aware that the times had changed in their societies. Both understood that their electorates were exhausted by ideological politics, first in the 1960s and again in the 1980s. No wonder they stood against the left and the right. Voters tended to identify neither with the revolutionaries of the 1960s nor the conservative ideologues of the 1980s. They preferred cultural peace to culture wars. Few in either the United States or Britain played a single role. Feminists were also mothers of both sons and daughters. Investors were also wage earners. Workers could simultaneously feel solidarity with members of their class and yearn to move up the class ladder. Most voters worried about more than one problem at a time.

Both Clinton's politics and Blair's reflected the declining influence of Marxist ideas after the end of the Cold War. Intriguingly, both Clinton and Blair searched for inspiration in a time that predated the rise of the Soviet Union, or even that of the Labour Party. Clinton looked to America's Progressive Era, Blair to the reforming 1906 Liberal government.[7] Clinton and Blair both sought to be and to present themselves as resolutely practical. They dealt with such questions as balancing responsibilities at home and at work, improving schools, paying for job training and university. And as sociologists who happened to be politicians, Clinton and Blair were acutely sensitive to the fact that the electorates whose votes they were seeking were not the same electorates that had voted for Franklin Roosevelt or Clement Attlee. Anthony Giddens, one of Britain's leading social theorists, became a great defender of Blair's Third Way and saw it responding to a decline of traditional class politics. "With the rapid shrinking of the working class and the disappearance of the bipolar world", he wrote in the *New Statesman*, "the salience of class politics, as well as the traditional divisions of left and right, has diminished".[8]

One should always be wary of predictions of the decline of class politics because such claims are so often used by those at the top of the heap to deny inequalities. In the United States and Britain, class differences in life circumstances have not disappeared. This point was graphically brought home in the United States by the sharp class and racial divide in how citizens fared in New Orleans after Hurricane Katrina. Indeed, Clinton and Blair both shared an awareness that they could not live with class politics, and could not live without it. Clinton was more populist and class oriented in his own campaigning than is usually recognized. Blair's majority (especially his narrowed 2005 margin in parliament) was still built on a foundation of Old Labour strength in Britain's working-class areas. Clinton and Blair even split the class difference when it came to their taste in American political consultants. Both at one point or another leaned on Stanley Greenberg, a Democratic pollster who has an acute sense of the imperative for centre-left parties to retain working-class loyalty, and Mark Penn, a rival Democratic pollster who emphasizes middle-of-the-road politics and middle-class votes. Clinton went first with Greenberg and then with Penn. In 2005, Blair hired both of them.[9]

Still, Giddens, Clinton and Blair were right that the manual working class, the base of traditional parties of the left, is shrinking as a percentage of the workforce and is being replaced by various kinds of service and white-collar workers. As class loyalties have diminished, so have party loyalties—or so it seemed until George W. Bush polarized the American electorate. Most political parties in the West are rooted in different times and circumstances (see Nicholas Allen in Chapter 3). Few still alive in Britain have personal experience of the socializing achievements of Atlee. Even fewer living Americans experienced Roosevelt's New Deal.

Thus were Blair and Clinton obsessed with the quest for suburban voters whose political loyalties are fluid, whose move away from urban centres weakened their ties to the traditional institutions of their parents, and who are influenced by mass media and their own search for information. The trans-Atlantic traffic between New Democrats and New Labour was not confined to learned policy conferences and papers. With the sharing of political consultants came the sharing of the most up-to-date techniques of voter contact and targeting, advertising, direct mail and other forms of persuasion.[10]

It is, finally, important to see both Blair and Clinton as responding to a long series of defeats. Both had a sense of urgency about the state of the Labour and Democratic parties. If the Third Way's approach seemed reactive, that is because it was. Labour had lost and lost and lost again, from 1979 forward. The Democrats had won but a single election between 1968 and 1992. Something needed to be done. The tone of a September 27, 1998, opinion article Blair wrote for the *Washington Post* perfectly captured the sense that Blair and Clinton both saw themselves as reacting to, or rising above, past failure.

> For many years in opposition, the British Labour Party was seen—
> however unfairly—as the party of big government, nationalization,
> anti-enterprise, soft on crime, unconcerned with family life, gripped by

pressure groups and favouring more tax and public spending across the board. We were also regarded as poor managers of public services, under the thumb of trade unions and producers' interests and too little concerned with choice and quality. The right was able to turn privatization and free markets into universal panaceas.

A false opposition was set up between rights and responsibilities, between compassion and ambition, between the public and private sectors, between an enterprise economy and the attack on poverty and exclusion.

New Labour has sought to move ahead and apply its values in a different way.[11]

Note those exquisitely balanced values ("rights and responsibilities", "compassion and ambition", "public and private"). The balancing act, which was actually quite rational and appealing, lay at the heart of the new creed for which Blair and Clinton were the leading evangelists.

It is entertaining, and sometimes even justified, to denigrate the Third Way and the achievements of Clinton in the United States and Blair in Britain. Neither fully resolved the tensions and contradictions of their doctrine. There was always a suspicion that Clinton and Blair were as interested in slogans as in ideas, that new forms of "progressive" politics were merely brilliantly veiled forms of capitulation to the right—the final triumph of Ronald Reagan and Margaret Thatcher. It seemed at times, as Anthony King suggests in his chapter, that Clinton and Blair were keen to distinguish themselves from some terrible "them" (the far right, the old left, etc.) without ever having to define who "we" were. As Ralf Dahrendorf put it, "when you define yourself in others' terms, you allow them to determine your agenda".[12]

Nor were the very words "Third Way" really so novel. Decades ago, the American journalist Marquis Childs described Swedish social democracy as embodying the "middle way" between American capitalism and Soviet communism. The new Clinton–Blair middle seemed to lie somewhere between Sweden and the United States, suggesting that the content of Third Wayism is relative, heavily determined by who sets the intellectual and political goalposts. Even Sid Blumenthal, a devout and effective defender of Clinton and Blair, acknowledged that the Third Way "is easily characterized as being the place equidistant between two points".[13]

Clinton and Blair also risked being seen as politicians who thought every problem could be solved if you just threw schooling and job training at it. And how sustainable was the politics they proposed? "The fear", Clinton's former Labour secretary Robert Reich once told the *Nation*'s David Corn, "is that Tony Blair and Bill Clinton, instead of charting a Third Way, will leave the progressive left in tatters and do little to rectify the social injustices experienced by modern capitalism".[14]

But Clinton and Blair seemed only to draw strength from the disappointment of their friends. Many of those friends, after all, had led the centre-left into a wilderness from which each had delivered their movement. If some of Labour's advertising during the 2005 campaign looked like a buddy movie—shot in intimate shadows—glorifying the vexed relationship between Blair and Gordon Brown, the smash hit of late 1990s was the Bill and Tony buddy movie that required no artifice.[15]

To get a sense of just how close Blair and Clinton, New Labour and the Democrats, really were, it is worth going back to September 21, 1998. It was a very odd day in American politics, the day that Bill Clinton's grand jury testimony from months before in the Monica Lewinsky case was made public and streamed over the American airwaves. That did not seem to concern Clinton or his friend Blair. They spoke before a crowd of intellectual well-wishers at New York University Law School on a grand theme: "Strengthening Democracy in the Global Economy". Clinton was replaying—successfully, as it turned out—the approach he had patented during the 1992 presidential primaries when scandals first started raining down on him. Clinton had told voters over and over: "This election is not about me, it's about you". And so while the rest of the political universe was focused on sex and sleaze, Clinton and Blair focused on problems and solutions, ideas and policies, hopes and plans, all aimed at raising up the forgotten middle class, the aspirational working class, and the poor who were no longer to be trapped in dependency. The cast stretched from Blair and Clinton to Prodi and Petar Stoyanov, Bulgaria's reformist leader. For Blair in particular, standing with his American friend on one of the most challenging days of his presidency was an act of solidarity that Clinton would one day repay.

For weeks, policy types had dubbed the gathering "The Third Way Meeting". Blair had the definitions down. The Third Way, he said, represented "the alliance between progress and justice", an effort to "take the basic value structure" of old progressive faith "minus the dogma". Blair, choosing an interesting word in the context of the day, said that government should be an "enabler" to help people do what they want through better education and training. It should not try to run people's lives. It offers "a different contract of citizenship" involving both "rights and duties". The happy conclusion from Blair: "We are witnessing, effectively, the rebirth of progressive politics".[16]

Clinton led off and moderated the meeting with the breezy informality he used so often when he had gotten the whole project—"the project" was a big phrase in those days—off the ground in 1992. Third Wayers, he said, wanted to be "modern and progressive", to avoid "false choices designed to divide people to win elections", to "moderate boom-bust cycles", to have an American foreign policy that would stand up for "collective responsibilities beyond our borders".[17] The last now looks ironic in light of the Iraq adventure. "I'm grateful", Clinton said, "that the Third Way seems to be taking hold".[18]

Hillary Rodham Clinton bravely did her part by presiding over a morning discussion among the Third Way's intellectuals. She offered what seemed, in light of what just about everyone outside the room was focusing on that day, a practical though hopeful stoicism: "We have to take the world as we find it and do what we can to improve upon it". It fell to Prodi, from the land of Machiavelli, to warn of the dangers of "walking in the clouds" and to highlight the need to acknowledge that the Third Way was a promising approach "not yet defined".

Blair and Bush: The Odd Couple

Before Democrats in the United States had a chance to offer further definition to the great project, Bush became president after the electoral fiasco in Florida. Al Gore, Clinton's vice president, won the popular vote, but lost the judicial war. Then came September 11, 2001, and a year and a half later, war in Iraq. The Third Way gradually disappeared as a phrase in the Blair lexicography. Blair became George W. Bush's staunchest friend and ally.

Blair's embrace of Bush, and especially of the adventure in Iraq, puzzled many of his long-time American friends.[19] Whereas virtually all of the Democratic Party, including the Clintonites, came to despise Bush, Blair seemed to like him.[20] Yes, Democrats split on the Iraq War, and the many Democratic politicians who supported it turned to Blair for ratification and justification. It was easier in some Democratic circles to support Blair's war than Bush's. And hawkish Democrats, in their polemics with the Democratic left, would cite Blair's steadfastness as the model for the party to follow. All this occurred before things began going badly in Iraq.

Conservatives who mistrusted Blair because he was Clinton's friend came to revere him when he offered a similar loyalty to Bush. Blair confounded all believers in the classic political rule: "The enemy of my enemy is my friend". Where American presidents were concerned, Blair chose only to have friends. He was "The Accidental American", as the British writer and broadcaster James Naughtie perceptively called him in the title of his book on the Bush–Blair relationship.[21] In an on-line conversation with the *washingtonpost.com*, Naughtie—who refers throughout to Blair as "TB"—neatly summarized why Clinton's friend became Bush's ally:

> TB was worried about terrorism before 9/11 and had discovered—to his surprise and enormous relief—that he could get on well, personally, with GWB. So after 9/11, TB's fears about terrorism, his natural sympathy with the US after the horror—emotions run high in his politics—meant that he became convinced (unlike most of his Cabinet) that the "war on terror" was a battle that had to be fought side by side with Washington. If you point out to him, as I have done . . . that he made common cause with neo cons who came from an entirely different perspective, he will simply assert that he believed that approach to Saddam was correct and was therefore willing to go along with anyone who shared that view, whatever part of the political forest they crept out from. This doesn't convince most of his party—who think he placed the value on the special relationship with Washington far above sensible foreign policy—but it is the way he operates. He drew from the Thatcher years a belief in conviction politics, as they become known,

and he rather enjoys being the PM who goes against the grain. All these factors mean it is a potent mix. . . . That's why we are where we are, and why the relationship is simultaneously so strong and so puzzling.[22]

Blair's Churchillian imprimatur on Bush's foreign moves won him an ardent following on the American right, particularly among the neo-conservatives who came to see Blair as one of their own. Joe Conason, a staunch American opponent of the neo-cons and Bush, noted in the *Guardian* in 2003 that "to American conservatives who still revere Churchill as the stalwart icon of the Second World War and the Cold War, Blair's unhesitating toughness in the war on terrorism was inspirational".[23] Conason continued: "For anyone convinced that the US is called to defend the values of western civilization in a worldwide conflict, the Anglo-American alliance carries an almost anthemic resonance. Americans longing for an echo of Churchill also heard it in Blair's lonely and rather defiant appeals to his divided cabinet, his furious party, his reluctant fellow Britons and Europeans. In ways that Bush never could, he provided a high-minded tone to the drive for war".[24] Conason also caught the ambivalent mood within large parts of the American centre-left: "The anti-war demonstrators lustily vented their contempt and hatred for Bush", he wrote, "but always seemed to feel something more akin to disappointment in Blair".[25]

There was nothing implicit or indirect about the comparisons to Churchill. William Kristol, who can fairly be described as this moment's leading American neo-conservative writer, began an editorial tribute to Britain and Blair after the July 2005 London bombings by citing Churchill's May 13, 1940, speech calling for "victory at all costs, victory in spite of all terror, victory, however long and hard the road may be; for without victory there is no survival". To drive the comparison home, Kristol closed with Blair's resolute declaration after the bombings: "We will show through our spirit and dignity that our values will long outlast theirs. The purpose of terrorism is just that, to terrorise people, and we will not be terrorised"—and he praised Blair's response, calling it "necessary, and admirable".[26]

Writing after Blair's 2005 victory for the *Weekly Standard*, the neo-conservative journal founded by Kristol, Irwin M. Stelzer said that "from a purely American point of view, last week's British election was a win".[27] Stelzer, close both to both Blair and to über-publisher Rupert Murdoch, continued: "The voters not only failed to unseat Tony Blair for siding with America, and for declaring that neoconservative foreign policy sounds to him like progressive politics with a different name, they handed him an unprecedented third victory, leaving in place America's staunchest ally".[28]

America's conservatives certainly noticed that Blair was fighting not only on their side but also against the tide of his own party. After the 2002 Labour Party Conference, Stelzer cited Blair's declaration that "the basic values of America are our values too . . . and they are good values".[29] Stelzer noted that to Americans, the statement "sounds uncontroversial, even banal. But to many of the rank-and-file members of his party, any praise of America, especially in the context of a statement of support for our position on Iraq, is praise too far. As the *Financial Times* put it, 'they listened politely if sulkily'. Few things warm the heart of an American conservative more than a Labour leader who makes the left 'sulk'".[30]

If Blair had been happy to come to Clinton's rescue in 1998, he came to Bush's defence after what became known in the United States as the "Downing Street memo" had been leaked. This document, dated July 23, 2002, and prepared by Matthew Rycroft, Blair's private secretary for foreign affairs, informed the British ambassador in Washington, "There was a perceptible shift in attitude. Military action was now seen as inevitable. Bush wanted to remove Saddam, through military action, justified by the conjunction of terrorism and WMD. But the intelligence and facts were being fixed around the policy".[31] The story of the memo had broken during Blair's re-election campaign and caused a stir but no lasting damage. The American press was slow to cover the memo. Many reporters insisted that it revealed nothing new, but anti-Bush bloggers argued that the memo proved that the administration's public arguments for the war, including Saddam's alleged possession of those never-found weapons of mass destruction, had been a fraud. Bush, they insisted, was hell-bent on war, and was willing to "fix" the intelligence to do it. Slowly, the memo worked its way into the mainstream press.

Blair, shortly after his 2005 victory, flew to Washington to meet with Bush and was asked at a joint news conference with the president what the memo's notion of fixed facts meant. Blair replied: "Well, I can respond to that very easily. . . . No, the facts were not being fixed in any shape or form at all. And let me remind you that memorandum was written before we then went to the United Nations. Now, no one knows more intimately the discussions that we were conducting as two countries at the time than me. And the fact is that we decided to go to the United Nations".[32] And on Blair went, concluding that the problem was "that there was no way Saddam Hussein was ever going to change the way that he worked or the way that he acted".[33] Bush was grateful and insisted that "both of us didn't want to use our military. Nobody wants to commit military into combat".[34] The two allies stuck together, to the consternation of many on the American left.

Was this Bush–Blair alliance something special between the two men or was it the product of a larger Blair project, different but related to "The Project" that was the Third Way? Consider these questions posed by David Hughes, writing in the *Daily Mail*: "Is the Prime Minister really the President's poodle, slavishly willing to jump through any hoops at the request of the White House? Or does his lone support of the U.S. military effort, which is coming under fire across the world, represent a more equal partnership?" These questions were not posed about Blair's relationship with Bush. Rather they appeared in an article published on December 18, 1998, about Blair's staunch support for Bill Clinton's air attacks on Iraq in which Blair ordered

British forces to participate and, as Hughes wrote, "put their lives at risk in the skies over Iraq".[35] Note, by the way, the word "poodle", which so many think was invented to describe Blair's relationship with Bush.

"Why", veteran Labour left-winger and former cabinet minister Tony Benn wanted to know, "do you do everything you are told to do by President Clinton?" Hughes offered his own answer to the question: "There is no doubt Mr Blair has a warm personal relationship with Mr Clinton", he wrote, "as close in its way as that of Margaret Thatcher and Ronald Reagan in the 1980s".[36] But that did not explain it all. In light of subsequent history, it is worth recalling what Hughes wrote in—it is important to remember—1998. Years later, with the Iraq War in mind, the sentences have an almost eerie ring:

> Mr. Blair is determined to make an impact in North America. He knows the only British Prime Ministers who have ever registered with the American public are Winston Churchill and Thatcher. He wants to be the third.

> But Mr Blair's rock-solid support for the American military effort goes further than that. He is deeply unimpressed with the ability of the European Union to take any kind of collective action on the military front. Bosnia, and more recently Kosovo, spelled that out with brutal clarity. Therefore, if a tyrant like Saddam is to be hauled into line, he knows the Americans have to play the key role. Mr Blair, affronted by the contempt Saddam has shown for the United Nations, is determined to be alongside them, no matter how much criticism it attracts from other countries.

> It was noticeable that the French with whom Mr Blair struck a new deal on defence cooperation just a couple of weeks ago were the first to register their coolness towards the air assault on Iraq. Mr Blair feels instinctively that he can rely more on the American allies than those in Europe and he is determined to show they can rely on him.[37]

The roots of Blair's friendship with Bush, in other words, lay in the strong bonds he built with Clinton. This may not have made sense to Bush's American critics, many of whom were Blair's friends, but it did make sense to a British prime minister determined to stand with America. Nor was Blair's Churchillian rhetoric during the Iraq War anything new. During the showdown between the west and Yugoslav President Slobodan Milosević over Kosovo, Blair sounded as tough as General Patton. "He's got to be in no doubt this is not brinkmanship by us", Blair said, speaking of Milosević for himself and Clinton. "We are prepared to see this thing through. We are prepared to use force if necessary".[38] During the crises in the Balkans in the 1990s, it was often *Blair* who urged Clinton to pursue the tougher course. And Blair's rhetoric on Iraq during the Bush years reflected the same devotion to humanitarian intervention he endorsed during the Balkan wars. "Ridding the world of Saddam", Blair declared shortly before the start of the Iraq War, "would be an act of humanity".[39] He might have said the same about Milosević.

What others saw as inconsistency—how in the world could Blair be loyal to Clinton's moderate progressivism and Bush's intense conservativism?—was quite consistent in Blair's terms. As Thomas Quinn points out in Chapter 1, Blair developed a "liberal interventionist foreign policy". His loyalty turned out *not* to be personal, and it was *not* primarily about a global political movement. Instead, Blair was loyal to the United States itself and to an assertive world role for an America that would work in partnership with Britain. The lessons he drew from the humanitarian military interventions in the 1990s was that more such interventions were required. The United States and Britain had the responsibility to alter bad regimes or their behaviour. Who was a more appropriate candidate for behaviour modification or ouster than Saddam Hussein? Hughes's analysis of Blair's motivations in 1998 was still operative in 2001 and beyond. "If a tyrant like Saddam is to be hauled into line, he knows the Americans have to play the key role. Mr Blair, affronted by the contempt Saddam has shown for the United Nations, is determined to be alongside them, no matter how much criticism it attracts from other countries".[40] Or from Blair's own country. Or from many of his progressive friends in the United States.

It is worth recalling that Blair was not alone among the Third Wayers and moderate progressives in supporting Bush on Iraq. Bill Clinton did, too. Many moderate Democrats—notably senators Joe Lieberman, Hillary Rodham Clinton and Joe Biden—also supported the invasion. But few among them demonstrated the loyalty to Bush that Blair did. Few seemed to trust him as much. Few played as prominent a role in offering public justifications for the action: "Iraq is not the only regime with WMD", Blair said on March 18, 2003, "But back away now from this confrontation and future conflicts will be infinitely worse and more devastating".[41] Few stuck with the policy more doggedly after it began to go sour.

By 2005, Blair, having pursued what was by his lights a thoroughly consistent course, had traded many of his old friends for new ones. His role in the world as a leader of the centre-left took second place to his commitment as a partner in a new global mission for democracy and against terror. While Blair's embrace of Bush and his adventure in Iraq bothered some of his American friends in the Democratic party, other early allies stuck with him. Particularly within the Democratic Leadership Council and in other centrist and hawkish circles, Blair continued to be hailed as a prophet. Bill Clinton not only stuck with him, but campaigned for Blair's re-election in 2005. It was certainly odd that Blair called upon a former *American* president to reassure disaffected left-of-centre Labour voters who disliked Blair's alliance with Bush. But there it was. "*Our people* get easily disillusioned", Clinton declared, piped in by satellite from New York to a rally at the Old Vic in London. "People fall into the trap of thinking it doesn't matter which party you vote for. If you believe that, you ought to look at the difference in the US between now and four years ago".[42] It was a neat bit of political jujitsu that perhaps only Clinton could pull off: the former American president was appealing to the crowd's *anti-Bush* sentiments ("look at the difference in the US between now and four years ago") in urging it to re-elect Bush's friend Blair. It could work because Clinton, despite his support for the Iraq War, was seen as Bush's antithesis in Britain no less than in the United States.

Many other American centrists continued to laud the Blair formula, praising Blair for sticking with the Clinton approach when many American Democrats were abandoning it. "Blair has left the right with no openings", marvelled Bruce Reed, the Democratic Leadership Council's president.[43] But on much of the American left, the most important event of the British election was not Blair's victory but the leaking of that Downing Street memo. The American left did not much take to Blair's defence of his and Bush's Iraq decisions. The memo had the lovely incidental effect of producing the most searching discussions of the differences between British and American English since George Bernard Shaw declared our two nations divided by a common language. Bush's defenders insisted that the left was misunderstanding that word "fixed". Writing in the conservative *Weekly Standard,* columnist Tod Lindberg insisted, "'Fix' here is clearly meant in its traditional sense, in the sort of English spoken by Oxbridge dons and MI6 directors—to make fast, to set in order, to arrange".[44] A brave effort, perhaps, but it did little to persuade Bush's critics, or Blair's.

Still, Blair retained an appeal to the American centre-left, as he did to enough of the British centre-left to win re-election. At times grudgingly, American liberals and Democrats appreciated in Blair the very trait that Anthony King identifies in Chapter 7: the skill to move progressive politics from an emphasis on old commitments to an engagement with new problems. The pragmatism that King identifies with Blair has been a core, if often contested, commitment of American liberalism going back to William James, John Dewey and Arthur Schlesinger Jr. "Rather than seeing life as being governed by fixed and permanent principles, as was the case in traditional philosophy", the historian John Patrick Diggins has written, "the pragmatists saw change and flux everywhere, and they looked to scientific philosophy to enable people to relate better to an environment of transition and transformation".[45] This openness to "transition and transformation", to "change and flux", was at the heart of Blairism. It was why the Democratic Centre stuck with Blair so ardently, and why American liberals and significant parts of the American left could not turn on Blair entirely, despite his friendship with a president whose defeat they so devoutly wished. In many ways, Blair's American friends on the left were much like his one-time sympathizers in Britain: they found him frustrating, they wondered about his unwavering commitment to Bush, but they did not want him to go. It is likely that many of Blair's early friends were happy he won again, and happy he got a come-uppance with a reduced majority.

For so many, Blair was still the leader who pushed centre-left parties everywhere to face the era's essential questions—again, it was as much about asking the right questions as about giving definitive answers. Will Marshall, president of the centrist Progressive Policy Institute, offered as good a list as anyone: "How can the left compete in this era of global markets? How do you find the right balance between enterprise and social conscience? How do you create a sustainable progressivism?"[46] It was, again, a matter of "the project", and Blair had pulled it off, electorally at least, better than anyone else around.

Writing shortly before the election in the *American Prospect*, the flagship magazine of the contemporary American liberal mainstream, James Ledbetter saw Blair as flawed, successful and a tragic figure, all at the same time. Ledbetter hinted at Blair's likely victory because of the competence of his (and Gordon Brown's) economic management. "If opposition to the war isn't enough to turn Blair out", he wrote, "it's because butter is ultimately more important than guns".[47] And he made clear that frustration with Blair *on* the American left is tempered by a belief that it is mightily difficult at this moment to govern *from* the left. "The tragic irony for Tony Blair, very much like it was for Bill Clinton", wrote Ledbetter, a senior editor at *Time* magazine, "is that the price of political success seems to be that you don't get to do very much, outside of running a good economy and keeping the right wing at bay while stealing its more palatable ideas".[48] But is that all there is to Blair and the Third Way—or whatever he would now wish to call his venture? The final irony may be that the failures of Blair's new friend George W. Bush may bring new lustre to the original project Blair and his old friend Clinton pioneered. Despite the ambiguities of their politics, Blair and Clinton always believed in a strong public sector that could empower individuals. They believed in a government that could create public goods and not just protect private interests. Bush's approach was badly dented by the failed response of the federal government to Hurricane Katrina and by his administration's poor planning and execution in Iraq.

If disillusionment with Bush gives rise to a call for a new approach to government, those inventing the alternatives are more likely to build on than reject what Blair tried to create. In his 1998 *Washington Post* article, Blair spoke of "the centre-left's traditional values of solidarity, social justice, responsibility and opportunity" and the dangers of "a new laissez-faire right championing narrow individualism and a belief that free markets are the answer to every problem".[49] These are themes likely to resonate again. The politics at the end of the first decade of the twenty-first century could well look like the politics of the last decade of the twentieth. Blair might come to hope that his legacy is defined not by his alliance with Bush but by his role in creating the alternatives to the Bush Era. But however Blair's legacy is judged, he is in so many ways—notably in his belief in both equality and achievement—quintessentially American. If Blair's purpose was, as the *Daily Mail's* David Hughes suggested, "to make an impact in North America", he has already succeeded.

Notes

1. David Miller, "Blair should read the polls", *Guardian*, October 3, 2001.
2. Clinton did not use the word "comrade", but addressing the 2002 Labour Party Conference, his opening words immediately struck a chord with the assembled throng: "Conference, Clinton, Bill. Arkansas CLP". See Simon Hoggart, "Swooning Blackpool surrenders to the seducer from Arkansas CLP", *Guardian*, October 3, 2002.
3. Clinton attended an early meeting of the new Labour cabinet and joked about wanting a 179-seat majority like Blair's. See Simon Hoggart, "They smiled and smiled and . . . ", *Guardian*, May 30, 1997.
4. For example, I first met Labour strategist Philip Gould at a Little Rock restaurant, where he was dining towards the end of the 1992 campaign with Clintonites James Carville and George Stephanopoulos.
5. See Sidney Blumenthal, *The Clinton Wars: An Insiders Account of the White House Years* (London: Penguin, 2005).
6. See Bill Clinton, *Between Hope and History: Meeting America's Challenges for the 21st Century* (New York: Time Books, 1996); and Tony Blair, *New Britain: My Vision of a Young Country* (London: Fourth Estate, 1996).
7. See David Marquand, *The Progressive Dilemma: From Lloyd George to Blair* (London: Phoenix Books, 1999); Neal Lawson and Neil Sherlock, *The Progressive Century: The Future of the Centre-Left in Britain* (Houndmills, Basingstoke: Palgrave, 2001). For example, Blair chose as his intellectual mentor Roy Jenkins, the biographer of Henry Herbert Asquith, the prime minister in that reforming Liberal government and also leading advocate of co-operation between parties on the centre-left. Lord Jenkins, as he later became, was the first leader of the Social Democratic Party (SDP), which broke away from Labour in 1980. He joined the Liberal Democrats, the result of the merger of the Liberal Party and SDP in 1988. He regularly met with Blair and chaired a commission on electoral reform, which reported in 1998. He died in January 2003. See Anthony Seldon, *Blair* (London: Free Press, 2005), chap. 20.
8. Anthony Giddens, "After the Left's paralysis", *New Statesman*, May 1, 1998.
9. Gerard Baker and Tom Baldwin, "Hail to the chiefs: how Americans lead the way in the dark art of politics", *The Times*, April 25, 2005.
10. See John Bartle and Dylan Griffiths, eds, *Political Communications Transformed: From Morrison to Mandelson* (Basingstoke: Palgrave, 2001).
11. Tony Blair, "Third way, better way", *Washington Post*, September 27, 1998.
12. E. J. Dionne Jr, "The Big Idea", *Washington Post*, August 9, 1998.
13. Dionne, "Big Idea".
14. Dionne, "Big Idea".
15. See Matthew d'Ancona, "Battered but unbowed, Mr Blair beckons us into unknown territory. The voters may think he is a liar, but they still acknowledge his charismatic leadership—as does Gordon Brown", *Sunday Telegraph*, May 1, 2005.
16. Rory Carroll, "Blair spells out vision for global partnership", *Guardian*, September 22, 1998.
17. Bill Clinton and Tony Blair, "Strengthening Democracy in the Global Economy: An Opening Dialogue". The full text of the New York Law School speeches is available at http://www.uhuh.com/laws/3w092198.htm.
18. Clinton and Blair, "Strengthening Democracy".
19. See Seldon, *Blair*, especially chap. 38; and Peter Riddell, *Hug Them Close: Blair, Clinton, Bush and the Special Relationship* (London: Politicos, 2005).
20. Seldon, *Blair*, chap. 38.

21. James Naughtie, *The Accidental American: Tony Blair and the Presidency* (Basingstoke: Macmillan, 2004).
22. The transcript is available at http://www.washingtonpost.com/wp-dyn/articles/A21050-2004Sep14.html.
23. Joe Conason, "Love ya Tony", *Guardian*, April 23, 2003.
24. Conason, "Love ya Tony".
25. Conason, "Love ya Tony".
26. William Kristol, "Victory in spite of all terror", *Weekly Standard*, July 18, 2005.
27. Irwin M. Stelzer, "Blair's last hurrah: America's staunchest ally hangs on to 10 Downing Street, weakened but not defeated", *Weekly Standard*, May 16, 2005.
28. Stelzer, "Blair's last hurrah".
29. Irwin M. Stelzer, "Tony Blair vs the Labour Party", *Weekly Standard*, October 14, 2002.
30. Stelzer, "Tony Blair vs the Labour Party".
31. See Michael Smith, "Blair planned Iraq war from start", *Sunday Times*, May 1, 2005.
32. Dana Milbank, "Seldom discussed elephant moves into public's view", *Washington Post*, June 8, 2005.
33. Milbank, "Seldom discussed elephant".
34. See "Transcript: Joint press conference with President Bush and Prime Minister Blair", *Washington Post*, June 7, 2005, http://www.washingtonpost.com/wp-dyn/content/article/2005/06/07/AR2005060701118_pf.html.
35. David Hughes, "Blair cements his Atlantic alliance", *Daily Mail*, December 18, 1998.
36. Hughes, "Blair cements his Atlantic alliance".
37. Hughes, "Blair cements his Atlantic alliance".
38. Mark Dowdney, "Rat on Nato and Face Blitz", *Mirror*, October 14, 1998.
39. See "Blair: UN must deal with Iraq", BBC News Online, February 15, 2003, http://news.bbc.co.uk/1/hi/uk_politics/2765151.stm.
40. Hughes, "Blair cements his Atlantic alliance".
41. See the Number 10 website, http://www.number-10.gov.uk/output/Page3294.asp.
42. Tania Branigan, "Parties unite to fight poverty: Clinton joins campaign", *Guardian*, April 25, 2005; emphasis added.
43. Dan Balz, "Democrats could profit from Blair's Labor", *Washington Post*, May 8, 2005.
44. Tod Lindberg, "A fix on Downing Street", *Weekly Standard*, June 20, 2005.
45. John Patrick Diggins, *The Promise of Pragmatism: Modernism and the Crisis of Knowledge and Authority* (Chicago: Chicago University Press, 1995).
46. E. J. Dionne Jr, "The Blair polarities", *Washington Post*, May 6, 2005.
47. James Ledbetter, "Tony Blair, a k a Bush's poodle, is not a beloved figure as British elections approach. But that still puts him above the competition", *American Prospect*, May 6, 2005.
48. Ledbetter, "Tony Blair, a k a Bush's poodle".
49. Blair, "Third way, better way".

9

New Labour's Hegemony: Erosion or Extension?

Ivor Crewe

Assessing the significance of the 2001 election result was relatively straightforward. It was a "no change" election, at which the main parties' share of the vote edged up or down by no more than a couple of percentage points, exceptionally few seats changed hands and Labour's massive parliamentary majority was barely dented. The only major discontinuity was the precipitous fall in turnout to the lowest level since 1918. That aside, the 2001 election consolidated New Labour's electoral dominance and suggested that the 1997 election might have been that rare phenomenon, a "realigning" election, which was to transform the electoral and party landscape for a generation.

Assessing the long-term significance of the 2005 election is considerably more difficult, for three reasons. First, the changes in 2005 were much more substantial than in 2001 but were not critical to the result or to the relative strengths of the parties in parliament. Stability of outcome was accompanied by much more turbulence in the electorate. Labour's parliamentary majority was slashed from 167 to 66 as a result of a 5.5 point fall in its national vote and the loss of 47 seats.[1] The Conservatives made 33 net gains, their first advance of any significance in over two decades, recapturing some of the ground they lost in 1997. The Liberal Democrats made 12 net gains and their tally of 62 seats constituted the largest centre-party block in parliament since 1923. Moreover, for the first time since the 1920s the Liberal Democrats gained more seats and votes from Labour than from the Conservatives, and they replaced the Conservatives as the main opposition to Labour in its urban heartlands. The fringe parties had their best election since 1918.

Second, although the electoral shifts were sharper than in 2001, they did not point to any clear conclusions about the long-term performance or prospects of the mainstream parties. Each party could find grounds for optimism, yet the election was notable for the undeniable sense of disappointment that all three main parties (and the Nationalists in Scotland and Wales) felt about the result. Labour under Blair may have won an unprecedented third consecutive term of office, but only with the aid of an electoral system whose huge pro-Labour bias converted a mere 35 per cent of the vote into 55 per cent of the seats. However, Labour will fight the next election under a new leader, almost certainly Gordon Brown, and thus without the handicap of Tony Blair's massive loss of trust among a large section of voters.

The Conservatives may have gained 33 seats, but they need to win another 127 seats to secure a bare overall majority: at this rate of progress it will take until some time after 2020 and another four elections. But the Conservatives will fight the next election under a new leader determined to find a strategy for accelerating the modest recovery of 2005.

The Liberal Democrats may be the strongest third party in parliament for over eighty years, but their vote share rose by only 4 points to 22 per cent, below the levels achieved by the Liberal–SDP Alliance in 1983 (25 per cent) and 1987 (23 per cent). This was despite the uniquely favourable circumstances of an unpopular government, a deeply distrusted prime minister, an uninspiring leader of the opposition and a Conservative party widely perceived to be unprepared for government. The general election of 2005 was the first in living memory to be dominated by an issue (Iraq) on which both Labour and the Conservatives took the unpopular position while the Liberal Democrats sided with the majority. Yet in votes, as well as seats, the Liberal Democrats remained very much the third party. They had their best chance in a generation to replace, or at least progress to being poised to replace, one of the major parties, and they blew it. However, at the next election the Liberal Democrats will have opened a second front as the main challenger in almost as many Labour as Conservative seats, which may prove the opportunity to make the parliamentary breakthrough which has eluded the political centre since the 1920s.

Third, interpreting the 2005 election is complicated by the absence of any consistent national pattern of change. Labour's loss of support was the most consistent feature of the election, but the scale and beneficiaries of the losses varied unpredictably from one constituency to another.[2] As Anthony King shows in Chapter 7, local factors seemed to matter more than usually in 2005. There was no single electoral battlefield, at which one party advanced and the other retreated in a uniform orderly fashion but instead, as in real war, a multiplication of battle sites and side skirmishes with unexpectedly successful assaults and defences from one locality to the next.

Unlike in 2001, the signals from the 2005 election are too weak, contradictory and particular to send a clear message about the durability of New Labour's electoral dominance. There is a case for interpreting the 2005 election as the beginning of the erosion of New Labour's short-lived dominance. There is also a case for interpreting it as a hiccup in the extension of what will prove to be New Labour's long-lasting hegemony. This chapter teases out the evidence for "erosion" versus "extension".

Interpreting Elections

How can one tell whether 2005 marks the erosion or extension of New Labour's hegemony? The short answer, of course, is that there is no way of knowing. The historical significance of an election is shaped by subsequent elections, whose results cannot be forecast.[3] The best-planned electoral strategies are waylaid by events beyond the control of government and parties, including wars, natural disasters, financial crashes and unexpected deaths. The only safe prediction about the next election is that in the intervening period the unpredictable will happen: when Labour was re-elected in May 2001 nobody forecast 9/11 and the chain of events that led to the government's backing of the US invasion of Iraq, which so influenced the 2005 election result.[4]

There is no way of knowing, but there are ways of arriving at credible probabilities. One useful approach is to think of any election result as the product of long-term "structural" factors and short-term "campaign" factors. The former consist of the enduring features of the political landscape, barely changing from one election to the next, which determine the underlying bedrock support for each party—their "normal" vote. They include the demographic composition of the electorate, in particular the class, religious and age structure; the parties' location on the ideological spectrum; the electoral system; and the partisan affiliations of the national media. The latter consist of powerful but short-lived influences on the vote which are limited to one election only but can supplement or erode a party's normal vote by a sufficient margin to make the critical difference to the result. They include the state of the economy; the policy issues of the campaign; the reputation of the party leaders and the parties' cohesion and organizational effectiveness.

In real elections the distinction between structural and campaign factors is not always as clearcut as described above. Some campaign factors are repeated in a second or even third election and may develop an enduring impact. For example, 2005 was the third successive election held in times of economic strength and stability, and this may have changed the traditional relationship between a government's economic record and its electoral reward or punishment.[5] Some structural factors imperceptibly but progressively change the balance of underlying party support: for example, the steady decline of the industrial working class from the 1960s eroded the natural electoral base of Old Labour. And some structural factors can be deliberately changed from one election to the next by the parties themselves, as the ideological re-positioning of the Labour Party under Tony Blair between 1994 and 1997 demonstrates.

Nonetheless, the model provides a framework for analysing the long-term meaning of the 2005 election result. It prompts the question of whether 2005 was a "transitional" election or a "deviating" election—or whether Labour's loss of support was a structural erosion of the party's electoral foundations or merely a sharp but short-term protest which does not threaten its underlying normal vote. It also encourages an analysis of the opportunities for the three parties to shift the underlying balance of party support between now and 2009/10 (when the next general election is likely to take place).

New Labour's Dominance: Foundations

To judge whether New Labour's electoral dominance was dealt a fatal blow in 2005 it is first necessary to understand how it came about.[6] The spectacularly successful electoral strategy that led to New Labour's landslide of 1997, and its consolidation in 2001, contained four elements. The first was the party's relocation on the ideological spectrum. It stopped being a traditional social democratic party, indisputably left of centre, and became a pragmatic, "progressive" party occupying a wide swathe of ground stretching all the way from the moderate left to the moderate right. Under Blair's driving leadership between 1994 and 1997, it ostentatiously ditched its time-honoured but increasingly unpopular support for nationalization, centralized economic planning, high taxation and the extension of trade-union rights—under Neil Kinnock's leadership it had already abandoned unilateral nuclear disarmament and withdrawal from the European Union. It embraced the pro-business principles of markets, competition and enterprise and accepted most of the Thatcher governments' economic reforms. It promised not to increase income tax or spend beyond the Conservative government's commitments. It claimed that social justice could be combined with the efficiency of market capitalism and that New Labour embodied the joining of the two.[7]

Second, it established closer relations with the Liberal Democrats. It initiated a cross-party partnership of support for constitutional reform, including devolved parliaments, reform of the Lords, freedom of information, a Human Rights Act and proportional representation for some elections—all dear to the hearts of Liberal Democrats—and hinted at the possible adoption of PR for Westminster elections too.

The third element of its strategy followed from the first two. By its clear shifts of position it sought to reach out to groups of the electorate who rarely if ever voted Labour, or even thought of it. In particular it made a pitch at the "middle England" of average-income, tax-paying, owner-occupying, aspirational, non-union families in the prosperous suburban and small-town South and Midlands. It believed it could become a one-nation party appealing to all classes, retaining the loyalty of its traditional blue-collar supporters while bringing in the vote of the swelling ranks of office workers, service staff, technicians and the professions.

Fourth, New Labour's electoral ascendancy was underpinned by an electoral system which became hugely biased in its favour. Much of the bias arose from population movement, but part was due to anti-Conservative tactical voting encouraged by New Labour's overtures to the Liberal Democrats.

In 1997 the strategy worked, although it was given a major boost by the failures and petty scandals of the 1992–97 Conservative government, in particular its severe loss of reputation for economic competence after Black Wednesday in September 1992 and its endless internal splits over Europe and Thatcher's legacy (see Philip Norton in Chapter 2).

Evidence of Erosion

A few features of the 2005 election result suggest that the electoral dominance New Labour so carefully constructed in 1997 may have been destroyed after only eight years. The first and most obvious is the sheer scale

of the haemorrhaging of the Labour vote. By historical standards the 5.5 percentage point drop in Labour's vote share is large: no Labour government has
incurred such a fall in a single election and the Labour governments of 1951,
1970 and 1979 were each ousted by smaller falls.[8] In the course of only eight
years the Labour vote has slumped from 13.5 million in 1997 (43.2 per cent)
to 9.6 million (35.2 per cent), a loss of almost four million or three out of
every ten people who voted Labour in 1997. If the 2005 rebuff to Labour was
a protest vote, it was a very large and deep-seated protest indeed. Expressed
as a proportion of the electorate, Labour's losses are even more dramatic—
from 30.8 per cent of all registered electors in 1997 to 21.6 per cent in 2005.
This was the lowest proportion of eligible voters on which any government
with a working majority has ever been elected. It is hardly a testimony to the
success of a "one nation" electoral strategy, intended to reach out to parts of
the electorate that Old Labour had been unable to penetrate. None of these
statistics demonstrate that Labour cannot recover at the next election,
although it is worth noting that the last occasion on which a government saw
its parliamentary majority significantly reduced at one election only to
recover at the next was the Liberal administration of 1859–65.

The second intimation of an unravelling of Labour's electoral dominance
comes from the geographical pattern of Labour's losses. Much attention has
been paid to the above-average falls in the Labour vote in constituencies with
concentrations of students and of Muslim voters. But this was almost certainly a protest vote against the government's record on Iraq, tuition fees and
anti-terrorist measures and benefited the Liberal Democrats and, in a few
places, Respect, the anti-war party, but never the Conservatives. More significant is the geography of Labour's losses of votes and seats to the Conservatives. The largest net swings from Labour to Conservative were in London,
the South East and the Eastern regions and within these regions in the London commuter belt of outer suburbs, New Towns and the M25 borderlands.[9]
These are the modestly affluent but far from posh slices of the Home Coun-
ties in which the Conservatives under Margaret Thatcher made deep inroads
into the Labour vote in 1979 and 1983 and which Blair snatched back with
his appeal to "middle England" in 1997.

It is not immediately obvious why compared with the rest of the country voters in these areas were even more alienated by Labour and more
attracted to the Conservatives. Indeed, it is something of a puzzle. The two
Blair administrations have presided over an unprecedented and uninter-
rupted period of low inflation, low unemployment, low interest rates and, by
historical standards, high economic growth. The areas which recorded the
largest swings from Labour to Conservative are economically the most
dynamic in the United Kingdom. Part of New Labour's electoral strategy was
to persuade middle-income voters that Labour, not the Conservatives, were
now the party of sound economic management, and the campaign polls of
2005 suggest that the electorate agreed. Why were voters in these high-swing
constituencies so ungrateful? One can but speculate. It may have been the

flip-side of prosperity: a combination of salary drift into the 40 per cent tax bracket, high property prices, higher property taxes, a congested and expensive public transport system. In some largely white skilled working-class constituencies, especially the New Towns, the Conservative play on asylum seekers may have paid off.[10] We simply do not yet know, and the erratic pattern of swings across similar and neighbouring constituencies makes firm conclusions impossible. But what we can infer is that a successful economic record and a long-standing reputation for economic competence, which has been a linchpin of New Labour's strategy for electoral dominance, was not enough to staunch a widespread loss of Labour votes in 2005. Stronger countervailing forces were at work.

The third indication of breakdown in Labour's electoral strategy is the success of the Liberal Democrats in Labour areas. This time Labour paid a price for its shift to the ideological centre. In 1997 and, more noticeably, 2001, the main impact was a decline in turnout in safe Labour areas, with almost no effect on Labour's tally of seats. This was well worth trading for the tactical votes of Liberal Democrats in marginal seats where Labour was in close contention with the Conservatives. In 2005, some traditional Labour supporters, especially in the big northern cities switched to the Liberal Democrats or, if they were Muslims in Muslim seats, to Respect. Some did so because of the Iraq War, tuition fees and related distrust of Tony Blair. But the Liberal Democrats' advance against Labour in local elections in the urban north, where they took over the town halls in Liverpool, Oldham, Newcastle and Sheffield, began well before the Iraq invasion and the controversy over university tuition fees, and reflected the new acceptability of the Liberal Democrats to some traditional Labour voters. Surveys showed that voters placed the Liberal Democrats to the left of Labour and that the views of Liberal Democrat supporters were similar to and sometimes to the left of Labour supporters.[11] On public services, taxation, the environment and human rights, as well as Iraq and fees, the Liberal Democrats have established themselves in the eyes of voters as the true party of the moderate left. In 2001 the Liberal Democrats gained one Labour seat and came within 15 points of winning ten more. In 2005 they gained twelve seats from Labour (including seven of its ten best prospects) and came within 15 percentage points of winning nineteen more. Unless New Labour can restore its informal anti-Conservative alliance with the Liberal Democrats it will be vulnerable on two flanks in 2009/10.

Evidence of Extension

In 2005 voters turned against Labour in large numbers and some features of the anti-Labour swing hint at the unravelling of New Labour's electoral strategy and the erosion of its dominance. But the balance of evidence suggests that Labour's underlying support and structural hegemony remained intact. The pollsters ICM found that voters overwhelmingly expected Labour to win, as shown in the following table:

Table 9.1 Expected General Election Results, 2005

Q. What do you think is the most likely outcome of the election?

	All	Lab	Con	Lib Dem
A clear Labour victory	26	43	14	27
A narrow Labour victory	52	51	59	56
A hung parliament	8	1	12	9
A Conservative victory	5	2	14	4

Source: ICM/Guardian polls, May 1–3, 2005.

Most voters were disappointed with the Labour government, particularly with its record on public services; and some voters, including Labour supporters, were very angry with the government over Iraq. They were determined to give the government a bloody nose and succeeded. But they did not want to land a knock-out punch.

Two features of public opinion strongly suggest that Labour significantly under-polled its natural vote in 2005. First, when people were asked the "forced-choice" question (would they prefer a Labour Government led by Tony Blair or a Conservative Government led by Michael Howard?), Labour led the Conservatives by 52 to 35 per cent.[12] Of course, in the actual election most voters did not see the choice in such stark terms, given the near-universal expectation that Labour would win, and record numbers opted to vote for the smaller parties that had no prospect of forming a government. But the figures suggest that in 2005 there remained many more anti-Conservative than anti-Labour voters in the electorate and that if the campaign polls had suggested a much closer result, Labour would have lost fewer votes to the Liberal Democrats and smaller parties on the left.[13] The voters Labour lost switched to other parties on the left, not to the Conservatives, and many would have stayed loyal if they had thought that the Conservative party had a serious prospect of winning power.[14]

The data on party identification in 2005 point to a similar conclusion. YouGov asked people to say, in addition to which party they intended to vote for, which party, if any, they "generally" identify with. The answer to this question (which was worded differently to that reported by Nicholas Allen in Table 3.2) was Labour 32 per cent, Conservative 24 per cent, Liberal Democrat 10 per cent, some other party 4 per cent, no party 30 per cent. Among the 70 per cent who identified with a party, Labour led the Conservatives by 46 to 34 per cent. If every voter had voted for the party they generally sympathized and instinctively sided with, Labour would have won with an even larger majority than in 1997. But in 2005, only 72 per cent of Labour identifiers voted Labour and of those that chose not to, almost half voted Liberal Democrat, largely out of opposition to the invasion of Iraq and their consequent disapproval of Tony Blair.[15] Thus Labour retains a substantially larger pool of potential voters than the Conservative party does, but it failed to mobilize them in 2005.

Many of the factors that fuelled the "progressive" voters' anti-Labour protest in 2005 will have disappeared by the next election. The Iraq invasion will be six years old and American and British troops will probably have ceased active operation there. Higher tuition fees will have been in place for three years and the government is unlikely to risk raising them again before the election. Most certain of all, Tony Blair has announced that he will *not* lead Labour into the next election. Of course, there will be new causes for disappointment among Labour identifiers by 2009/10, such as an economic downturn or unsatisfactory public services perhaps, but they are unlikely to pack the same emotional charge as the Iraq War and its plausible but misleading advocate, Tony Blair, did in 2005.

The New Labour hegemony is partly based on a favourable underlying distribution of "natural" Labour and Conservative predispositions in the electorate (or, it would probably be more accurate to say, anti-Labour and anti-Conservative predispositions) and polls suggest that this distribution did not shift in 2005. As mentioned earlier, it is also dependent on the marked bias of an electoral system, which since 1997 has delivered many more seats to Labour than to the Conservatives (let alone the Liberal Democrats) for the same number of votes. In 1997 Labour won 63.4 per cent of the seats (in the United Kingdom) with 43.2 per cent of the vote and in 2001 62.5 per cent of the seats with 40.7 per cent of the vote. In 2005 the bias was only fractionally less: Labour won 55.1 per cent of the seats on a 35.2 per cent vote. Expressed another way, it took 96,378 votes to elect a Liberal Democrat MP, 44,521 votes to elect a Conservative MP but only 26,877 votes to elect a Labour MP. The bias comes about because Labour seats typically have smaller electorates and lower turnout than Conservative seats and because since 1997 the Labour Party has distributed its vote across constituencies more efficiently, winning a larger number with small majorities.[16] This has been aided by a modest level of anti-Conservative tactical voting by Labour and Liberal Democrat supporters willing to support the other party where it was clearly better positioned to defeat a Conservative MP or hold off a Conservative challenge (see Anthony King in Chapter 7).

As a result, if the next election were held on the current constituency boundaries, Labour would again enter the race with a huge advantage over the Conservatives. This is evident from Table 9.2, which estimates the impact of a uniform national swing from Labour to Conservative on the distribution of seats.

Table 9.2 shows, first, that it would not be enough for the Conservatives to draw level with Labour in the national vote (each winning 33.8 per cent) to have a prospect of office. Labour would remain firmly in government with an overall majority of twenty-four, which, while modest, is sufficient to survive a full parliamentary term. John Major's 1992 government lasted five years with an initial overall majority of twenty-two. Second, for Labour to lose its overall majority the Conservatives would need a swing of 2.3 per cent and a lead of 1.7 per cent. But Labour would remain by far the largest party,

Table 9.2 Relationship Between Seats and Votes, 2005

Swing from Lab to Con	Con lead	Percentages				Seats								Outcome
		Con	Lab	LD	Other	Con	Lab	LD	Nat	Other	Majority	Lab minus Con		
0	-2.9	32.3	35.2	22.1	10.4	197	356	62	9	22	Lab 66	159	Lab Government
1.0	-0.9	33.3	34.2	22.1	10.4	216	340	59	9	22	Lab 34	124	Lab Government
1.5	0.0	33.8	33.8	22.1	10.4	221	336	58	9	22	Lab 24	115	Lab Government
2.0	1.1	34.3	33.2	22.1	10.4	229	327	58	10	22	Lab 8	98	Lab Government
2.3	1.7	34.6	32.9	22.1	10.4	234	322	58	10	22	Lab -2	88	Hung: Lab–Lib Dem Government
3.0	3.1	35.3	32.2	22.1	10.4	247	309	58	10	22	Lab -15	62	Hung: Lab–Lib Dem Government
4.0	5.1	36.3	31.2	22.1	10.4	262	293	59	10	22	Lab -31	31	Hung: Lab–Lib Dem Government
4.8	7.1	37.5	30.4	22.1	10.4	279	277	58	10	22	Con -45	-2	Hung: Con in office?
5.0	7.1	37.3	30.2	22.1	10.4	282	274	59	9	22	Con -42	-8	Hung: Con in office?
6.0	9.1	38.3	29.2	22.1	10.4	300	258	57	9	22	Con -24	-42	Hung: Con in office?
7.0	11.1	39.3	28.2	22.1	10.4	313	245	57	9	22	Con -11	-68	Hung: Con in office?
7.4	11.9	39.7	27.8	22.1	10.4	324	234	57	9	22	Con 2	-90	Con Government
8.0	13.1	40.3	27.2	22.1	10.4	329	227	59	9	22	Con 12	-102	Con Government
9.0	15.1	41.3	26.2	22.1	10.4	344	213	57	9	23	Con 42	-131	Con Government

Notes: The table assumes a uniform national swing. The Liberal Democrat, Nationalists and other parties' votes are assumed not to change. The Speaker's seat is counted as Labour.

with eighty-eight more seats than the Conservatives (322 as against 224) and could thus continue in office by winning the support of one or more of the smaller parties (probably the Liberal Democrats).

Third, to become the largest party in the House of Commons, the Conservatives would need a swing of 4.8 per cent and a lead of 7.1 per cent. This is a sizeable swing, achieved by the Conservatives only twice since the war, in 1970 and 1979. Moreover, the Conservatives would fall far short of an overall majority. It would not be enough to catapult the Conservatives into office unless they outbid Labour for the support of fifty-eight Liberal Democrat MPs. Finally, the Conservatives would need a swing of 7.4 per cent and a lead of 11.9 per cent for a bare overall majority in parliament. For a more secure overall majority it would need a swing of between 8 and 9 per cent. Swings on this scale are well beyond anything the Conservatives have achieved at a single election since the war (although Labour did in 1945 and 1997).

The next election will be fought on new boundaries, but these are unlikely to correct the bias more than marginally. The reason is that the continuing population drift from north to south and from urban Labour areas to small town and rural Conservative areas will again generate smaller-sized electorates in Labour than Conservative seats. According to a recent analysis, if the 2005 election had been fought on the new boundaries, Labour's majority would have only fallen from sixty-six to fifty-two and even this small correction may diminish further as a result of further population drift in the years up to 2009/10.[17] The Conservatives will therefore still require an 11 per cent lead and 7 per cent swing from Labour to gain a bare overall majority.[18] Such is the Everest that the Conservatives must climb to win the next election.

But Everest is conquered from time to time, as 1997 showed. Strongly-led, disciplined parties, with a realistic analysis of their electoral situation and a clear strategy for change, can alter the party landscape. The 2005 election presents each of the three mainstream parties with opportunities and challenges for a significantly better result at the next election. Each party's prospects will be explored in turn.

The Promise and Pitfalls of a Gordon Brown Government

Barring accidents, Gordon Brown will be prime minister and Labour leader at the next election. He brings promise and danger to Labour's electoral prospects in almost equal measure. On the one hand, he is a politician of formidable public standing; on the other, he is associated, accurately or otherwise, with "Old Labour" values and policies, which may re-enthuse Labour Party members but alienate the voters whom New Labour under Tony Blair attracted in 1997 and 2001.

By 2005 Gordon Brown had presided over an exceptionally strong economy for eight years as chancellor of the exchequer, and was widely credited with its success. His public ratings as chancellor were exceptionally high— fully 66 per cent considered he had done a "good job", only 25 per cent a "bad job". More significantly, they were much better than Tony Blair's ratings as prime minister, which had been as high as Gordon Brown's until the Iraq War but fell sharply thereafter: in April 2005 slightly more people thought Blair was doing a "bad job" (50 per cent) than a "good job" (46 per cent).[19] As a result Gordon Brown and Tony Blair were seen together throughout the campaign, doing a double act in the television studios, at the press conferences and on walkabouts. It was a skilful tactic which almost certainly contributed to Labour's gradual recovery during the campaign. An eve-of-election poll reported that Labour's 4-point 36 to 32 lead over the Conservatives would have increased to a 13-point 42 to 29 lead if Gordon Brown had been the Labour leader.[20] Never before in post-war British politics has a senior minister been so much more respected than his prime minister.

The hypothetical boost to Labour's lead under a Gordon Brown premiership does not automatically translate into a runaway Labour win at the next election. A serious downturn in the economy could tarnish Gordon Brown's reputation as chancellor and Labour's credibility as a government. The qualities and personality that have made Gordon Brown a success at Number 11 may be unsuitable for Number 10. Gordon Brown is frequently portrayed as a dour Scot—a brooding, introspective man, happiest among a small coterie of friends. Voters might prefer someone who is sunnier, more outgoing, emotionally more engaged, as leader of the nation.

But the electoral consequences of Gordon Brown will depend most on whether voters perceive his government as moving away from the pragmatic centre and back to the left. Gordon Brown is usually depicted, by supporters and detractors alike, as being to the left of Tony Blair.[21] It is true that his Labour roots go deeper than Tony Blair's and his Labour Party networks stretch wider.[22] The Labour discourse of poverty and exclusion comes more naturally to him. He is part of the Labour tribe whereas Tony Blair is not. Yet the policy and philosophical differences between him and Tony Blair are exaggerated. Gordon Brown was the leading architect of New Labour's conversion to the values of enterprise, innovation, competition, flexible labour markets, financial incentives and fiscal prudence—in a word, to the acceptance of economic globalization. He is more enthusiastic than Tony Blair about US-style corporate capitalism and American-influenced welfare-to-work schemes. He is equally determined to subject public services to the management disciplines of targets and performance indicators. It is only on the role of markets and the private sector in the delivery of public services that he has taken an "Old Labour" position in contrast to Tony Blair (see Thomas Quinn in Chapter 1).

Whatever the reality, as prime minister Gordon Brown will come under pressure to revert to Old Labour policies: more public expenditure, higher taxation, centralized and standardized public service delivery and an extension of welfare rights. If he yields it would be popular with the Labour Party's members and traditional voters as well as with his close parliamentary supporters. It would bring back many of those who deserted Labour in 2005. But it would confirm to an expectant media, egged on by the Conservatives, that

Labour had reverted to its old ways. It would provide an opening for a regalvanized Conservative opposition to reclaim the centre and offer itself as a party of modernization and reform. Yet if Gordon Brown resists the pressure to tack to the left, and pursues the New Labour reform agenda, he risks disappointing many of Labour's traditional voters and workers, some of whom stayed loyal at the 2005 election on the promise of Gordon Brown as prime minister, and who may be tempted to switch to the Liberal Democrats or smaller parties on the left. The challenge for a Gordon Brown premiership will be to speak a language and adopt policies which re-connect the government with Labour's traditional base without frightening the new groups of largely middle-class voters who flocked to Labour in 1997. As chancellor, Gordon Brown initiated a number of measures that achieved that balance, such as the minimum wage, family tax credits, educational maintenance allowances and Sure Start childcare programme.[23] These probably had a limited impact on the vote in 2005, being swamped by the Iraq War, but similar measures may hold the key to the maintenance of New Labour's ascendancy under Gordon Brown.

Strategies for Conservative Recovery

The Conservative Party too will contest the next election under a new leader; their fourth in as little as nine years. How might he succeed, where William Hague, Iain Duncan-Smith and Michael Howard have so evidently failed, to win back the 5.3 million Conservative voters lost since 1992, and to win the additional 127 seats needed to form a Conservative government?

The 2005 election leaves the Conservative Party in almost as desperate a position as they were after their 1997 defeat, with a formidable electoral mountain to climb and no clear path to the top. Although the election produced more Conservative MPs and reduced Labour's lead to only 3 percentage points, by no stretch of optimism does it constitute a stepping stone to government in 2009—or even 2013. The Conservatives have only covered a fifth of the ground they need to travel. Even this modest progress was illusory in the sense that it owed more to the capacity of the Liberal Democrats to win over disaffected Labour supporters. The Conservatives failed entirely to profit from voters' disillusion with the government and their dislike of the prime minister: for the third election running the Conservative share of the popular vote remained stuck at less than a third. The doctrine of "one more push"— doing little different from before other than attacking the government, keeping the party united, avoiding rash commitments and waiting patiently for the Labour government to implode—is not a recipe for success. Much bigger changes are required. More than that, the Conservative Party needs to persuade the electorate that it has made these radical changes, just as the Labour Party re-invented itself in the 1990s after four consecutive election defeats.

Although there are parallels with Labour's electoral predicament in the 1990s, the creation of New Labour is not a particularly helpful model to the

Conservatives. The Labour Party was able to convince the public it had fundamentally changed by jettisoning a raft of unpopular policies and by conspicuously distancing itself from unpopular organizations, such as the trade unions. The Conservative Party, despite its electoral difficulties, is not saddled with an equivalent set of unpopular policies and organizational alliances. The abolition of Clause 4 of the Labour Party constitution (which entrenched a commitment to full-scale nationalization) and the "block vote" at the party conference (which entrenched trade-union power) provided the Labour Party with its "symbolic moment" of change. But the Conservative Party has no iconic equivalent: there is no single act or decision that is likely to convince voters that the party has fundamentally changed. The Labour Party was able to create an informal alliance with the Liberal Democrats because it was toying with electoral reform and the two parties were converging ideologically. The Conservative Party, by contrast, cannot make common cause with the Liberal Democrats because it has no truck with electoral reform and the two parties are ideologically more distant than at any time since the 1920s. Rebranding the Conservative Party will be much more difficult than it was for the Labour Party.

A strategy for electoral recovery needs a clear-eyed analysis of the causes as well as scale of the Conservatives' electoral problems. A memo to the new Conservative leader on his first day in office should make seven points:

> *Point 1:* Simply changing the leader is neither a sufficient nor necessary condition for electoral success. The personal attributes and image of the leader are far less important than people imagined.[24] The Conservative Party elected three men of very different personalities, abilities, age and appearance between 1997 and 2005 and none of them took the party closer to power. It was not the leader's personal defects that made the Conservative Party unpopular but the party's political weaknesses that made the leader unpopular. The new leader should cease to worry about his image and concentrate on devising a clear strategy and mobilizing the party behind it.

> *Point 2:* The Conservative party should not preoccupy itself with policy details. It did not lose the 2005 and 2001 elections because voters disagreed with its policy positions. On the contrary, the Conservatives were in tune with the public on Europe in 2001 and on asylum seekers, crime and pensions in 2005. But only a minority of voters choose a party on the basis of their particular policies on specific issues. The majority judge a party on what and whom it stands for and on its general capacity to govern. It is in these respects that the Conservatives have conspicuously failed since 1997.

> *Point 3:* The Conservative party has a huge image problem. Polls consistently report that, irrespective of their policies and leaders,

the Conservative Party's popular image is much less favourable than the Labour Party's.[25] People regard the Conservatives in 2005 as the same party as the one that lost under John Major in 1997, as having failed to move on, as stuck in the past, as hankering after a better yesterday and uncomfortable with modernity. Voters see it as a party of, and for, people very different from themselves; as exclusive and divisive, unconnected with the lives of ordinary people, sectional rather than national; as a party for the rich, for business and for rural England (see Anthony King in Chapter 7).

Point 4: Image change cannot be achieved overnight. But the party would make some headway if many more of its MPs (and councillors) were women, young, from "ordinary" backgrounds speaking in ordinary accents and a few more were openly homosexual and from ethnic minorities; if its language was less censorious and divisive; and if it distanced itself from unpopular minority causes (such as hunting).

Point 5: The party has a second, more critical, image problem: it fails to inspire any confidence in its ability to govern. It simply does not look like a government-in-waiting. Voters no longer know what the party stands for because the party itself does not appear to know: its policies chop and change (see Philip Norton in Chapter 2). Despite being disillusioned with the Labour government's record, voters are even less convinced that a Conservative government would deliver. The central task for the new leader is to make the idea of a Conservative government credible as well as attractive, but this raises acute dilemmas about the party's broad policy stance, which all three previous leaders failed to resolve.

Point 6: Since 1997 the Conservative opposition has grappled with a difficult choice: should it compete with New Labour on vision or on delivery? There is no easy answer. Putting "clear blue water" between itself and New Labour, differentiating itself not just on policy details but on principles and philosophy, would have the advantage of making it clear to voters what the party stood for and of enthusing party members. But because New Labour occupies a wide strip of centre ground it would require the Conservatives to place themselves well to the right on the ideological spectrum. And that might make it clear to voters that where the party stood was a long way from where most of them stood. Alternatively, the Conservatives could set up camp on New Labour's ideological patch, promote the same objectives as the government, but claim to be more efficient at achieving them. This would have the advantage of placing the Conservative Party closer to the average swing voter, but the drawback of leaving voters unclear about the difference that a Conservative government would make. It is particularly difficult for an opposition to persuade voters that it would be more efficient than the government because doing so often involves going into quite technical and off-putting policy detail. The opposition is only trusted to govern more competently when the government has had such a spell of spectacular blunders, failures and scandals that voters decide that "it couldn't do any worse; its time for a change"— and there is no knowing, or controlling, when that time will come.

Point 7: The choice should not be fudged. In 2005 the Conservatives tried to finesse the dilemma by differentiating itself from Labour on the "liberal versus popular authoritarian" policy dimension while claiming to be better at delivery on the "public spending versus tax cuts" policy dimension. On the first, it was the party that would crack down on illegal immigrants, illegal gypsy sites, unruly pupils and dirty hospital wards. On the second, it was the party that would spend as much as or more than the government on public services, but make a modest cut in taxes by cutting waste and bureaucracy. This compromise did not work. The Conservatives made some headway on the issue of asylum seekers, placing it high on voters' agenda and establishing itself in their eyes as the party more in tune with their concerns. But the policy mainly appealed to committed Conservatives and apart from (probably) helping to gain some working-class votes in outer London and the South East, it did not harvest a significant reward. The question of public services and tax cuts was of concern to many more voters, but the Conservative Party's sophisticated balance of limited tax cuts and more selective, slower-growing, public spending left them perplexed: were the Conservatives a tax-cutting party or were they not? The lesson of 2005 for the Conservatives' recovery strategy is that it will need to decide well before the next election whether it is a low-tax/low-spend or current-tax/current-spend party and not try to dodge the issue.

There is one other feature of the Conservative Party's electoral situation which requires some difficult strategic decisions and has been entirely neglected until now. The party is aware of the scale of recovery required to form a government: 127 gains and a record 7.4 swing. But it is in denial about the small chance of this occurring at a single election. As Table 9.2 shows, a net Labour to Conservative swing anywhere within the normal post-war range of 2 to 6 per cent will produce a hung parliament.[26] A good result for the Conservatives is much more likely to mean minority or coalition government than a Conservative government in overall control. Yet the Conservative Party lacks any strategy for a hung parliament. It thinks in the bi-polar terms of the 1980s rather than the three-party reality of the 2000s. If after the next election it becomes the largest party in parliament—and even this would require as large a swing as Margaret Thatcher secured in 1979, after the "Winter of Discontent"—it will have to decide whether to take office in formal or tacit partnership with the Liberal Democrats or stay in opposition. It may at that time make a tactical decision to remain in opposition in the expectation of a second election within a short period which it would win. But that would be a considerable gamble. It may also wish to be in a position to take office immediately, and therefore with Liberal Democrat support, with a view to seeking a stronger mandate from the electorate at a second election after a short period during which it demonstrated its fitness to govern. Yet currently there seems little prospect of the Liberal Democrats supporting the Conservatives in preference to Labour in government. In his strategy for electoral recovery the new Conservative leader will need to think whether it makes sense to allow this situation to continue.

The Liberal Democrats: Fighting on Two Fronts

The 2005 election marked the point at which the Liberal Democrats became a third party in the fullest sense of the term, challenging both the major parties with broadly equal force. For much of the post-war period the Liberal Democrats, or the Liberals as they were formerly known, competed asymmetrically with the two main parties. Disillusioned Conservatives regarded the Liberals as a more acceptable refuge than Labour, but the reverse was not the case: disillusioned Labour supporters tended to defect straight over to the Conservatives. Thus the Liberal Democrats prospered more during periods of Conservative than Labour government and more in Conservative than Labour territory. The minority of MPs facing serious challenge from a Liberal/Liberal Democrat candidate were almost invariably Conservatives. In most of the country the constituency battle was between the Conservative and Labour parties; in a few areas, notably the rural South West and rural Scotland, it was between the Conservative and Liberal parties but almost nowhere was it between Labour and the Liberals. The Conservatives needed to worry about a Liberal resurgence, which would not only elect Liberal MPs but help Labour snatch Conservative marginal seats, whereas Labour did not.

The 2005 election was notable for breaking the normal pattern. After eight years of Labour government, disillusioned supporters were four times more likely to defect to the Liberal Democrats than to the Conservatives.[27] The Liberal Democrats advanced further in Labour areas, where they increased their vote by 5.2 points, than in Conservative areas, where it rose by 2.1 points (although usually from a higher base). They made a net gain of twelve Labour seats but a net loss of two seats to the Conservatives. They were also responsible for nine of Labour's thirty-one losses to the Conservatives.[28] And, for the first time since the war, they were the runner-up in more Labour seats than Conservative seats. These gains reflected the relocation of the Liberal Democrats, in the eyes of voters, to the left of Labour rather than half way between the two main parties. They were the party that, in contrast to New Labour, opposed the creeping privatization of public services, opposed the Iraq invasion, defended civil liberties in times of terrorism and wanted to abolish university tuition fees. The Liberal Democrats had swapped places with Labour on the ideological spectrum. What was surprising was that it had taken so long for traditional Labour supporters to notice.

The Liberal Democrats may well feel encouraged by their 2005 successes to continue their two-front strategy of challenging the Conservatives in the shires and suburbs and challenging Labour in the big cities. They may even opt to concentrate more on their Labour flank, as the inevitable mid-term disillusion with the government sets in and they take more seats from Labour in local elections. But such a strategy is not without risk, for four reasons. First, the appeal of the Liberal Democrats to natural Labour voters in Labour areas is very different to their appeal to natural Conservatives in Conservative areas.[29] In the first they win votes by appearing as a party of the principled left, in the second by appearing as a party of the moderate centre. To some degree the difference can be ignored because local candidates will tailor their message to the constituency and modern marketing and communications make that easier. But the more distinct the Liberal Democrats' national profile the more difficult it is to fight equally effectively on both fronts.[30] Second, the Conservative front remains the more important theatre of war. The Liberal Democrats are in close contention in more Conservative seats than Labour seats. And in the seats they hold they are more vulnerable to a Conservative than a Labour challenge.[31] To achieve a breakthrough to a hundred or more MPs they must capture more Conservative seats and beat back Conservative insurgents.

Third, by promoting themselves as a party of the moderate left, similar to the old Labour Party but without the trade-union connection, they risk retreat in Conservative areas. The Liberal Democrats win in traditionally Conservative areas by squeezing the Labour vote and attracting moderate ex-Conservatives. But there are as many of the latter as the former and they are more liable to revert to type. In 2005, the Liberal Democrat advance in Conservative areas stalled: their vote stayed put, they lost two more seats than they gained and they failed to "decapitate" all but one of their target senior Conservatives.[32] It seems likely that the Liberal Democrats' much sharper national profile as a party of the left was a factor. Had the Liberal Democrats taken as many votes from Conservative incumbents as they did from Labour incumbents, they would have gained an additional nineteen seats. Fourth, although the Liberal Democrats have been adept at holding on to the seats they capture at general elections, they may find it more difficult to hang on to their gains from Labour if, as seems likely, the Iraq War and tuition fees cease to be issues, and a Gordon Brown government persuades its traditional supporters that the Labour Party is returning to its roots.

Charles Kennedy, the Liberal Democrat leader, told his party conference in 2002 that the Liberal Democrats need not be a third party for ever and should aim to replace the Conservatives as the main opposition to the Labour government.[33] At the time the Conservatives, led by the uninspiring Iain Duncan-Smith, were dipping below 30 per cent in the polls. By 2004, the Liberal Democrats, buoyed up by their by-election victories in the hitherto safe urban Labour seats of Brent East and Leicester South and by their local election advances in Labour areas, turned their sights on Labour. Moves by a group of able, young MPs from the 1997 cohort to wean Liberal Democrat social and economic policy away from centralized state solutions were rebuffed.[34] By contesting the 2005 election as a left-of-centre party the Liberal Democrats gained enough seats to give them the illusion of significant progress and to mask a missed opportunity. They changed the shape of the party system, but its contours suggest that continuation of their 2005 strategy may not serve their interests.

Conclusion

The significance of the 2005 election is unusually difficult to judge. It offered each party some grounds for optimism about their future prospects but more grounds for disappointment and concern. In each case the election could be interpreted as a vindication of at least one of their tactics. The Labour Party benefited from inviting Gordon Brown to join Tony Blair in a dual leadership. The Conservatives probably benefited from highlighting immigration and adopting a clearly differentiated and populist position on the issue. The Liberal Democrats increased their tally of seats by promoting themselves as a left-of-centre party. But in each case the limitations and dangers of turning these tactics into an electoral strategy are apparent. The two major parties will contest the next election with different leaders, who in the light of the election result will be under pressure to take or keep their parties away from the broad centre of the policy spectrum, as will the Liberal Democrats' Charles Kennedy. As this chapter has shown, moving the parties in this direction carries considerable electoral dangers for each.

One feature of the 2005 election is clear: the country turned sharply against the Labour government, in particular Tony Blair, partly out of disappointment on the slow progress in the public services, but mainly because of the invasion of Iraq and the manner in which the decision was taken and justified. Elements of New Labour's electoral strategy unravelled but the balance of evidence suggests that the foundations of its electoral ascendancy remain intact. The 2005 election was a strong but safe protest: the electorate got the result it wanted, including many who did not vote Labour. In all probability it will turn out to have been a deviation from the norm rather than the new norm or the transition to a new party configuration.

There is one further verdict to come to about the election: it was a dispiritingly poor advertisement for the democratic process. Electioneering concentrated even more ruthlessly than before on bombarding a tiny group of supposedly volatile voters with carefully tailored (and sometimes contradictory) messages in a hundred or so highly marginal seats. The rest of the electorate had to make do with the national media's reporting of the utterances of the party leaders. The leaders largely controlled the agenda and they chose to ignore many of the major long-term problems for the country's future, with which government will have to grapple: climate change, the provision of pensions, the place for nuclear energy, the proper balance between civil liberties and security against terrorism and the expansion of the European Union to name but some.[35] Turnout barely recovered from its historically low level of 2001, despite easier postal voting and the hotter political temperature of the campaign. The United Kingdom has one of the lowest participation levels in Europe for its election to the nation's parliament. The relationship between votes was grossly disproportionate and biased: Labour won 55 per cent of the seats with 35 per cent of the vote. Four out of five electors did not vote for the party that will govern the United Kingdom with a comfortable parliamentary majority for up to five years. It would be gratifying if a large majority of the electorate turned out to vote at the next election, galvanized by a vigorous debate on the critical choices facing a British government, and confident that the distribution of their votes would be fairly reflected in the result. This is extremely unlikely to happen.

Notes

1. Labour lost ten seats as a result of the reduction in the number of constituencies in Scotland from seventy-two to fifty-nine. Had Scotland retained its 2001 constituency boundaries, as the rest of the United Kingdom did, Labour's majority would probably have been seventy-six. See David Denver, Colin Rallings and Michael Thrasher, *Media Guide to the New Scottish Westminster Parliamentary Constituencies* (London: BBC, ITN, PA News and Sky News, 2004), p. 7.
2. Labour's share of the vote fell in 593 of the 628 constituencies on the mainland of the United Kingdom. Most of the constituencies in which the Labour vote share increased were seats held or once held by the Liberal Democrats, where a previous tactical squeeze on the Labour vote had slightly loosened.
3. This does not stop political scientists from trying to forecast election outcomes. See James E. Campbell and James C. Garand, *Before the Vote: Forecasting American National Elections* (Thousand Oaks: Sage, 2000).
4. See Samuel Brittan, "The irresistible folly of crystal-gazing", *Financial Times*, January 4, 2001: "Winston Churchill said that a young person entering politics needs 'the ability to foretell what is going to happen, tomorrow, next week, next month and next year. And to have the ability afterwards to explain why it didn't'."
5. See Anatole Kaletsky, "It's not the economy, stupid", *Prospect*, May 2005, pp. 18–20.
6. For a fuller account, see Ivor Crewe, "A New Political Hegemony?" in Anthony King, ed., *Britain at the Polls, 2001* (New York: Chatham House Publishers, 2002), pp. 207–32, especially pp. 212–18.
7. See Tony Blair, *New Britain: My Vision of a Young Country* (London: Fourth Estate, 1996).
8. Since 1945 the only governments to have incurred a sharper drop in vote share are the Conservatives in 1964 (-6.0 per cent), the Conservatives in February 1974 (-8.5 per cent) and the Conservatives in 1997 (-11.2 per cent).

9. Setting aside university/student and Muslim constituencies, where the "swing" from Labour to Conservative is artificial, the seats with Labour to Conservative swings of over 7.0 per cent were: Enfield Southgate (8.7 per cent), Crawley (8.5 per cent), Bedfordshire South West (8.1 per cent), Welwyn Hatfield (8.0 per cent), Castle Point (7.7 per cent), Romford (7.5 per cent), Hertford and Stortford (7.2 per cent), Wimbledon (7.2 per cent), Bexleyheath and Crayford (7.2 per cent), Brent North (7.1 per cent) and Hertsmere (7.1 per cent).

10. The prominence of the fast-expanding new towns, with a largely white working-class population, among the high Labour-to-Conservative swing seats is noticeable. In addition to Crawley and Welwyn Hatfield (see n. 4), there were swings of 6.9 per cent in Peterborough, 6.9 per cent in Swindon South, 6.7 per cent in Swindon North, 6.4 per cent in Harlow, 6.4 per cent in Hitchin and Harpenden, 6.3 per cent in Stevenage and 5.8 per cent in Basildon.

11. See Peter Kellner, "Clearing the Fog: What Really Happened in the 2005 Election Campaign", *Political Quarterly*, 76 (2005): 323–32 (p. 331); and Geoffrey Evans, "The Working Class and New Labour: A Parting of the Ways?" in Roger Jowell, John Curtice, Alison Park, Katrina Thompson, Lindsey Jarvis, Catherine Bromley and Nina Stratford, eds, *British Social Attitudes: The 17th Report* (London: Sage Publications, 2000), pp. 51–70 (especially pp. 61–7).

12. Peter Kellner, "Clearing the Fog", p. 324. The full question wording was "If you *had* to choose between a Labour Government led by Tony Blair and a Conservative Government led by Michael Howard, which would you vote for?" The poll was conducted by YouGov on May 3–4, 2005, immediately before the election.

13. The same poll showed that Liberal Democrat voters and Nationalists in Scotland and Wales preferred a Blair/Labour government to a Howard/Conservative government by two-to-one.

14. Another particle of supporting evidence is the apparent absence of "tactical unwind". Before the election it was widely expected that many Liberal Democrat supporters who in 1997 and 2001 had tactically voted Labour in Conservative–Labour and Labour–Conservative marginal seats would refuse to do so in 2005. This does not appear to have occurred. Although there was a swing from Labour to Liberal Democrat in these marginal seats, it was no higher than average. See also Stephen Fisher and John Curtice, "Tactical Unwind?" (paper presented to the Elections, Public Opinion and Parties (EPOP) Conference, University of Essex, September 2005), who report "little sign of change in the level or pattern of tactical voting" (p.1).

15. See Kellner, "Clearing the Fog", p. 326.

16. See, for example, John Curtice and Michael Steed, "Appendix 2: An Analysis of the Results", in David Butler and Dennis Kavanagh, eds, *The British General Election of 2001* (London: Palgrave, 2002), pp. 304–38 (esp. pp. 328–32).

17. Electoral Reform Society, *5 May 2005, Worst Election Ever: A Preliminary Report* (London: Electoral Reform Society, 2005), p. 8.

18. Electoral Reform Society, *5 May 2005, Worst Election Ever: A Preliminary Report*, p. 8.

19. See Kellner, "Clearing the Fog", p. 328.

20. There are reasons, of course, to take such findings with a pinch of salt. See John Bartle and Ivor Crewe, "The Impact of Party Leaders in Britain: Strong Assumptions, Weak Evidence", in Anthony King, ed., *Leaders' Personalities and the Outcomes of Democratic Elections* (Oxford: Oxford University Press, 2002), pp. 70–95, at p.74.

21. A YouGov poll conducted April 19–21, 2005, asked its respondents to place politicians on a left–right scale, scored from -100 to +100. Gordon Brown scored of -20 (as did Charles Kennedy) whereas Tony Blair scored +7.

22. See Paul Routledge, *Gordon Brown: The Biography* (London: Simon and Schuster, 1998), chaps. 2 and 3.
23. See Polly Toynbee and David Walker, *Did Things Get Better? An Audit of Labour's Successes and Failures* (London: Penguin, 1997); Polly Toynbee and David Walker, *Better or Worse? Has Labour Delivered?* (London: Bloomsbury, 2001).
24. See King, *Leaders' Personalities and the Outcomes of Democratic Elections.*
25. See, for example, Anthony King, "The Tories are stuck with an image problem", *Daily Telegraph*, May 2, 2005, p. 8; and John Curtice, "Historic Triumph or Rebuff: The 2005 UK General Election", *Politics Review*, 15:1 (September 2005), 2–7, Table 7.
26. The swing between the two major parties has exceeded 6 per cent in only one of the sixteen post-1950 elections (1997). See Colin Rallings and Michael Thrasher, *British Electoral Facts, 1832–1999* (Aldershot: Ashgate, 2000), p. 74.
27. Kellner, "Clearing the Fog", p. 326.
28. By which is meant that the difference between the increase in the Liberal Democrat share of the vote and the Conservative share of the vote was larger than the Conservative percentage majority.
29. Peter Riddell, "The Lib Dems must decide who their enemy will be", *The Times*, March 16, 2005.
30. Unusually, the Liberal Democrats in 2005 had sufficient funds for an extensive national poster and media advertising campaign, which focused on their policy positions and reinforced their image as a left-of-centre party. Moreover, they did not make as much use of geo-demographic databases as the Labour and Conservative parties did to send different political messages to different target groups of voters. See Tom Baldwin, "A New Style of Campaign which Left Too Many Voters Outside", in *The Times Guide to the House of Commons 2005* (London: Times Books, 2005), pp. 41–43, at p. 43.
31. The Liberal Democrats were less than 15 per cent behind in nineteen Labour seats and twenty-nine Conservative seats. Of the Liberal Democrat seats the Conservatives were less than 15 per cent behind in twenty-eight, Labour in thirteen. By this measure the Conservatives and Liberal Democrats are in close contention in fifty-seven seats, Labour and the Liberal Democrats in thirty-two seats.
32. Liberal Democrat strategists claimed to have a "decapitation" strategy, aimed at removing senior Conservative MPs. In the event, the only senior Conservative to lose his seat was Tim Collins in Westmorland and Lonsdale.
33. Greg Hurst, "Kennedy steps up pace in an effort to overtake Tories", *The Times*, September 27, 2002.
34. See David Laws, "No need to fear liberalism", *Liberator*, September 14, 2004.
35. Anthony King, "Economy fails to stretch Labour poll lead", *Daily Telegraph*, April 8, 2005.

Appendix: Results of British General Elections, 1945–2005

| Year | Turnout | Percentage of popular vote | | | | | | Seats in House of Commons | | | | | |
		Con	Lab	Lib[a]	Nat[b]	Other	Swing[c]	Con	Lab	Lib	Nat	Other	Government majority
1945	72.8	39.7	47.7	9.0	0.2	3.4	-12.2	210	393	12	0	25	146
1950	83.9	43.3	46.1	9.1	0.1	1.4	+2.6	297	315	9	0	4	5
1951	82.6	48.0	48.8	2.6	0.1	0.5	+1.0	321	295	6	0	3	17
1955	76.8	49.6	46.4	2.7	0.2	1.1	+2.0	344	277	6	0	3	60
1959	78.7	49.4	43.8	5.9	0.4	0.5	+1.2	365	258	6	0	1	100
1964	77.1	43.3	44.1	11.2	0.5	0.9	-3.2	303	317	9	0	1	4
1966	75.8	41.9	47.9	8.5	0.7	1.0	-2.6	253	363	12	0	2	96
1970	72.0	46.4	43.0	7.5	1.7	1.4	+4.7	330	287	6	1	6	30
1974 (Feb)	78.8	37.8	37.2	19.3	2.6	3.1	-1.2	297	301	14	9	14	-34[d]
1974 (Oct)	72.8	35.7	39.3	18.3	3.4	3.3	-2.1	276	319	13	14	13	3
1979	76.0	43.9	36.9	13.8	2.0	3.4	+5.3	339	268	11	4	13	43
1983	72.7	42.4	27.6	25.4	1.5	3.1	+3.9	397	209	23	4	17	144
1987	75.3	42.2	30.8	22.6	1.7	2.7	-1.7	375	229	22	6	18	102
1992	77.7	41.9	34.4	17.8	2.3	3.6	-2.0	336	271	20	7	17	21
1997	71.4	30.7	43.2	16.8	2.5	6.8	-10.0	165	418	46	10	20	179
2001	59.4	31.7	40.7	18.3	2.5	6.8	+1.8	166	412	52	9	20	167
2005	61.5	32.3	35.2	22.1	2.2	8.2	+3.1	198	355	62	9	22	66

Source: House of Commons Library Research Papers 04/61 and 05/53

a. Liberal Party, 1945–79; Liberal/Social Democrat Alliance, 1983–87; Liberal Democrat Party, 1992–2005.

b. Combined vote of Scottish National Party (SNP) and Welsh Nationalist Party (Plaid Cymru).

c. "Swing" compares the results of each election with the results of the previous election. It is calculated as the average of the winning party's percentage point increase in its share of the vote and the losing party's decrease in its percentage point share of the vote. In the table, a positive sign denotes a swing to the Conservatives, a negative sign a swing to Labour.

d. Following the February 1974 general election, the Labour Party was 34 seats short of having an overall majority. It formed a minority government until it obtained a majority in the October 1974 election.

Index